The Feminist Companion to the Bible

(Second Series)

5

Editors
Athalya Brenner and
Carole R. Fontaine

Sheffield Academic Press

Exodus to Deuteronomy

A Feminist Companion to the Bible
(Second Series)

edited by Athalya Brenner

Published by Sheffield Academic Press Ltd
Mansion House
19 Kingfield Road
Sheffield, S11 9AS
England

www.SheffieldAcademicPress.com

Printed on acid-free paper in Great Britain
by Bell & Bain Ltd
Glasgow

British Library Cataloguing in Publication Data

A catalogue record for this book is available
from the British Library

ISBN 1-84127-079-2

To the memory of

_____

Fokkelien van Dijk-Hemmes

תּ·נ·צ·ב·ה·

CONTENTS

Part III
THIRD REVISIT: DAUGHTERS

ABBREVIATIONS

ABD	David Noel Freedman (ed.), *The Anchor Bible Dictionary* (New York: Doubleday, 1992)
BARev	*Biblical Archaeology Review*
BN	*Biblische Notizen*
BR	*Bible Review*
CBC	Cambridge Biblical Commentary
CBQ	*Catholic Biblical Quarterly*
CTC	Commission on Theological Concerns
ICC	International Critical Commentary
JBL	*Journal of Biblical Literature*
JBQ	*Jewish Biblical Quarterly*
JSOT	*Journal for the Study of the Old Testament*
JSOTSup	*Journal for the Study of the Old Testament*, Supplement Series
JSS	*Journal of Semitic Studies*
NCBC	New Century Bible Commentary
OTL	Old Testament Library
OTP	James Charlesworth (ed.), *Old Testament Pseudepigrapha*
SBLDS	SBL Dissertation Series
SBS	Stuttgarter Bibelstudien
SCI	*Scripta Classica Israelica*
SE	*The Standard Edition of the Complete Psychological Works of Sigmund Freud* (trans. and ed. James Strachey; 24 vols.; London: Hogarth Press and Institute of Psycho-Analysis, 1953–74).
TDOT	G.J. Botterweck and H. Ringgren (eds.), *Theological Dictionary of the Old Testament*
VT	*Vetus Testamentum*
WBC	Word Biblical Commentary
ZPE	*Zeitschrift für Papyrologie und Epigraphik*

LIST OF CONTRIBUTORS

Alice Bach, Department of Religion, 105 Mather House, Case Western Reserve University, Cleveland, OH 44106-7112, USA

Athalya Brenner, Department of Theology and Religious Studies, Faculty of Humanities, University of Amsterdam, Oude Turfmarkt 147, 1012 GC Amsterdam, The Netherlands

Leila Leah Bronner, 180 N. Las Palmas Ave, Los Angeles, CA 90004, USA

Irmtraud Fischer, Altes Testament und Theologische Frauenforschung, Universität Bonn, Regina Pacis-Weig 1a, D-53113 Bonn, Germany

Tal Ilan, Reuven Arazi 34/7, Pisgat Zeev East, Jerusalem 97822, Israel

Cheryl Kirk-Duggan, Center for Women and Religion, Graduate Theological Union, 2400 Ridge Road, Berkeley, CA 94709, USA

Helen Leneman, 10 Defoe Ct., Rockville, MD 20850, USA

Ilona Rashkow, Department of Comparative Studies, State University of New York at Stony Brook, NY 11794-3355, USA

Susanne Scholz, Department of Religious Studies, The College of Wooster, Wooster, OH 44691-2363, USA

Phyllis Silverman Kramer, 6848 Palmetto Circle South 1215, Boca Raton, FL 33433, USA

Harold C. Washington, Saint Paul School of Theology, 5123 Truman Road, Kansas City, MO 64127, USA

INTRODUCTION

Athalya Brenner

The chief, underlying concerns of Hebrew Bible feminist critics who read Exodus texts (that is, texts of the Torah beyond Genesis) seem to be: the reassessment of liberation theology issues in the Exodus texts; woman figures in matters of textual and so-called law authority; midrashic elaborations old and new and their applicability/relevance to textual and feminist concerns; and ongoing cultural (art) transmissions of Exodus 'events' and textual personalities. These concerns can be thematized in the following clusters: (I) the Exodus from Egypt, including Moses's textual role, (II) Miriam, and (III) other woman figures in the same texts, especially defined as 'daughters'.

Therefore, this second *Feminist Companion to Exodus to Deuteronomy* is organized around the concept of three 'revisits' to the seemingly *terra cognita* of the Exodus. Each 'revisit' corresponds to one of these clusters.

Part I
First Revisit: Exodus and Moses

In 'The Complexities of "His" Liberation Talk: A Literary Feminist Reading of the Book of Exodus', Susanne Scholz writes:

> The story of the oppression and the liberation of Israel posed considerable difficulties, once feminist perspectives guided the exegesis. When feminists examine biblical texts, they usually focus on historical, literary, and theological representations of women. The problem with the book of Exodus, however, is that it contains few female characters and issues of feminist concern. Only the initial chapters, the middle part, and several brief comments throughout the book refer to women. As a result, not many feminist scholars have dealt with Exodus. If they did, they interpreted only the few sections about women and disregarded the rest.

Consequently, she sets out to 'remedy the situation' by reinterpreting the Exodus from a feminist viewpoint, thus reassessing and re-vision-ing the liberation tradition from a fresh angle (and see Fischer's article below). Her article is an overview of the book of Exodus, to be followed by more specific elaborations on Exodus traditions.

In 'Signifying on Exodus: Reading Race and Culture in Zora Neale Hurston's *Moses, Man of the Mountain*', Harold C. Washington first explains why he has turned to Zora Neale Hurston's 1939 novel, *Moses, Man of the Mountain*, in order to illustrate a feminist reading *and* interrogate his own subject position, that of a US Southern-born male, as a reader of Hurston's reading of Exodus. Washington then sets out to describe Hurston's achievement in terms of biblical criticism and social criticism, as relevant to her time and location, through 'defiant humor' and literary skill. In a 'Womanist midrash', Hurston treats Moses' figure as a trickster, thus subverting Scripture by using the practice of 'signifying'. Her retelling of female voices in the Exodus, her life and her legacy reflect the suppression and silencing of women in the biblical text and require further studying.

How do images and symbols such as snakes, serpents, penis, Phallus, and Isis relate to Moses, to the Israelite god, to Yhwh's Rod'? In the biblical narrative, the relationship between Moses and God exposes displacements, and his relationship of Moses and God's rod lasts beyond Egypt. In 'Oedipus Wrecks: Moses and God's Rod', Ilona Rashkow applies herself to these intriguing questions from literary and psychoanalytic perspectives. The fundamental themes of the Oedipal conflict—desire, the meaning of the father figure, law and guilt—characterize the relationship of Moses and God's rod. In Rashkow's reading, the Egyptian sacralization of female sexuality has been displaced by Israelite male sexuality, symbolized by the circumcised penises of the Israelites, the manifest symbol of the relationship of Moses and God's rod. However, she concludes, 'Moses may wield God's rod, but never its power'.

In 'Divine Puppeteer: Yahweh of Exodus', Cheryl Kirk-Duggan continues to question God's character and Moses' character and their mutual relationship in the Exodus narratives. Moral and ethical problems abound in these narratives. How should one read the 'hardening of Pharaoh's heart', for instance? Or that God's chosen will be oppressed, notably so that God can rescue them? Or how the 'other' is oppressed in order to facilitate the delierance from oppression of Yhwh's people? How does the god of promise (Exod. 3–4) turn into another god altogether in the Exodus process? What are women's roles in the story? How can one define the relationship between Yhwh and Moses—ultimately, is Moses a puppet and God a divine puppeteer? Such questions have been asked before, and are also touched upon in

Scholz's article. But Kirk-Duggan's perspective is different: she reads from the perspective of Womanist biblical theory and theology (see also Washington), hence she also arrives at conclusions that are otherwise nuanced.

Part II
Second Revisit: Miriam

The figure of Miriam has always held fascination for feminist readers. 'Miriam', by Phyllis Silverman Kramer, is a classified overview of 'Miriam studies' in two, seemingly disparate sources of learning and reception that are often linked by the willingness to use midrash as a means for transmission and updating. Kramer begins by looking at Miriam in the Hebrew Bible itself. She then proceeds to look for her in rabbinic interpretation, under the headings of name, personality, role as sister, leader and prophetess, the song (Exod. 15), slander (Num. 12), Miriam's well (see Bach below), her death, and gender issues. The same classification obtains for feminist readings, with the addition of sections about Miriam as daughter, perpetuator of family continuity, her relationship with God, and her punishment. The comparison of these two types of learning are gratifying for their obvious differences as well as surprising similarities.

Miriam is, according to Exod. 15.21-22, a poet and a musician. In 'Miriam Reimagined, and Imaginary Women of Exodus in Musical Settings', Helen Leneman begins by writing:

> Music is a universal art, a form of midrash (creative re-writing,) and the most emotional medium for transmitting a story. Composers set biblical stories because they were inspired by the story and characters; their music brings new dimensions to both. This article will explore the texts of various musical settings written for Miriam and for imaginary women of Exodus. These texts will be translated, discussed, and compared. Each will be treated as a 'musical midrash' which amplifies women's voices and gives their character new dimensions.

Leneman proceeds to retell Miriam and other Exodus women, textual or imagined, in song (*Miriam's Song* by Charles Avison; *Miriams Siegesgesang* by Franz Schubert; *Miriams Siegesgesang* by Carl Reinecke), oratorio (*Israel in Egypt* by Georg Frederic Handel; *Il Mosé* by Lorenzo Perosi; *Mosé* by Adolph Mar) and in opera (*Mosé in Egitto* and *Moïse et Pharaon* by Gioacchino Rossini; *Il Mosé* by Giacomo Orefice). The emphasis is, of course, on the librettos. These are extensively quoted and partly translated by the article's author herself. An appendix supplies several German originals.

In 'Dreaming of Miriam's Well', Alice Bach takes up one of the themes mentioned by Kramer as existing in both rabbinic and feminist midrashim on Miriam. In her own words:

> Midrashic storytelling, revisioning the biblical narrative from one's own perspective, points toward a contrapuntal, nomadic style of reading. Such a reading eludes the borders of accepted reading conventions and makes no claims for historical truth. As a student of modern midrash, I am challenged by the power of narrative expansion—and as a student of ancient haggadic midrash I feel constrained by scholarly reliance upon the dating and provenance of each text in determining its authenticity—and value.

After problematizing the relevance, methodology and usefulness of the midrash genre and its contemporary offspring, including short discussion of the film the *Prince of Egypt* as a visual midrash, Bach proceeds to present an ostensibly 'ancient midrash' called the *Book of Miriam*, again ostensibly from the middle ages and translated by Leonard Angel. She concludes by saying:

> The *Book of Miriam* is a true midrash of the Other. As such it debates the historical and political construction of identities and Self/Other relations. It allows the voice of the Other to come through the level of the doxa text. This Miriam has been de-doxified, and as such she has sung a revolutionary Song of the Sea.

In 'The Authority of Miriam: A Feminist Rereading of Numbers 12, Prompted by Jewish Interpretation', Irmtraud Fischer re-examines the narrative of Numbers 12 about the conflict between Aaron and Miriam on the one hand, Yhwh and Moses on the other. A close reading indicates that there are tensions in the story's present form. Fischer rejects a source-critical solution for explaining the tensions away. Instead, she opts for an explanation of tensions as reflecting narrative intentionality. Ultimately, she asks, Who is behind the three textual 'siblings' at the time of the text's composition? Or, differently put, what is the sociohistorical location of the conflict described? And what is the link made in the Numbers 12 story, with its internal tensions, between prophecy, Torah, time/location, and gender relations? After giving some surprising answers to these questions, Fischer concludes with a fresh look at the story's mixed message for contemporary womanly readers.

Part III
Third Revisit: Daughters

The issue of biblical daughterly inheritance is quite a popular one for feminists, and over the past decades attempts have been made to view it as an actual if sometimes conditioned practice in the Hebrew Bible as well as in several cognate cultures. In 'The Daughters of Zelophehad and Women's Inheritance: The Biblical Injunction and Its Outcome', Tal Ilan continues the discussion back from the perspective of Jewish studies. In her view, the biblical law of inheritance is clearly spelt out. Its successor, the rabbinic deed of gift as a Jewish legal tool, is an innovation. Therefore, in their legal discussions the rabbis had to make sure that their formulation of the latter did not appear to be a violation of the former. In effect, deeds of gift, particularly those formulated so as to be executed after the death of their author, were the forerunners of the Jewish will. Yet all Jewish deeds of gift from the Judean Desert and all those found in the much earlier Jewish archive of Elephantine, dating from the Persian period, were written on behalf of women—wives and daughters. Clearly, the ramifications of the daughters of Zelophehad's episode were at work here

The final article of this collection is about 'Seraḥ and the Exodus: A Midrashic Miracle', by Leila Leah Bronner. Seraḥ daughter of Asher is not a prominent Exodus woman. Her name appears three times in lists (Gen. 46.17; Num. 26.46; 1 Chron. 7.30), and there is no story linked to her name. Curiously enough, the midrash fills her figure in by allocating liberating functions to this figure. Thus, she facilitates the Exodus by finding Joseph's bones, without which the Exodus cannot commence, and is accredited with divine inspiration, wisdom, and longevity.

> The midrashic stories about Seraḥ bat Asher are the most astonishing, both in content and presentation. No other biblical woman sparks an equivalent interest in the rabbis. From three appearances of her name in the Scriptures, they fashion a multifaceted woman who is without parallel in Jewish literature.

writes Bronner. And she continues:

> But Seraḥ is not the only woman of the Exodus made exceptional in the Midrash… [T]he Talmud also claims heroism for every woman in the days of Exodus, saying that 'as the reward for the righteous women who lived in that generation [Exodus] were the Israelites delivered from Egypt'. For women of our time, the legends of these women are a gift to reclaim.

But this last assertion, on which Bronner concludes her contribution, is for each reader to contemplate, together with the opposite view about rabbis, women, and gender issues in the Bible and in ancient Judaisms.

Part I

FIRST REVISIT: EXODUS AND MOSES

THE COMPLEXITIES OF 'HIS' LIBERATION TALK:
A LITERARY FEMINIST READING OF THE BOOK OF EXODUS*

Susanne Scholz

The book of Exodus has inspired the imagination of writers, artists, musicians, and theologians throughout the centuries. The tale of oppression suffered by the Israelites in Egypt and their subsequent escape to Mount Sinai is the most well known of biblical stories. People who know little of the Bible have heard of the revelation of God in the burning bush, the plagues against the Egyptians, the parting of the Reed Sea, the giving of the Ten Commandments, and the dance around the golden calf. Even they know that Moses rescued the Israelites from slavery and personally conversed with God.

During the twentieth century the book of Exodus received significant attention from Christian biblical scholars and liberation theologians. Historical critics, such as Martin Noth and Gerhard von Rad, valued the Exodus narrative as the historical and theological starting point of ancient Israel. Latin American and black American liberation theologians grounded their theologies on the Exodus story, identifying with the oppressed people of Israel.[1] Feminist theologians, too, related the narrative to their situation as women in the churches. For instance, in 1972, Mary Daly encouraged women to become an 'Exo-

---

*   This article is a slightly revised translation of my German essay: 'Exodus: Was Befreiung aus "seiner" Sicht bedeutet...', in Luise Schottroff and Marie-Theres Wacker (eds.), *Kompendium Feministische Bibelauslegung* (Gütersloh: Gütersloher Verlag, 1997), pp. 26-39.

1.   See, e.g., Albert J. Raboteau, 'African-Americans, Exodus, and the American Israel', in Paul E. Johnson (ed.), *African-American Christianity: Essays in History* (Berkeley: University of California, 1994), pp. 1-17; Peter Hebblethwaite, 'Let My People Go: The Exodus and Liberation Theology', *Religion, State and Society* 21.1 (1993), pp. 105-14; Bas van Iersel and A. Weiler (eds.), *Exodus: A Lasting Paradigm*, (Edinburgh: T. & T. Clark, 1987); James A. Loader, 'Exodus, Liberation Theology and Theological Argument', *Journal of Theology for Southern Africa* 59 (July 1987), pp. 3-18; M.J. Oosthuizen, 'Scripture and Context: The Use of the Exodus Theme in the Hermeneutics of Liberation Theology', *Scriptura* 25 (1988), pp. 7-22.

dus Community' and to leave their male-dominated religion, Christianity.[2]

Despite this general interest in the Exodus story feminist biblical scholars approached the book only reluctantly. The story of the oppression and the liberation of Israel posed considerable difficulties, once feminist perspectives guided the exegesis. When feminists examine biblical texts they usually focus on historical, literary, and theological representations of women. The problem with the book of Exodus, however, is that it contains few female characters and issues of feminist concern. Only the initial chapters, the middle part, and several brief comments throughout the book refer to women. As a result, not many feminist scholars have dealt with Exodus. If they did, they interpreted only the few sections about women and disregarded the rest.[3]

Remedying the situation, this article offers a feminist interpretation of the whole book and particularly integrates the feminist work. The article is based on the belief that female characters in the Bible are male constructs and, as such, they illuminate issues of sexism, racism, ethnocentrism, or classism.[4] Disclosing the androcentric perspective of the book of Exodus, the article offers a literary reading of the final form of the text.[5] Two parts structure the 40 chapters. The first part establishes Moses as the leader of the people of Israel (1.1–18.27). The second part describes how the Israelites learn to acknowledge God as their savior (19.1–40.38). Since the historicity of the Exodus events has occupied scholarly attention for some time, the recent study of Keith W. Whitelam should at least be mentioned. Whitelam's work exam-

2. Mary Daly, 'The Women's Movement: An Exodus Community', *Religious Education* 67 (Sep.–Oct. 1972), pp. 327-35. See also Dianne Bergant, 'Exodus as a Paradigm in Feminist Theology', in Iersel and Weiler, *Exodus*, pp. 100-106.

3. For a prominent feminist treatment of Exodus, cf. Drorah O'Donnnell Setel, 'Exodus', in Carol A. Newsom and Sharon H. Ringe (eds.), *Women's Bible Commentary: Expanded Edition with Apocrypha* (Louisville, KY: Westminster/John Knox Press, 1998), pp. 26-35. See also Tikva Frymer-Kensky, 'Forgotten Heroines of the Exodus: The Exclusion of Women from Moses' Vision', *BR* 13 (December 1997), pp. 38-44.

4. J. Cheryl Exum, 'Second Thoughts about Secondary Characters: Women in Exodus 1.8–2.10', in Athalya Brenner (ed.), *A Feminist Companion to Exodus to Deuteronomy* (Sheffield: Sheffield Academic Press, 1994), pp. 75-87; Renita Weems, 'The Hebrew Women Are Not Like the Egyptian Women: The Ideology of Race, Gender and Sexual Reproduction in Exodus 1', *Semeia* 59 (1992), pp. 25-34.

5. For the definition of 'androcentrism', see Ina Praetorius, 'Androzentrismus', in Elisabeth Gössmann *et al.* (eds.), *Wörterbuch der feministischen Theologie* (Gütersloh: Gütersloher Verlag, 1991), pp. 14-15.

ines the epistemological difficulties of reconstructing the history of ancient Israel. Whitelam demonstrates that political and religious convictions of biblical scholars decisively shaped their histories, a situation that pertains also to the book of Exodus.[6] A literary reading is thus a legitimate and desirable alternative for understanding the content and form of the Exodus narrative.

Part One: Exodus 1.1–18.27
The Establishment of Moses as the Leader of the Israelites

In Part One four sections describe the birth of Moses, his call to leadership, the escape from Egypt, the rebellion of the Israelites against Moses, and the wandering in the wilderness to Mount Sinai (1.1–2.25; 3.1–6.30; 7.1–15.21; 15.22–18.27).

Exodus 1.1–2.25: The Birth and Early Life of Moses
Arranged in a chiasm, seven literary units depict the circumstances at the time of Moses' birth and his early life. The first unit (1.1-7) summarizes briefly the situation (A). The second unit (1.8-14) reports a change (B). The third (1.15-21) describes an imminent danger (C). The fourth (1.22–2.10) depicts the circumstances of the birth of Moses (D). The fifth (2.11-15) mentions another imminent danger (C'). The sixth (2.16-22) reports another change (B'). The seventh (2.23-25) contains another summary (A'). The whole segment centers on the birth of Moses. He is surrounded by different women who rescue him and other sons. The following literary structure emerges:[7]

6. Keith W. Whitelam, *The Invention of Ancient Israel* (New York: Routledge, 1996). For further discussions on the historical reconstructions of ancient Israel, see, e.g., Marc Vervenne, 'Current Tendencies and Developments in the Study of the Book of Exodus', in Marc Vervenne (ed.), *Studies in the Book of Exodus* (Leuven: Leuven University Press, 1996), pp. 21-59; Jonathan Adler, 'Dating the Exodus: A New Perspective', *JBQ* 23 (1995), pp. 44-51; Baruch Halpern, 'The Exodus from Egypt: Myth or Reality', in Hershel Shanks *et al.* (eds.), *The Rise of Ancient Israel* (Washington, DC: Biblical Archaeology Society, 1992), pp. 86-117.

7. See Lawrence Boadt, 'Divine Wonders Never Cease: The Birth of Moses in God's Plan of Exodus', in Frederick C. Holmgren and Herman E. Schaalman (eds.), *Preaching Biblical Texts: Exposition by Jewish and Christian Scholars* (Grand Rapids: Eerdmans, 1995), pp. 46-61; Ina Willi-Plein, 'Ort und literarische Funktion der Geburtsgeschichte des Mose', *VT* 41 (1991), pp. 110-18; *idem, Das Buch vom Auszug: 2. Mose (Exodus)* (Neukirchen–Vlyun: Neukirchener Verlag, 1988); Beat Weber, ' "Jede Tochter aber sollt ihr am Leben lassen!" Beobachtungen zu Exod. 1, 15–2, 10 und seinem Kontext aus literaturwissenschaftlicher Perspektive', *BN* 55 (1990), pp. 47-76.

A Summary (1.1-7)
  B Change (1.8-14)
    C Danger (1.15-21)
      D Birth of Moses (1.22–2.10)
    C' Danger (2.11-15)
  B' Change (2.16-22)
A' Summary (2.23-25)

1.1-7 (A): The first summary links the events to Joseph and his broth-ers in Genesis. After Jacob moved to his son Joseph in Egypt (Gen. 50.22-23) where the family prospered, Exod. 1.1-7 reports the deaths of the male family members. The wives and daughters of Joseph and his brothers are not mentioned. From the beginning male pronouns and verbal constructions indicate that men are more important than women.

1.8-14 (B): The privileged situation of the Israelites soon changes. The time of harmonious coexistence in Egypt is over when a new pharaoh begins to rule. The pharaoh does not know Jacob or Joseph and com-mands his people to persecute the Israelites. The new ruler believes that their population growth threatens his own people (v. 9). He thus forces them into slavery. The enslavement is supposed to discourage the Israelites from reproduction but they continue to give birth in high numbers (v. 12). Consequently, the Egyptian taskmasters mistreat the Israelites even more and make 'their lives bitter with hard service in mortar and brick and every kind of field labor' (v. 14). The Israelites, however, do not revolt. Silently, they submit to their fate, enduring their enslavement and building Egyptian cities. A subtle literary fea-ture emphasizes the pharaoh's position of power in contrast to the powerlessness of the Israelites. He speaks directly (vv. 9-10) whereas the Israelites do not. Only narrated discourse describes their situation (v. 13).

1.15-21 (C): Since the enslavement does not reduce the Israelite birth rate, the new king devises another measure. He talks to the midwives Shifrah and Puah whose national identities remain grammatically am-biguous. Are they Hebrew or Egyptian? The grammar allows for either possibility. Yet for the first time two women appear. They have names that emphasize their importance. A nameless king faces the midwives Shifrah and Puah.

Although feminist interpreters have highlighted this inequality that favors the female characters,[8] Shifrah and Puah appear in roles typical

---

8. Renate Ellmenreich, '2. Mose 1, 15-21: Pua und Schiphra—Zwei Frauen im

for women. They care for and save babies, the proper tasks for women in an androcentric perspective. Although the narrative stresses their significance, they do not cross gender-specific roles. As long as they act according to these roles, the androcentric storyteller allows them even to outwit the Egyptian king.

The prominent position of the midwives is problematic for another reason. The unusual emphasis on the women allows the storyteller to characterize the pharaoh as particularly despicable: he is foolish enough to be tricked by women. The narrator twists the story even more. Not only midwives but also 'daughters', including his own, outwit the pharaoh. He commands all his people to kill the male newborns while females—young and old, Egyptian and Hebrew—rescue the babies. In fact, the king misjudges the situation so severely that his biggest enemy survives with the help of women, who are the lowest valued members of society. This twist is the real irony of the androcentric tale.

The midwives take advantage of royal prejudice. To defend themselves they refer to ethnic differences between Egyptian and Israelite women. Presupposing those prejudices, the king is at their mercy. He is unable to prevent the birth of his true opponent. However, the narrative does not criticize the national, ethnic and gender stereotypes that emerge in the description of the royal impotence.[9]

1.22–2.10 (D): Twelve women guarantee Moses' well-being during his youth and early adulthood. Indeed, they ensure his very survival.[10] At the time of his birth he owes his life to four women: the two midwives, his mother, and his sister. Eight more women help him during infancy and early adulthood. The pharaoh's daughter disobeys her father and raises the infant as her son. According to 2.16-22 seven women support him years later. One of them, Zipporah, even marries him.

Widerstand', in Eva Renate Schmidt, Mieke Korenhof and Renate Jost (eds.), *Feministisch gelesen*, I (Stuttgart: Kreuz, 1988), pp. 39-44; Cresy John *et al.* 'An Asian Feminist Perspective: The Exodus Story (Exodus 1.8-22; 2.1-10): An Asian Group Work', in R.S. Sugirtharajah (ed.), *Voices from the Margin: Interpreting the Bible in the Third World* (Maryknoll, NY: Orbis Books, 1991), pp. 267-79.

9.   Weems, 'Hebrew Women', p. 32.

10.   Jopie Siebert-Hommes, 'But if She Be a Daughter… She May Live! "Daughters" and "Sons" in Exodus 1–2', in Brenner (ed.), *Exodus to Deuteronomy*, pp. 62-74, 71. See also her monograph *Let the Daughters Live! The Literary Architecture of Exodus 1–2* (Leiden: E.J. Brill, 1998).

Feminist scholars have long suggested that the third attempt by the king to reduce the Israelite birthrate takes a central place in 1.1–2.25. The literary structure of the story about Moses' birth centers on Moses. His mother and sister surround the pharaoh's daughter. She surrounds the newborn Moses. Jopie Siebert-Hommes delineated the following literary structure:[11]

> Introduction: the man, the daughter, the Levite (2.1)
> A Birth of the *Son* (2.2)
>   B *Mother* lets child go (2.3)
>   C *Sister* looks from a distance (2.4)
>   D Pharaoh's *Daughter* sees basket (2.5)
>   E the *Child* (2.6a)
>   D' Pharaoh's *Daughter* has compassion (2.6b)
>   C' *Sister* negotiates (2.7-8)
>   B' *Mother* gets child back (2.9)
> A' adoption of the *Son* (2.10)

The literary unit begins and ends with Moses. He is also its center. All women involved care actively for his well-being. Their presence and cooperation protect him against the imminent threat of the pharaoh. In contrast to the named midwives (1.15-21), the women of this passage are nameless. Only their relationships to men give them identity. The daughter of the pharaoh remains doubly anonymous: she is a nameless daughter of a nameless pharaoh. Her social and ethnic background is more important than her name. Among all these nameless women only the male infant Moses has a name.

The Hebrew text contains an interesting detail that blurs the boundaries between the mother of Moses and the daughter of Pharaoh. In 2.10b the daughter of the pharaoh is explicitly called 'daughter of Pharaoh'. The mother is described only with the pronoun 'she': 'And she took him to the daughter of Pharaoh' (v. 10b). The following sentence declares that 'Moses was to her like a son' (v. 10c). Although the pronoun 'her' relates to the pharaoh's daughter, the narrator creates an intentional ambiguity. Except for v. 10b the narrator uses only third person feminine pronouns in v. 10 to refer both to the pharaoh's daughter and the mother. This multiple use of feminine pronouns creates a certain ambiguous identity between daughter and mother. For instance, the pronoun in v. 10c is feminine singular as in v. 10b ('she'). The ambiguity indicates that the narrator does not clearly dis-

---

11. Jopie Siebert-Hommes, 'Die Geburtsgeschichte des Mose innerhalb des Erzählzusammenhangs von Exodus I und II', *VT* 42 (1992), pp. 398-404.

tinguish between mother and daughter. They are represented as one in caring for Moses.

Another literary observation supports the conclusion that the individual identities of the women do not matter much to the storyteller. Even if one assumes that Moses receives his name from the pharaoh's daughter, the name makes sense only figuratively. Not the daughter herself but a servant draws the infant out of the water (2.5). Arguably, it could mean that the mother also draws Moses out. She places the basket in the river and thus provides the opportunity for his rescue (2.3). In other words, both women participate in saving Moses since the literal sense of the name does not apply to either one.

Another detail related to the name of Moses elucidates the androcentrism of the narrative. Some interpreters proposed that the pharaoh's daughter chooses a name similar to the Egyptian Tutmoses, Amoses or Ramoses. Others emphasized that v. 10 explains the Hebrew origin of the name that is incongruous with Hebrew grammar. Since the name 'Moses' consists of an active and not a passive participle, the name really means 'the one who pulls out' and not 'the one who is pulled out'. In other words, the name points already toward the future role of Moses as the savior of Israel. The actual meaning of the name focuses on Moses and lessens the contribution of the women to the survival of Moses.[12]

The high number of women in chapters 1 and 2 has prompted feminists to emphasize the significance of women in the history of ancient Israel. Without these women the Exodus could not have happened, and so their efforts helped all Israelites.[13] This enthusiastic response, however, does not take into account that the women are only concerned about male infants and one male infant in particular. The commitment of the women enables the male protagonist to survive and to grow into his leadership position. After the days of childcare and special support for Moses are over, women disappear from the story.

Many feminists have cherished 1.22–2.10 as a prototype story because it teaches women to live in solidarity with each other.[14] Over-

---

12. J. Cheryl Exum, 'You Shall Let Every Daughter Live: A Study of Exodus 1:8-2:10', *Semeia* 28 (1983), pp. 63-82.

13. E.g. Ellmenreich, 'Pua und Schiphra'; Exum, 'You Shall Let Every Daughter Live'; Esther Gebhardt, '2. Mose 2:1-10: Frauen für das Leben', in Schmidt, Korenhof and Jost (eds.), *Feministisch gelesen,* II (Stuttgart: Kreuz, 1989), pp. 55-62; Siebert-Hommes, 'But if She Be a Daughter', in Brenner (ed.) *Exodus to Deuteronomy*, pp. 62-74.

14. E.g. Canny Aratangi, 'Born Into A Living Hope: The Role of the Midwives

coming ethnic, religious, and social differences, mother, sister and the pharaoh's daughter care for the infant who eventually escapes the cruel order of the king. However, the characterization of these women as heroines is problematic. The women stay within traditional gender boundaries that are never challenged or subverted by the narrative.

2.11-15 (C'): From this point on the narrative attends only to the immediate events concerning Moses. The element of danger returns (cf. 1.15-21). Moses is an adult now who is curious about the welfare of his 'brothers'. The story does not explain how Moses knows that the Israelites are his 'brothers'. He witnesses an Egyptian guard killing an Israelite man. In turn, Moses kills the guard. Shortly afterwards, Moses fails to make peace between two Israelite men. They accuse him of killing an Egyptian and question his right to interfere into their affairs. Moses becomes afraid. Neither an Egyptian nor an Israelite, he finds himself in limbo. He flees Egypt when the pharaoh seeks his life. The incident demonstrates that Moses is far from being the leader of Israel. The two Israelite men not only question his leadership qualities, they consider him an Egyptian. But women do not appear in the narrative. Egyptian and Israelite men dominate the events.

2.16-22 (B'): The element of change (cf. 1.8-14) reappears. Moses escapes to Midian where he rests at a well. In the genre of the betrothal scene, the passage describes how Moses meets his future wife, Zipporah.[15] When the seven daughters of the priest of Midian arrive at the scene, Moses helps them to give water to their sheep. In return, they invite him to their home and introduce him to their father as an 'Egyptian' man (2.19). Thereupon Reuel, who is called Jethro elsewhere, offers him his daughter Zipporah as a wife (2.21b). The next verse skips at least nine months. Verse 22 reports that Zipporah gives birth to a son whom Moses, his father, calls Gershom, because 'I have been an alien resident (גֵּר) in a foreign land'. The mother does not speak. Moses remains at the center. Even the name of his son relates to him.

2.23-25 (A'): Similarly to 1.1-7, this unit describes the ensuing events in a short summary. The king who enslaved the Israelites dies. They

Shiprah and Puah: Exodus 1:15-21', *Pacific Journal of Theology* 4 (1990), pp. 41-44; Kristina Kerscher, 'God's First Instrument of Liberation', *Bible Today* (1995), pp. 359-63; Elizabeth S. Tapia, 'The Story of Shiphrah and Puah: Disobedient or Subservient Women?' *CTC Bulletin* 10 (May–Dec. 1991), pp. 398-404.
    15.   Robert Alter, *The Art of Biblical Narrative* (New York: Basic Books, 1981).

groan and cry to God who responds in remembrance of the covenant with the patriarchs Abraham, Isaac and Jacob. The text does not include the matriarchs Sarah, Rebecca, Leah and Rachel. The androcentric perspective validates only the men.

Descriptions about the situation of the Israelites in Egypt frame the report of the birth of Moses and his escape to Midian. The literary structure of 1.1–2.25 emphasizes the centrality of Moses (D) who will shape the future of the Israelites. Without further digression the next section turns to this center.

Exodus 3.1–6.30: The Call of Moses as the Leader of the Israelites and his Objections

3.1–4.17: Appearing 14 times, the Hebrew root 'to see' is the keyword of the passage. The root links this unit to the previous one. As God 'saw' (ראה) the sons of Israel (2.25) so, for example, Moses sees the burning bush (3.2), God appeared to Moses (3.16, ראה, *nif.*), and God did not appear to Moses (4.2, ראה, *nif.*). Other repetitions further connect the call narrative with the previous unit. The names of 'Abraham, Isaac and Jacob' appear in the summary of 2.24 and in the speech of God in 3.6 (cf. also 3.15-16; 4.5). The Hebrew root of 'to know' (ידע) appears in 2.25 and 3.7. The latter verse explains what remains unspoken in 2.25. In 3.7 God knows the 'sufferings' of the Israelites. Another Hebrew root, ענה (here 'to oppress', *pi.*), is repeated in 1.11 and 3.7, and so links 3.1–4.17 to 1.1–2.25.

God appoints Moses as the leader of the Israelites to bring them to the land flowing with milk and honey (3.17). The speech (3.14-22) mentions the women of Israel. They are asked to get jewelry and clothing from the Egyptian women and to dress the sons and daughters of Israel (3.22). After the earlier description as mothers and caretakers of infants, women now appear in the context of fashion. Moses continues to be the center of the speech.

The future leader recognizes immediately that he has problems with the call. Five times he attempts to change God's mind (3.11, 13; 4.1, 10, 13). Five times God responds (3.12, 14-22; 4.2-9, 11-12, 14-17). The answers encourage Moses to accept the call. In 3.12 God tries to comfort Moses: 'I will be with you.' Several verses later God promises again to be on his side: 'I will be with your mouth and with his [i.e. Aaron's] mouth and will teach you what you shall do' (4.15). Moses, however, remains hesitant. He does not trust God's promise. He devises three further objections until God becomes angry (4.14) and simply commands Moses what to do (4.16). A hierarchical solution ends the debate.

From a theological perspective one answer is particularly significant. It includes an explanation for the name of God that contains an image of God beyond androcentrism: 'I will be what I will be' (3.14). Although the storyteller uses elsewhere only male pronouns and verbal constructions for God, the definition in v. 14 imagines God beyond male vocabulary. Moreover, the explanation does not presuppose the divine as fixed and unchangeable. On the contrary, the image is dynamic and flexible. Due to the characteristics of the Hebrew tense system,[16] the verbs in v. 14 can be translated into the future tense ('I will be what I will be') as well as the present tense ('I am what I am'). A combination of present and future tense is also possible: 'I am what I will be' or 'I will be what I am'. In Hebrew the relative pronoun does not differentiate between things ('which') and persons ('who'), and so the sentence could also be translated: 'I will be *who* I will be.' The divine answer in v. 14, then, offers an important alternative to the male-dominated discourse in the rest of the book of Exodus.[17]

4.18-26: After his call Moses decides to move with his wife and son to Egypt. His father-in-law encourages him to do so in direct discourse. His wife, however, does not speak. Another speech of God (vv. 21-23) instructs Moses that the pharaoh has to release the Israelites because Israel is God's 'first-born son'. If the pharaoh does not allow them to leave, God threatens to kill all first-born males of Egypt. The doublet in v. 19 and v. 20 as well as the unclear sequence of vv. 18-26 suggested to historical critics that the passage consists of two sources (J, E).[18] Scholars also proposed that the unit is a secondary addition because of the dubious content.[19] However, for the first and only time Zipporah speaks. She says: 'Truly you are a bridegroom of blood to

16. For the Hebrew tense system see, e.g., Thomas O. Lambdin, *Introduction to Biblical Hebrew* (New York: Charles Scribner's Sons, 1971), p. 100.

17. Stanley A. Dreyfus, 'The Burning Bush Through the Eyes of Midrash: God's Word Then and Now', in Holmgren and Schaalman (eds.), *Preaching Biblical Texts*, pp. 62-75; Ee-Kon Kim, 'Who is Yahweh: Based on a Contextual Reading of Exodus 3:14', *Asia Journal of Theology* 3 (April 1989), pp. 108-17.

18. For a brief summary of the issues involved, see, e.g., Brevard S. Childs, *The Book of Exodus: A Critical, Theological Commentary* (Philadelphia: Westminster Press, 1974), pp. 94-95.

19. Josiah Derby, 'Why Did God Want to Kill Moses?', *JBQ* 18 (1989), pp. 222-29; Terry John Lehane, 'Zipporah and the Passover', *JBQ* 24 (1996), pp. 46-50; Pamela Tamarkin Reis, 'The Bridegroom of Blood: A New Reading', *Judaism* 159.40 (1991), pp. 324-31; Gisela Schneemann, 'Die Deutung und Bedeutung der Beschneidung nach Exodus 4, 24-26', *Communio viatorum* 32.1-2 (1989), pp. 21-37.

me' (v. 25), and 'A bridegroom of blood by circumcision' (v. 26). Saving Moses, Zipporah is the agent. But the androcentric storyteller transmits an unintelligible fragment that erases the meaning of Zipporah's words and thus her significance.

4.27–6.30: Aaron supports his brother when Moses tries to persuade the people with several signs (4.27-31). The ensuing negotiations with the Egyptian king, however, lead only to increasingly severe circumstances for the Hebrews. The pharaoh orders the taskmasters: 'You shall no longer give the people straw to make bricks, as before; let them go and gather straw for themselves. But you shall require of them the same quantity of bricks' (5.7-8). Finally, God calls Moses another time (6.2-8). The vocabulary 'to know' (6.7) and 'Abraham, Isaac and Jacob' (6.8) link this passage to the earlier call (3.1–4.17). Moses and Aaron go again to the Egyptian king to demand the release of the Israelites.

An extensive genealogy interrupts the events. Strengthening the authority of Moses (6.14-25), the list legitimates him as the leader of the people of Israel. The passage includes his male and a few female ancestors. The women are characterized as daughters, wives and mothers. Again, women are significant only in their relationship to men (cf. 1.27–2.10). Jochebed, the mother of Moses, is named (6.20) but not Moses' sister and wife. Instead, Aaron's wife Elisheba (6.23) and the daughters of Putiel are listed. One of the daughters marries Eleazar and gives birth to a son (6.25).

Sending Moses to the pharaoh, two speeches of God (6.10-13, 26-30) frame the genealogy. Divine authority surrounds the origins of Moses. Still, Moses resists. A final expression of Moses' hesitation ends the unit. In 6.30 Moses rejects the call a last time: 'Since I am a poor speaker, why would Pharaoh listen to me?' However, the question remains unanswered. God does not respond anymore. The next section simply describes the negotiations between Moses and Pharaoh.

Exodus 7.1–15.21: The Defeat of Egypt and the Victory Songs of Moses and Miriam

7.1–13.16: The pharaoh adheres to Moses' demand after ten plagues afflicted nature and humans in Egypt. The plagues fall into three groups, each containing three plagues. Only the tenth plague stands by itself.[20] The severity of the plagues increases steadily. From the

20.   Gunther Plaut, *The Torah: A Modern Commentary* (New York: Union of Amer-

first group (bloody waters, frogs, lice) to the second (insects, pestilence, boils) to the third (hail, locusts, darkness), the last and tenth plague is the worst: God kills all Egyptian first-born males.[21]

The duel between Moses and Pharaoh is severe. Hardened by God (4.21; 7.3), the pharaoh does not release the Israelites for the duration of nine plagues (e.g. 7.22; 8.15, 28; 9.7). After the tenth plague God softens the heart of the pharaoh (11.1) so that the pharaoh 'knows' God (7.17; 8.6). Only then the pharaoh agrees to let the Israelites go (12.31). The violent struggle between the Egyptian magicians and Moses finds an end. While the Israelites wait in their houses and celebrate Passover for the first time, the Egyptians scream in anguish, pain and despair (12.29-30). According to God's announcement, first-born males of poor and rich, of humans and animals are killed (11.5) while Israelite men implement the Passover (12.3-20). Protected or killed, men stand at the center of the narrative.

13.17–14.31: The story continues to narrate the escape of the people from Egypt. As 'a mixed crowd' (12.38) they head towards the desert. God leads them as a pillar of fire or clouds. Moving to the Reed Sea, they try to escape the Egyptian army. In great fear the people cry to God while they accuse Moses: 'For it would have been better for us to serve the Egyptians than to die in the wilderness' (14.12). God, however, does not respond to the people. God speaks only to Moses. Special powers of Moses and the forces of nature enable the Israelites to escape. When the soldiers pursue them on the dry ocean ground, the waves return. Washing on the shore (14.30), the dead bodies convince the people of the power of God. Finally, they 'believe' in God and 'his servant Moses' (14.31).

15.1-21: The victory song of Moses (vv. 1-18) and the short song of Miriam (v. 21) follow the victory against Egypt. Miriam is even called a 'prophet' (v. 20). However, Rita Burns maintains that this title was added secondarily since other references to Miriam do not support her in this position.[22]

---

ican Hebrew Congregations, 1981). For a different numbering of the plagues, see Pss. 78.43-51 and 105.26-36, which mention only seven plagues.

21. Terence E. Fretheim, 'The Plagues as Ecological Signs of Historical Disaster', *JBL* 110 (1991), pp. 385-96.

22. Rita J. Burns, *Has the Lord Indeed Spoken Only Through Moses? A Study of the Biblical Portrait of Miriam* (SBLDS, 84; Atlanta: Scholars Press, 1987).

Feminist scholars have highlighted the significance of Miriam's song as one of the oldest songs in the Hebrew Bible.[23] For example, Burns claims that the song preserves an old liturgical tradition, which celebrated God as a divine warrior. J. Gerald Janzen changes the literary order of the events. He suggests that the song of Miriam preceded the song of Moses. Originally, Miriam's song followed the events in 14.16-30, and Moses' song followed the reaction of the people in 14.31.[24] Marie-Theres Wacker stresses another intriguing detail. She translates the song of Miriam: 'Sing to the LORD/for he has triumphed gloriously/horse and chariot (ורכבו סוס)/ he has thrown into the sea' (v. 21). Her interpretation tackles the ethical problem that Miriam seems to celebrate the death of the Egyptian soldiers ('riders'). She translates the consonants *rkb* (רכב) as 'chariot' (רֶכֶב) and not as 'rider' (רָכָב). According to Wacker, Miriam celebrates only the destruction of war materials, whereas Moses' song celebrates the death of the Egyptian men.[25]

The appearance of Miriam at this crucial juncture encouraged feminist exegetes to follow the literary traces of Miriam in the Hebrew Bible. Miriam is mentioned in Num. 12.1-15; 20.1; 26.59; Deut. 24.8-9; 1 Chron. 5.29; and Mic. 6.4. Some consider her as an equal leader next to Moses and Aaron.[26] Others claim her as a role model for Jewish and Christian women.[27] However, Miriam emerges as a different

23. E.g. Ana Flora Anderson and Gilberto Da Silva Gorgulho, 'Miriam and Her Companions', in Marc H. Ellis and Otto Madura (eds.), *The Future of Liberation Theology: Essays in Honor of Gustavo Gutiérrez* (Maryknoll, NY : Orbis Books, 1989), pp. 205-21; Brazilian Pastoral Workers, 'Miriam', *Estudos Biblicos* 29 (1991), pp. 37-39; George J. Brook, 'A Long-Lost Song of Miriam', *BARev* 20 (May–June 1994), pp. 62-65; Elisabeth Lüneburg, '2. Mose 15,20f: Schlagt die Trommeln, tanzt und fürchtet euch nicht!', in Schmidt, Korenhof and Jost (eds.), *Feministisch Gelesen*, II, pp. 45-52; Phyllis Trible, 'Subversive Justice: Tracing the Miriamic Traditions', in Douglas A. Knight and Peter J. Paris (eds.), *Justice and the Holy: Essays in Honor of Walter Harrelson* (Atlanta: Scholars Press, 1989), pp. 99-109; Marie-Theres Wacker, 'Miriam: Kritischer Mut einer Prophetin', in Karin Walter (ed.), *Zwischen Ohnmacht und Befreiung: Biblische Frauengestalten* (Freiburg: Herder, 1988), pp. 44-52.

24. J. Gerald Janzen, 'Song of Moses, Song of Miriam: Who Is Seconding Whom?' *CBQ* 54 (1992), pp. 211-20 (reprinted in Brenner (ed.), *Exodus to Deuteronomy*, pp. 187-99).

25. For the ambiguous grammar of this verse, see also R. Ficker, '*rkb* to ride, drive', in Ernst Jenni and Claus Westermann (eds.), *Theological Lexicon of the Old Testament*, III (Peabody, MA: Hendrickson, 1997), p. 1238.

26. See, e.g., Trible, 'Subversive Justice'.

27. E.g. Penina V. Adelman, *Miriam's Well: Rituals for Jewish Women Around the Year* (Fresh Meadows, NY: Biblio, 1986); Heidemarie Langer and Herta Leistner,

character in an interpretation that focuses on the androcentric aspects. Miriam's song is only one verse long and describes her as the leader of women. In contrast, 19 verses contain Moses' song and describe him as the leader of the whole people. In addition, v. 20 characterizes Miriam as Aaron's and not as Moses' sister. The omission conceals her relationship to Moses and her imminent role in his survival. Miriam is a marginal figure. In accordance with the androcentric perspective of the entire book, Moses figures prominently in chapter 15.

Exodus 15.22–18.27: The Complaints of the Israelites against Moses and the Recognition of his Leadership

15.22–18.27: After the events at the Reed Sea Moses guides the Israelites in the wilderness. Three times they resist his leadership for lack of water and food (15.22-25; 16.1-36; 17.1-7; cf. also Num. 14.1-4; 17.6). In all three stories Moses functions as the mediator between the people and God. At first the Israelites arrive at Marah where the water is undrinkable (15.22-26). Although the people cried to God during their enslavement (2.23) and later at the Reed Sea (14.10), this time they turn to Moses and not to God (15.24). God, however, responds only to Moses with a first set of commandments. The speech introduces God as a healer (15.26). The speech also announces that the people will become sick if they do not keep the commandments. The narrative does not describe the reaction of the people to this threat.

In the second story which takes place in the wilderness of Sin (16.1-36) the people criticize Moses and Aaron for their poor leadership (16.2-3). Again they turn to Moses and Aaron. Again God responds only to Moses (16.4). Thereupon Moses and Aaron explain to the people when they should collect the bread. Moses defends himself against the people's accusation (v. 8; cf. v. 7) and promises the appearance of God's glory to them. God indeed appears (v. 10).

After the heavenly bread revokes the threat of a famine, the people complain a third time (17.1-7). In Rephidim they are short of water. Again the people accuse Moses and not God. This time, however, Moses explains that their resistance against him compares to resisting God. After the people criticize his leadership one more time (17.3) and Moses 'cries out' to God again (17.4), God advises him to do a miracle in front of the elders (masc., pl., 17.5-6) to consolidate his authority. Moses strikes water from the rock. Afterwards the people do not revolt anymore.

Elisabeth Moltmann-Wendel, *Mit Mirjam durch das Schilfmeer: Frauen bewegen die Kirche* (Stuttgart: Kreuz, 1982).

17.8-16: The unit describes how Moses gains complete acceptance as the leader of Israel. The men of Israel defeat the Amalekites (17.9) because Moses lifts his arms for the duration of the battle. Aaron and Hur help him to keep his arms up while Joshua leads the Israelites. Men continue to dominate the events.

18.1-27: Without a transition the passage describes the visit of Moses' father-in-law, Jethro. The unit mentions twice that the wife of Moses, Zipporah, and his sons Gershom and Eliezer also visit (18.2-5). Jethro's speech mentions them a third time (18.6). However, Moses greets and kisses only Jethro (18.7). After Jethro praised God for the rescue of the people (18.10-11), Aaron and the elder of Israel join for a meal. Zipporah and the sons seem not to participate. The report of the departure specifies again Jethro but not wife and children (18.27). Men populate the narrative in which Moses is the central character. When Jethro advises Moses to select several men and to share the responsibilities with them, Moses and his work are the focus (18.25-26). At the end of the first part (chs. 1–18), Moses is the established leader of the people of Israel.

Part Two: Exodus 19.1–40.38
The Acknowledgment of God as the Savior of the Israelites

Part Two describe in four sections how the Israelites learn to acknowledge God as their savior after Moses is the recognized leader of the Israelites (19.1–24.18; 25.1–31.18; 32.1–34; 35.1–40.38).

Exodus 19.1–24.18: The Arrival of the Israelites at Mount Sinai and the Revelation of God

19.1-25: After the Israelites arrive at Mount Sinai, Moses climbs up 'to God' and receives God's words (19.3-6). God is represented as an eagle, like in Deut. 32.11, caring for her brood. God offers a covenant to the people to become a holy people (19.6). Judith Plaskow bases her Jewish-feminist theology upon this verse which includes women.[28]

Moses reviews God's offer with the elders (masc., pl.) of the people whereupon the elders and the people accept the convenant. God then promises to Moses that God will appear in a cloud and speak to him so that the people 'believe' Moses 'forever' (19.9). In his reiteration of God's speech, Moses continues to play a central role.

28. Judith Plaskow, *Standing Again at Sinai: Judaism from a Feminist Perspective* (New York: Harper & Row, 1992).

In preparation for the revelation God demands the people's sanctification. According to the words of Moses, the event presupposes that three days prior to the revelation no man touches a woman (19.15). The verse thus clarifies that in Moses' speech the noun 'people' refers only to the men of Israel. Moses excludes the women from the revelation.

20.1-21: During the revelation of God through thunder and lightening, a thick cloud and the sound of a trumpet (20.16), the male Israelites are not allowed to be near God. Only Moses is permitted to be close. He receives the Ten Commandments that contain only male pronouns (cf. Deut. 5.6-21). The grammatical androcentrism has led Athalya Brenner to doubt that the Ten Commandments address women indirectly.[29] So, for example, the male addressee is advised that he shall not covet his neighbor's (masc., sing.) house, wife, male and female servant, ox, donkey, or anything else he owns (20.17). A female neighbor or her husband are not imagined. Also, the slave woman and daughter are mentioned in the Sabbath commandment, but not the wife. In addition, the stipulation of the fourth commandment lists the mother only after the father (20.12). In other words, the decalog assumes a society based on slavery, classism and misogyny.

The revelation causes a strong reaction among the people. They run away and plead with Moses to speak to God so that they will not die (20.19). Fearing God, the people accept Moses as their leader. Moses tries to calm them and then approaches God.

20.22–23.19: The text continues, however, with a divine speech that presents a set of laws. Called the Book of the Covenant, these laws regulate property, theft, and protection rights. Several laws exemplify the androcentric perspective prevalent in this ancient code. The laws about Hebrew slaves are particularly revealing (20.2-11) despite Mayer I. Gruber's claim that they represent the origins of Jewish matrilineal lineage.[30] Women are mentioned as the wives of enslaved men. Either the women followed their husbands into slavery or the male slave owner married them to his male slaves (21.3-4). In the latter case wife

29. Athalya Brenner, 'An Afterword: The Decalogue—Am I an Addressee?', in Brenner (ed.), *Exodus to Deuteronomy*, pp. 255-58.

30. Mayer I. Gruber, 'Matrilineal Determination of Jewishness: Biblical and Near Eastern Roots', in David P. Wright, David Noel Freedman and Avi Hurvitz (eds.), *Pomegranates and Golden Bells: Studies in Biblical, Jewish and Near Eastern Ritual, Law, and Literature in Honor of Jacob Milgrom* (Winona Lake, IN: Eisenbrauns 1995), pp. 437-43.

and children belong to the slave owner should he free a married male slave. If the slave does not want to leave his family, the slave 'shall serve him for life' (21.6). To Gruber this law proves that the mother, and not the father, determines the identity of the children. Above all, however, the law assumes the existence of slavery as a social and economic institution. It identities women as slaves while men appear as both slaves and slave owners.[31]

The Book of the Covenant discusses the particular situation that a father sells his daughter as a slave (21.7). The law stipulates that she cannot be released into freedom like other slaves. If the slave owner does not like her as a slave anymore, he cannot sell her (21.8). He has to redeem her or he can give her to his son (21.9). If he buys another female slave, he has to take care of the physical needs of the other enslaved woman (21.10-11). In general, then, the code imagines men as independent subjects who rule over enslaved women and men. Males buy and sell, decide and take care. Sometimes they are also enslaved. Restricting men to a certain degree, the law imagines them as the decision makers. In contrast, women appear as potential slaves only.

The Book of the Covenant does not criticize the existence of slavery. Rather, the laws legitimate this societal structure. Another passage elucidates the problems of such a law code. In 21.20-21 the law orders the punishment of a slave owner only if he beats his male or female slave to death. If they, however, survive for one or two days, the owner has to pay merely a monetary fine (cf. 21.26-27). In other words, the Covenant code supports the rights of the slave owners and discriminates against the slaves.

Other regulations reveal the same androcentric view. If a woman has a miscarriage because she was pushed during a fight between her husband and another man, her husband determines the amount of the financial compensation (21.22). Even the seduction of a young woman by a man concerns only her father and the man. The woman does not participate in the legal procedures that compare to the laws on rape (e.g. Deut. 22.22-29). Moreover, the Book of the Covenant imposes the death penalty for female sorcerers (22.18), sex with animals (22.19),

---

31. For a recent discussion about the treatment of '(slave) wife', 'daughter', 'widow' or 'bondswoman' in Exod. 21.2-11, see Carolyn Pressler, 'Wives and Daughters, Bond and Free: Views of Women in the Slave Laws of Exodus 21.2-11', in Victor H. Matthews, Bernard M. Levinson and Tikva Frymer-Kensky (eds.), *Gender and Law in the Hebrew Bible and the Ancient Near East* (Sheffield: Sheffield Academic Press, 1998), pp. 147-72.

and worshipers of other gods (22.20). Male sorcerers are not mentioned.

Several laws protect women and children who submit to this androcentric order. If a husband or father dies, his wife and children have the right to financial help. God threatens the male Israelites to keep this law because God hears the 'cries' of widows and orphans (22.23-24). If a man violates this regulation, he himself will die so that his own wife becomes a widow and his children become orphans. Since only men matter in the androcentric perspective, the legal code assumes that God's commandments address only male Israelites. If they obey these laws, they are protected.

The Book of the Covenant presupposes poverty as a social condition. The regulations do not implement strict measures to abolish poverty. They only criticize unfair interest rates (22.25) and emphasize the right of the poor (23.3, 6).[32]

23.20-33: The epilog of the Book of the Covenant elucidates the problems of the androcentric view. God promises the entry into the land if the Israelites keep God's covenant. However, God also announces the annihilation (23.23) of other peoples whom God plans 'to throw into confusion' (23.27). 'Little by little I will drive them out from before you, until you have increased and possess the land' (23.30; cf. also 23.31; 33.2). In other words, vv. 20-33 express a militant extermination policy in the name of God. The androcentric view links to other ideas that stabilize hierarchy and oppression.[33]

24.1-18: The people of Israel accept the regulations unanimously (24.3). In response Moses builds an altar and, with the young men, he offers burnt offerings (24.5). Moses performs the ritual that celebrates the covenant between God and the people (24.8). Afterwards Moses climbs up the mountain together with Aaron, Nadab, Abihu and 70 elders (masc., pl.), where the men see God (24.10, cf. also 2.25: 'God sees'; 3.2: 'Moses sees'). In contrast to 20.19, the people do not flee God anymore. They acknowledge God as their savior. After a meal together Moses leaves them. On the seventh day God appears to Moses in a fire (24.18). Moses stays on the mountain for 40 days and 40 nights.

32. For a different interpretation, see George V. Pixley, *On Exodus: A Liberation Perspective* (Maryknoll, NY: Orbis Books, 1987).

33. For this idea, see especially Robert Allen Warrior, 'A Native American Perspective: Canaanites, Cowboys, and Indians', in Sugirtharajah (ed.), *Voices from the Margin*, pp. 287-95.

Exodus 25.1–31.18: The Envisioned Institutionalization of God's Presence
During these 40 days and nights, Moses receives detailed instructions about the building of the tabernacle. Led by Aaron and his sons (Exod. 28; 29), the priests also receive their orders. God's presence among the Israelites requires meticulous regulation so that the Israelites 'know that I am Yhwh their God, who brought them out of the land of Egypt that I might dwell among them; I am Yhwh their God' (29.46).

Exodus 32.1–34.35: The Doubts of the People of Israel
The people wait in vain for Moses to return from the mountain (32.1). To assure themselves of God's presence the Israelites build a golden calf made of the gold of their wives, sons and daughters. Aaron leads them (32.2). As in 35.22, women are mentioned in the context of jewelry (32.2). However, the wrath of God (32.7-11) and the wrath of Moses (32.19-21) restore the envisioned structure. Moses commands the sons of Levi to kill 3000 men (32.27-28), and also God punishes the people (32.34). The punishment is huge although the numerical extent of God's action is not spelled out (32.35). During the next conversation between God and Moses (33.1–34.28), Moses receives a second set of two tablets. When Moses returns from the mountain, his facial skin color has changed (34.29-32). He conceals the shining with a veil (34.33-35).

Exodus 35.1–40.38: The Institutionalization of God's Presence
The upheaval that followed the building of the golden calf vanished. In a final step Moses institutionalizes the presence of God among Israel. He commands the people to build the tabernacle. In 35.20-29 women and men contribute to the completion. The noun 'woman' appears four times: 35.22, 25, 26, 29. Women donate jewelry and linen. According to 38.8 women donate their mirrors to build the altar. Manfred Görg believes that this remark is based on a memory of an ancient life-giving cult entertained particularly by women.[34] Wacker claims that the donation of the mirrors indicates a form of 'cultic chastity' among the participating women.[35] Although these scholars highlight the prominence of women, the narrator refers to women

---

34. Manfred Görg, 'Der Spiegeldienst der Frauen (Exod. 38:8)', *BN* 23 (1984), pp. 9-13.

35. Marie-Theres Wacker, ' "Religionsgeschichte Israels" oder "Theologie des Alten Testaments": (k)eine Alternative?', *Jahrbuch für biblische Theologie* 19 (1995), pp. 129-55.

again in gender-specific roles. The women are concerned with jewelry, clothing and beauty items. The passage also demonstrates that the narrator deliberately chooses where to include women. He attributes to them gender roles that conform to an androcentric view.

The narrative describes the completion of the building in great detail, with the same vocabulary that describes God completing the creation of the universe. Genesis 2.2 states that 'God finished the work' just as Exod. 40.33 concludes: 'So Moses finished the work.' The central role of Moses could not be more powerfully expressed. The narrative culminates in God's appearance in the tabernacle that accompanies Israel in the wilderness (40.34-38).

Conclusion: A Feminist Quintessence

Understanding the book of Exodus as a liberation story is problematic if we are conscious of the text's androcentric perspective. The narrative supports the establishment and the stabilization of a hierarchical society and various forms of domination.

Women play a secondary role. They are few in number. When they appear, they are marginal to the literary composition. They are only portrayed in gender-specific roles. They care for children, own jewelry, and appear in economically vulnerable positions. Divine speeches add to the marginalization of female characters. God speaks only to male Israelites and does not address the women.

The narrative itself, as well as social laws and regulations, indicates that the book of Exodus represents, at best, an enormously complicated liberation story. The violent and bloody conflict with the Egyptian population, the slave laws, the death penalty, or the references to other peoples describe oppressive and hierarchically structured interactions among people. The establishment of Israelite male dominance over others is the goal and not the liberation from such dynamics.

The description of God does not even liberate the Israelites. Rather, they themselves become alarmed of their God (e.g. 20.19). God commands, decides, is angry, and punishes. Only one passage reveals a less authoritarian and hierarchical image of God (3.14). Usually, God does not speak to the Israelites, but only to Moses. Although God frees the Israelites from slavery, God demands their submission. The reaction of the people to such a God is not surprising. They do not dare to speak to God, in contrast to the time of their enslavement (2.23). Instead, they complain to Moses (15.22-17.7). Only after the people accept the laws, do the Israelites acknowledge God as their savior (24.1-18).

The focus on the androcentric elements demonstrates that Moses, and not actual liberation, is the center of the narrative. The events create faith among the people to Moses and God (4.16; 14.31). Although the well-being of the people depends on Moses as well as on God, Moses is the center. He mediates between God and the people.

The exposure of the androcentrism, however, does not imply that the book of Exodus is irrelevant to Christian or Jewish feminists. As long as androcentric structures dominate Western societies and as long as our culture transmits biblical images and stories, the book of Exodus is a significant source for theological reflection. The critical thinking about the role of women, the laws regarding society and economics, the image of God, and the position of Moses teach that the collective trauma of oppression is not simply an issue of liberation. Those who were formerly oppressed often re-enact the oppression after the supposed liberation. Androcentrism persists despite freedom. The Exodus narrative is, then, a profound metaphorical reminder that it is hard to escape the patterns of collective or individual trauma. Feminist theologians cannot afford to neglect this insight in their quest for theologically responsible theory and practice.

SIGNIFYING ON EXODUS: READING RACE AND CULTURE IN ZORA NEALE HURSTON'S *MOSES, MAN OF THE MOUNTAIN*

Harold C. Washington

Zora Neale Hurston, A Genius of the South, 1901–1960,
Novelist, Folklorist, Anthropologist
(Epitaph in the Garden of Heavenly Rest, Fort Pierce, Florida)

Autobiographical Preface: Why Zora?

Several years ago I was asked to contribute to a panel discussion on the question: What Makes a Feminist Reading Feminist?[1] 'Great question', I thought, but if I answered with an appropriate focus on women's experience, I ran the risk of presuming to speak for others, which could rightly invalidate whatever I had to say.[2] The way out I chose was to give up categorical pronouncements and to opt for strategically chosen particularity. I turned to Zora Neale Hurston's 1939 novel, *Moses, Man of the Mountain*,[3] and illustrated feminist reading by interrogating my own subject position as a reader of Hurston's

1. Earlier versions of this paper were given at sessions of the SBL Feminist Theological Hermeneutics Group on 21 November 1993: 'What Makes a Feminist Reading Feminist? Reading Exodus with Zora Neale Hurston'; and the SBL History of Interpretation Group, 24 November 1996: 'Reading Exodus Differently: Political and Cultural Critique in Zora Neale Hurston's *Moses, Man of the Mountain*'. My thanks to both groups for their helpful responses.

2. 'The practice of speaking for others', writes Linda Alcoff, 'is often born of a desire for mastery, to privilege oneself as the one who more correctly understands the truth about another's situation or as one who can champion a just cause and thus achieve glory and praise' ('The Problem of Speaking for Others', *Cultural Critique* 20 [Winter 1991–92], pp. 5-32, 29).

3. Originally published by J.B. Lippincott (New York: 1939), Hurston's *Moses* is the finest of several African-American literary retellings of the Exodus story. The book has appeared in several editions. Page references below are to the new critical edition edited by Cheryl A. Wall, *Zora Neale Hurston: Novels and Stories* (Library of America, 74; New York: Literary Classics of the United States, 1995), pp. 335-595.

reading of Exodus. I found Hurston helpful for the occasion because —decades before feminist theory's problematizing of essentialist notions of gender—she sends deep, dislocating shock waves through monolithic constructs of 'woman' and 'experience', and she mixes race and class up with this trouble as well.

I got more than I bargained for when I turned to Hurston, for I am a son of the South, born and raised on the white side of a racially segregated town on the Tennessee River in the north of Alabama. Mine is the same town, in fact, where Hurston's younger brother, Clifford Joel, was the principal of the Negro High School in the decades before the Second World War.[4] As a child I experienced a bizarre split consciousness, witnessing, for example, national grief at the assassinations of John F. and Robert Kennedy, and Martin Luther King, Jr, while some of my white playmates celebrated the deaths of these civil rights champions. Years later I saw the Ku Klux Klan show interest in recruiting my football player brother (not athletic myself, I presumably didn't fit their ideal of white manhood). As I write at the turn of the millennium, militant white supremacists prepare for 'race war' in armed training camps located a few miles from my hometown. All this is to say that Hurston's work with the Bible strikes very close to home for me. Zora Hurston, born in Alabama too,[5] is not only a witness to the racist and sexist culture that confronted me as a child, but also a model for readings of the Bible that subvert that culture.

But enough about me. Although I find recent inroads of autobiographical criticism into biblical scholarship most enlivening, I will not continue in that vein here.[6] With this note of how I became interested in Hurston, I will now retreat behind the cover of conventional academic exposition. My aim is simply to urge broader appreciation of Zora Hurston as a biblical interpreter, and in particular to show how Hurston's reading of Exodus in *Moses, Man of the Mountain* problematizes dominant constructions of racial, class, and gender difference in the US society of her day. A key figure of the Harlem Renaissance literary movement of the 1920s, Hurston was also a pioneering scholar

---

4. Wall (ed.), *Novels and Stories*, p. 1017.
5. Wall (ed.), *Novels and Stories*, p. 1013.
6. For examples of the autobiographical trend in literary criticism and in biblical scholarship, see H.A. Veeser (ed.), *Confessions of the Critics* (London: Routledge, 1996); J.L. Staley, *Reading with a Passion: Rhetoric, Autobiography and the American West in the Gospel of John* (New York: Continuum, 1995); J.C. Anderson and J.L. Staley (eds.), *Taking it Personally: Autobiographical Biblical Criticism (Semeia,* 72; Atlanta: Scholars Press, 1995); and I.R. Kitzberger (ed.), *The Personal Voice in Biblical Interpretation* (London: Routledge, 1999).

of African-American folklore. She trained with anthropologist Franz Boas at Columbia University and conducted extensive field research in the African diaspora traditions of the American South and the Caribbean. Hurston lived before the American civil rights movement, at a time when US feminism was not an influential cultural force, a generation before self-identified Womanist writing emerged in American letters. Her work suffered critical neglect through the postwar period into the 1970s, but today Zora Hurston is recognized as a major American author. Against all odds, Hurston created a singular literature that embodies her irrepressible self-respect, delight in her blackness, and fierce devotion to the African-American cultural legacy. Elemental to that legacy is a tradition of African-American biblical interpretation that runs against the grain of the larger society.

'Signifying' as Cultural Critique

Hurston was a classic American renegade, and a key strategy of hers was defiant humor.[7] She lived as a veritable performance artist (before there was such a term), parodying the conventions of white US society. She would, for example, gain access to an exclusive 'whites-only' restaurant by wrapping her head in exotic scarves and passing as an African princess. Her self-promotion amounted to social-class piracy, as she vigorously cultivated wealthy white patrons to support her research financially. Said to be capable of taking any social gathering by storm with her legendary wit, Hurston was a bit of a gender outlaw. She brazenly smoked cigarettes in settings where 'polite' women wouldn't dare, and delighted in cross-dressing with outfits of trousers, boots and big hats.[8]

Hurston's humorous subversion of social norms exemplifies the African-American folk practice of 'signifyin(g)'. Historically rooted in the classic traditional cultures of West Africa, signifying is, as Henry Louis Gates, Jr, has shown, not only a key mechanism of African-American cultural survival but also an indispensable critical matrix

7. Alice Walker captures this quality in the quotation with which she titles a Hurston anthology: *I Love Myself When I Am Laughing… and Then Again When I Am Looking Mean and Impressive: A Zora Neale Hurston Reader* (Old Westbury, NY: The Feminist Press, 1979).

8. For these aspects of Hurston's life, see R.E. Hemenway, *Zora Neale Hurston: A Literary Biography* (Urbana: University of Illinois Press, 1977); and also the Foreword to Hemenway's volume by A. Walker, 'Zora Neale Hurston: A Cautionary Tale and a Partisan View', pp. xi-xviii.

for understanding African-American literature.[9] The 'Signifying Monkey', a folktale character who models the practice, is according to Gates a reflex of the Yoruba divine trickster figure, Esu-Elegbara. Gates describes the function of the figure in African-American folklore as an 'ironic reversal of a received racist image of the black as simianlike, the Signifying Monkey, he who dwells at the margins of discourse, ever punning, ever troping, ever embodying the ambiguities of language'.[10] In African-American traditional culture, signifying can involve both speech and gesture:

> Signifying... certainly refers to the trickster's ability to talk with great innuendo, to carp, to cajole, needle, and lie. It can mean in other instances the propensity to talk around a subject, never quite coming to the point. It can mean making fun of a person or situation. Also it can denote speaking with the hands and eyes, and in this respect encompasses a whole complex of expressions and gestures. Thus it is signifying to stir up a fight between neighbors by telling stories; it is signifying to make fun of a policeman by parodying his motions behind his back; it is signifying to ask for a piece of cake by saying, 'my brother needs a piece of cake'.[11]

Seizing upon the term 'signify' to denote such sly and disruptive actions is in itself a gesture of African-American linguistic rebellion. As Gates observes, ' "Signification", in standard English, denotes the meaning that a term conveys, or is intended to convey'.[12] But in black vernacular, the term 'signifyin(g)' is a subversive 'homonymic pun of the profoundest sort', because here 'signifyin(g)' has to do with the *diversion* or *misdirection* of meaning, usually humorously, often at the expense of the one who is being 'signified on'.[13] Only in black popular usage could one say, 'What *are* you signifying?', with the meaning, 'What is it that you are studiously refusing to express in a straightforward manner?' Only in an African-American vernacular would a command to 'stop signifying!' be intelligible.[14] A complex and subtle rhetoric of indirection, 'signifyin(g) is black double-voiced-

---

9. H.L. Gates, Jr, *The Signifying Monkey: A Theory of African-American Literary Criticism* (Oxford: Oxford University Press, 1988).

10. Gates, *The Signifying Monkey*, p. 52.

11. R.D. Abrahams, *Deep Down in the Jungle: Negro Narrative Folklore from the Streets of Philadelphia* (Chicago: Aldine Publishing, 1970), pp. 51-52, 66-67, 264; as quoted by Gates, *The Signifying Monkey*, p. 54.

12. Gates, *The Signifying Monkey*, p. 46.

13. Gates, *The Signifying Monkey*, p. 47.

14. Cf. Gates, *The Signifying Monkey*, p. 81.

ness'; as a literary technique, it always involves 'formal revision and an intertextual relation'.[15]

Hurston's writing offers consummate examples of this African-American parodic art of 'signifyin(g)'. *Moses, Man of the Mountain* displays Hurston as a trickster interpreter, undermining the white, patriarchal, middle- and upper-class respectability of US society with her irreverent, indirect humor and wily refashioning of the biblical text. In 1939, when Hurston published *Moses*, the USA was struggling to pull out of economic depression and the Second World War was breaking out abroad. Ostensibly a humorous retelling of the biblical Exodus–Deuteronomy narrative, Hurston's novel takes on US white racism and economic injustice, as well as American complacency at the rise of antisemitism and the Third Reich abroad. Even if the book does not attain the heights of Hurston's masterpiece, *Their Eyes Were Watching God*,[16] as cultural criticism *Moses, Man of the Mountain* is a tour de force.

'Womanist Midrash': Hurston's Approach to the Bible

Before writing *Moses, Man of the Mountain*, Hurston had treated biblical themes in several shorter works. Her 'Book of Harlem', a short story written around 1921 in the form of an apocryphal biblical chapter with numbered verses and introductory glosses, satirizes black life in New York, referred to here as 'the city of Babylon, which is ruled by the tribe of Tammany'.[17] As the story begins, 'a pestilence visiteth the land of Hokum, and the people cry out: ..."We are verily the dry-bones of which the prophet Ezekiel prophesied." ' The 'pestilence'

---

15. Gates, *The Signifying Monkey*, p. 51. Gates adds the following definitions of 'signifying' by R.D. Abrahams: '[It is] a *technique* of indirect argument or persuasion...a language of indirection...[it means] to imply, goad, beg, boast, by *indirect* verbal or gestural means; [it is] a language of implication' (*Deep Down in the Jungle*, pp. 51-52, 66-67, 264; quoted by Gates, pp. 54, 75). Cf. the following eight characteristics of signifying identified by G. Smitherman: indirection or circumlocution; use of metaphorical-imagistic language rooted in daily life; humor and irony; rhythmic fluidity and sound; teaching but not preaching; direction toward someone present; punning; and use of the unexpected (*Talkin' and Testifyin': The Language of Black America* [Boston: Houghton Mifflin, 1977], p. 121; cited by J. Lowe, *Jump at the Sun: Zora Neale Hurston's Cosmic Comedy* [Urbana University of Illinois Press, 1994], p. 59).

16. Z.N. Hurston, *Their Eyes Were Watching God*, in Wall (ed.), *Novels and Stories*, pp. 173-333.

17. See Hemenway, *Zora Neale Hurston*, p. 31. Quotations below are from 'Book of Harlem' in Wall (ed.), *Novels and Stories*, pp. 979-84.

lamented here is Prohibition, the failed US attempt to outlaw alcoholic drinks. The protagonists of the story are two sons 'of the tribe of Ham' named Toothsome and Mandolin, the latter of whom 'goeth to a hall of dancing, and meeting a damsel there, shaketh vehemently with her'. Hurston pokes fun at a prominent white patron of the Harlem Renaissance cultural scene, Carl van Vechten, dubbing him 'Chief of the Niggerati...(which being interpreted means Negro literati)'. The story concludes as Mandolin proclaims:

> 53. 'In my early days in Babylon was I taught to subscribe to Vanity Fair, and to read it diligently, for no man may know his way about Babylon without it'.
> 54. Then did a great light dawn upon him called Toothsome, and he rushed forth to subscribe to the perfect magazine.
> 55. And of his doings and success after that, is it not written in the Book of Harlem?

This early story has the hallmarks of Hurston's later work with the Bible in *Moses*: her skill in adapting biblical forms for humorous effect, her strategy of 'signifying' both on the foibles of her African-American contemporaries and on the perils of defining black culture in uneasy alliance with white patronage. Giving the name 'Babylon' to New York of the Harlem Renaissance era, she points to the cultural exile of black literary figures at the time.

Hurston's 1926 play, *The First One*, is a comic retelling of the Ham legend (Gen. 9.18-27), which has long been used to justify slavery and racial discrimination in the USA. 'In effect,' writes Robert Hemenway, 'the play pokes fun at all those who take seriously the biblical sanction for racial separation.'[18] In 1934 Hurston published a short story, 'The Fire and the Cloud', depicting Moses on Mount Nebo just before his death, an early version of the final scene of *Moses, Man of the Mountain*.[19] Hurston's first novel, *Jonah's Gourd Vine*, is the tragic story of an illiterate black working man named John Pearson, who finds his calling as a preacher but dies in disrepute, trying in vain to recover from his failings.[20] Biblical strains echo through the black church life depicted in this novel, and John Pearson's climactic sermon on Zech. 13.6 (interpreted as a reference to the wounds of Christ) is a vivid record of African-American biblical preaching.[21]

18. Hemenway, *Zora Neale Hurston*, p. 68.
19. Z.N. Hurston, 'The Fire and the Cloud', in Wall (ed.), *Novels and Stories*, pp. 997-1000; cf. *Moses*, pp. 588-95.
20. In Wall (ed.), *Novels and Stories*, pp. 1-171.
21. Hurston, *Jonah's Gourd Vine*, pp. 145-51. The sermon, arranged strophically

From her work as a folklorist, Hurston understands the traditional process through which diverse oral legends were incorporated into the biblical narrative. Hurston carries this folk process forward in her creative retelling of the Exodus–Deuteronomy story. Her introduction to *Moses, Man of the Mountain* asserts that the biblical portrayal of Moses is only one of numerous 'concepts of Moses abroad in the world'. The Bible contains the 'old man with a beard', 'the great lawgiver' who, she observes in wry tones, 'had some trouble with Pharaoh about some plagues and led the Children of Israel out of Egypt'. But, she adds, 'Asia and all the Near East are sown with legends of this character', and 'then Africa has her mouth on Moses' (p. 337).

Hurston draws on this diverse lore to create a Womanist midrash of Exodus, interweaving the biblical plot with African diaspora traditions such as the Caribbean association of Moses with the Haitian serpent god Damballah, revered for his magical powers. As in the book of Exodus, Hurston's Moses performs wonders at Pharaoh's court (notably, he turns his rod into a serpent; cf. *Moses*, pp. 469-70; Exod. 4.1-4; 7.8-12), and he effects the plagues upon the Egyptians. But unlike the biblical account, Hurston's Moses derives his magical power from an encounter with a sacred Egyptian snake (pp. 386-88, 447-49). Portraying Moses as the 'finest hoodoo man in the world' (p. 443), Hurston highlights a magical element of West African spirituality that has endured in African-American folk religion. [22]

'Womanist midrash', an incongruous term at first glance, is not so far-fetched here. Alice Walker, who coined the term 'Womanist' to denote 'a black feminist or feminist of color', drew great inspiration from Zora Hurston.[23] Hurston, in turn, was a serious student of Jewish texts, keenly interested in the creative freedom and organic inter-

---

to represent the preacher's phrasing, is drawn from Hurston's field notes of preaching by the Reverend C.C. Lovelace of Eau Gallie, Florida, 3 May 1929 (Hemenway, *Zora Neale Hurston*, p. 197).

22. Hurston studied Haitian magical religion and was initiated by followers of the legendary New Orleans priestess Marie Leveau (Hemenway, *Zora Neale Hurston*, pp. 118-23, 246-50; C.A. Wall [ed.], *Zora Neale Hurston: Folklore, Memoirs, and Other Writings* [Library of America, 75; New York: Literary Classics of the United States, 1995] pp. 176-267; 376-532). On traditional West African magical discourse as a symbolic means of mapping and managing the world, and on 'biblical conjure' as a transformative African-American cultural practice, see T.H. Smith, *Conjuring Culture: Biblical Formations of Black America* (Oxford: Oxford University Press, 1994); on Hurston, esp. pp. 32-35.

23. Cf. A. Walker, *In Search of Our Mothers' Gardens: Womanist Prose* (San Diego: Harcourt Brace Jovanovich, 1983), p. xi; and 'A Cautionary Tale and a Partisan View', pp. xi-xviii.

textuality of black folklore and midrashic literature alike.[24] Thus she augments the biblical Exodus narrative not only with African-Caribbean traditions but also with Josephus' account of Moses' Egyptian military exploits against the Ethiopians.[25] Hurston had completed at the end of her life a fictional work titled *Herod the Great*, based principally on Josephus (along with material from Livy, Eusebius, Strabo, and Nicolas of Damascus). She had also proposed to write for Scribners a 'history and philosophy of the Hebrews', improbably titled *Just Like Us*, which she hoped would 'bring about a revision of our Sunday School literature, and alter the slovenly and inimical attitude towards the modern Jew'.[26]

In *Moses, Man of the Mountain*, Hurston deals with peculiarities of Exodus such as the two names for the holy mountain, Sinai and Horeb. Given the breadth of her reading, Hurston may have known of the 'four sources' (J, E, D, P) documentary hypothesis of Pentateuchal criticism.[27] Hurston's solution, however, is closer to the traditional rabbinical commentaries: Hurston's Moses asks, 'What is the name of that mountain?', and he is told, 'It's according to where you live. The people on one side of it call it Horeb. On the other side they call it Sinai' (p. 415). Likewise Hurston appears to imitate the traditional midrashic harmonization of the various names of Moses' father-in-law. Is he Jethro, Reuel, or Hobab (cf. Exod 3.1; 2.18, Num 10.29, Judg. 4.11)? Hurston's character explains:

> Jethro is the name my father named me. As chief of my clan I am chief Jethro. Otherwise, I am Ruel. Among the Kenites a priest has a ceremonial name, too. Pretty general habit all over the land of Midian. But I guess you already know that.[28]

24.   For a proposal of feminist midrash as an interpretive strategy, see J. Plaskow, *Standing Again at Sinai: Judaism from a Feminist Perspective* (San Francisco: Harper & Row, 1990), pp. 53-56.

25.   *Ant.* 2.238-253; cf. *Moses*, pp. 380-91.

26.   Hemenway, *Zora Neale Hurston*, pp. 343-44.

27.   I cannot establish that Hurston read Wellhausen, but it would not be surprising. It has been suggested that Hurston's depiction of Moses as an Egyptian is influenced by S. Freud's *Moses and Monotheism* (New York: Knopf, 1939). Freud's volume appeared in English the same year as Hurston's novel, but she is thought possibly to have encountered the work two years earlier when it was published in the German psychoanalytic journal *Imago* (Hemenway, *Zora Neale Hurston*, p. 257).

28.   Hurston, *Moses*, p. 419. For modern historical-critical and traditional Jewish interpretive solutions to the Sinai/Horeb, Jethro/Reuel/Hobab variants, compare Brevard S. Childs, *The Book of Exodus: A Critical, Theological Commentary* (OTL; Philadelphia: Westminster Press, 1974), p. 79, with further references; J.H. Hertz (ed.), *The Pentateuch and Haftorahs: Hebrew Text, English Translation, and Commentary*

'Dislocating the Color Line': Black Moses?[29]

Hurston's *Moses* is sometimes described simply as a retelling of the Exodus story in African-American dialect, but the novel's treatment of race is much more complex and unsettling than this. On one level, Hurston clearly takes up the historical African-American identification with the Exodus story. The prominent Moses/Exodus/Egypt/Promised Land typologies of the classic African-American slave narratives, black fictionalizations of slavery, and black preaching run deep through *Moses, Man of the Mountain*.[30] The futility of African-American experience in slavery, for example, is evoked in Hurston's version of Pharaoh's preposterous decrees (cf. Exod 1.8-22; 5.6-9):

> Israel, you are slaves from now on. Pharaoh assumes no responsibility for the fact that some of you got old before he came to power. Old as well as young must work... No sleeping after dawn. Fifty lashes for being late to work. Fifty lashes for working slow. One hundred lashes for being absent. One hundred lashes for sassing the bossman. Death for hitting a foreman. Babies take notice. Positively no more boy babies allowed among Hebrews.[31]

As Lillie Howard observes, American blacks are unmistakably transplanted to an 'Old Testament' milieu when Hebrew workers strain under the demands of the 'bossman', and when Moses' mother Jochebed says, as she lowers the baby's basket into the water: 'Nile, youse such a great big river and he is such a little bitty thing, show him

---

(London: Soncino, 2nd edn, 1960), pp. 212-213; and N. Sarna, *Exodus* (JPS Torah Commentary; Philadelphia: Jewish Publication Society of America, 1991), pp. 12-14.

29. I am borrowing a phrase from S. Kawash, *Dislocating the Color Line: Identity, Hybridity, and Singularity in African-American Narrative* (Mestizo Spaces/Espaces Métissés; Stanford: Stanford University Press, 1998). Kawash's chapter on Hurston's autobiography, *Dust Tracks on a Road* (in Wall [ed.], *Folklore, Memoirs, and Other Writings*, pp. 558-808), focuses on Hurston's 'refusal of race' as an essential category of identity (pp. 167-209).

30. Lowe, *Jump at the Sun*, p. 209. On the Exodus motif in African-American religious history, see A. Raboteau, *Slave Religion: The 'Invisible Institution' in the Antebellum South* (New York: Oxford University Press, 1978), pp. 250, 311-12; Smith, *Conjuring Culture*, pp. 55-80. On Exodus in African-American biblical interpretation, see the following in C.H. Felder (ed.), *Stony the Road We Trod: African American Biblical Interpretatation* (Minneapolis: Fortress Press, 1991): T. Hoyt, Jr, 'Interpreting Biblical Scholarship for the Black Church Tradition', pp. 17-39, 30-31; D.T. Shannon, '"An Ante-bellum Sermon": A Resource for an African American Hermeneutic', pp. 98-123; C.B. Copher, 'The Black Presence in the Old Testament', pp. 146-64, 155-56.

31. Hurston, *Moses*, pp. 341-42.

some mercy please'.[32] When the wilderness-weary Hebrews long for the food they enjoyed back in Egypt, they recall diets typically associated with black folk: 'the nice fresh fish…nice sweet-tasting little pan-fish…[of which] a person could get all they could eat for five cents—and the nice fresh cucumbers, and the watermelons'.[33] Howard continues:

> Not only do the language and diets give the novel a distinctive Negro folk flavor, but the housing situation in Goshen also strongly resembles the big house–shanty house habitats characteristic of plantation days. Pharaoh, of course, lives in his palace (the equivalent of the huge white mansions of the agrarian South), while the Hebrews live in hovels which strongly resemble the cabins from plantations of the antebellum South.[34]

It is impossible, however, to read *Moses* as a simple allegory of black experience under slavery, because Hurston destabilizes the racial identifications of the novel's characters, Hebrew, Egyptian, and Midianite alike. This must be understood in the context of Hurston's controversial, and in the eyes of many, self-contradictory, racial politics.[35] On the one hand, she bears acute witness to the experience of US racism in essays such as 'How It Feels to Be Colored Me', and 'My Most Humiliating Jim Crow Experience'.[36] On the other hand, Hurston remains aloof toward the first stirrings of a political civil rights struggle: 'Negroes [are] supposed to write about the Race Problem. I was and am thoroughly sick of the subject'.[37] She repudiates her contemporaries' embrace of race pride and race solidarity as means of resistance. 'Race pride,' writes Hurston, 'is a sapping vice. It has caused more suffering in the world than religious opinion and that is saying a lot.'[38]

---

32. L. Howard, *Zora Neale Hurston* (Boston: Twayne Publishers, 1980), p. 116; cf. Hurston, *Moses*, p. 362; Exod. 2.3.

33. Hurston, *Moses*, p. 563; cf. Exod. 16.3; Num. 11.5.

34. Howard, *Zora Neale Hurston*, p. 116

35. I draw here on Samira Kawash's discussion, 'Racial Consciousness and the Trouble with Zora', in *Dislocating the Color Line*, pp. 172-85; cf. Hemenway, *Zora Neale Hurston*, ch. 11, 'Ambiguities of Self, Politics of Race', pp. 273-300.

36. In Wall (ed.), *Folklore, Memoirs, and Other Writings*, pp. 826-29, 935-36.

37. Hurston, *Dust Tracks on a Road* (New York: HarperCollins, 1991), p. 151, as quoted by Kawash, *Dislocating the Color Line*, p. 172. Subsequent quotations from *Dust Tracks on a Road*, are from Wall (ed.), *Folklore, Memoirs, and Other Writings*, pp. 558-808.

38. Hurston, *Dust Tracks on a Road*, p. 783.

Hurston's anthropological studies quicken her conclusion that race is a cultural construct—not a biological 'fact'—and naturally she applies her devastating humor to this scientific question. An essay titled 'Now Take Noses', published the same year as *Moses*, lampoons biological explanations for cultural differences.[39] Her essay, 'How It Feels to Be Colored Me', opens with a joke targeting the notion of essential black identity:

> I am colored but I offer nothing in the way of extenuating circumstances except the fact that I am the only Negro in the United States whose grandfather on the mother's side was *not* an Indian chief.[40]

The remainder of the essay repeatedly implies, notwithstanding the force of racism, that US 'colored' identity is a contingent product rather than a stable property: 'I remember the very day that I became colored', she writes. Or, 'but I am not tragically colored... I do not always feel colored... I feel most colored when I am thrown against a sharp white background... At certain times I have no race, I am *me*'.[41] A similar sense of fractured, unstable racial identity, with the added contingency of gender, appears in Hurston's autobiography: 'I maintain that I have been a Negro three times—a Negro baby, a Negro girl, and a Negro woman.' Yet from this experience emerges no 'clear cut impression of what the Negro in America is like'. In fact, Hurston concludes, 'there is no *The Negro* here'.[42]

Hurston's observation of Nazism's rise in Europe during the years that she is working on *Moses* further confirms her aversion to essentialist racial theories and the violent nationalisms they inform. 'In an effort to end or escape this violence,' writes Samira Kawash, 'Hurston repudiates not only nationalism but race consciousness, a truly risky practice for a black woman in the 1940s but perhaps no less so today.'[43] Challenging any people's presumption to 'racial purity', Hurston therefore rejects Exodus as a story of organic national

---

39. See Hemenway, *Zora Neale Hurston*, pp. 290, 357; Wall (ed.), *Hurston: Novels and Stories*, p. 1024.

40. 'How It Feels to Be Colored Me', p. 826.

41. 'How It Feels to Be Colored Me', pp. 826-29; cf. B. Johnson, 'Threshholds of Difference: Structures of Address in Zora Neale Hurston', in H.L. Gates, Jr and K.A. Appiah (eds.), *Zora Neale Hurston: Critical Perspectives Past and Present* (Amistad Literary Series; New York: Amistad, 1993), pp. 131-33; and C.A. Wall, *Women of the Harlem Renaissance* (Bloomington: Indiana University Press, 1995), p. 25.

42. *Dust Tracks on a Road*, p. 733.

43. *Dislocating the Color Line*, p. 168.

unity.[44] Above all, she subverts ethnocentric reading of the biblical narrative by placing Moses' ethnicity in question.[45] In Hurston's rendition of Exodus ch. 2, Miriam fails to watch what happens to the baby set adrift in the basket. She falls asleep on the river bank, and waking 'with a guilty start' she discovers to her dismay that the child and his basket are gone (p. 363; cf. Exod. 2.4). When Jochebed demands, 'What happened to my child, Miriam?', the girl first replies, 'Oh—er—...I—I don't know, mama'. Eventually, to cover her lapse, she makes up the story of Pharaoh's daughter saving the Hebrew infant. Miriam's story inspires rumors of Hebrew origins that follow Moses through his career, but the reader, like Moses himself, never knows for sure, 'Is he Hebrew or Egyptian?'

The irony that Moses, leader of the Hebrews, is not clearly Hebrew himself is sharpened by the fact that one cannot ascertain whether Moses is black or white.[46] Nor is it clear what 'difference' this would make: skin color does not work as a racial-ethnic marker in this narrative. Although the Hebrew people speak black dialect, Moses' putative Hebrew mother, Jochebed, has a 'white face' and 'thick red hair' (p. 350). Meanwhile black non-Hebrews appear, for example, among the party attending Pharaoh's daughter at the Nile, or among caravan travelers from the Sudan (pp. 364, 413). Moses' Midianite wife seems to have an African appearance: 'Zipporah of the tawny skin...night-black eyes...luxuriant, crinkly hair...full, dark red lips... [and] warm, brown arms' (p. 433).

In other writings Hurston makes fun of the use of skin color as a basis for racial classification. For example, her autobiography, *Dust Tracks on a Road*, contains the following passage:

> Who are My People?... They range in color from Walter White, white through high yaller, yaller, Punkin color, high brown, vaseline brown, seal brown, black, smooth black, dusty black, rusty black, coal black, lam black and damn black... Still and all, you can't just point out my people by skin color.[47]

44. See L.E. Donaldson, 'Rereading Moses/Rewriting Exodus: The Postcolonial Imagination of Zora Neale Hurston', in Donaldson, *Decolonizing Feminisms: Race, Gender, and Empire Building* (Chapel Hill: University of North Carolina Press, 1992), pp. 102-17.

45. Howard, *Zora Neal Hurston*, pp. 119-20; D. McDowell, 'Lines of Descent/Dissenting Lines', Foreword to Z.N. Hurston, *Moses, Man of the Mountain* (New York: HarperCollins, 1991), pp. xv-xvi; Donaldson, 'Rereading Moses/Rewriting Exodus', pp. 106-110.

46. Howard, *Zora Neale Hurston*, p. 120.

47. *Dust Tracks on a Road*, p. 774.

Thus despite Hurston's African-American characterization of the Hebrews in *Moses, Man of the Mountain*, the novel frustrates any attempt to construe Moses as a black hero. Jethro says to Moses when he joins up with the Midianites (cf. Exod. 2.15-22): 'Moses, I never saw anybody who looked more like what he was than you do' (p. 422). Yet 'what he is' as a racial subject remains unsettled throughout the novel.

As Deborah McDowell observes, Hurston's novel creates a multi-layered typology in which oppression of the Hebrews in Egypt portends black slavery in America, which in turn parallels persecution of the Jews in the Third Reich.[48] This complex scheme allows Hurston, in one sweep, both to ridicule white America's attempts to segregate the races (seeing that the antebellum plantation was commonly a site of forced miscegenation through rape or other means), and to make fun of the rumors of Hitler's Jewish ancestry. Both jibes are at play when the Hebrew slaves comment on Pharaoh's house:

> There is plenty of Hebrew blood in that family already. That is why that Pharaoh wants to kill us all off. He is scared somebody will come along and tell who his real folks are... The higher-ups who got Hebrew blood in 'em is always the ones to persecute us. I got it from somebody that ought to know, that the grandmother of Pharaoh was a Hebrew woman.[49]

Hurston plays on a double sense of 'passing' as legislation, that is, passing laws, and as racial camouflage, or crossing the color line undetected.[50] A Hebrew says of Pharaoh, 'he figures that it makes a big man out of him to be passing and passing laws and rules' (pp. 344-45). As rumor spreads that Pharaoh's daughter has adopted a Hebrew boy, Israelites joke among themselves: 'Ho, ho! Pharaoh hates Hebrews, does he? He passes a law to destroy all our sons and gets a Hebrew child for a grandson. Ain't that rich?' (p. 369).

Once the baby Moses leaves his Hebrew parents, the novel becomes a sustained 'signifying' play on the theme of passing. In a passage that is often described as the rhetorical high point of the novel, Hurston recounts Moses' first crossing of the Red Sea in the insistent cadences of a black preacher:

> So Moses felt himself moving Godward with an understanding of force and time. So he walked out with clean feet on the other side. Moses had

48. McDowell, 'Lines of Descent/Dissenting Lines', p. xvi. McDowell points out that even these relatively clear lines of typology quickly become crossed and confused.

49. Hurston, *Moses*, p. 370.

50. McDowell, 'Lines of Descent/Dissenting Lines', p. xv.

crossed over. He was not in Egypt. He had crossed over and now he was not an Egyptian… He had crossed over so he was not of the house of Pharaoh. He did not have a palace because he had crossed over… He had crossed over. He felt as empty as a post hole for he was none of the things he once had been. He was a man sitting on a rock. He had crossed over.[51]

In this decisive moment Moses, no longer an Egyptian, does not 'cross over' into Hebrew identity. He is not yet headed to the Promised Land but to Midian. Neither Egyptian, Hebrew nor Midianite, neither black nor white, Moses is not here confirmed in a stable identity but rather is suspended, indeterminate, 'empty'. He is a transgressor of boundaries, outlawed from Egypt, exiled among the Midianites.

Laura Donaldson comments on the 'oscillating' quality of Moses' ethnicity in Hurston's novel:

> The nationalist subject depends upon the hierarchies of inside and outside, native and alien, and finds his or her natural habitat in the structure of metaphysical opposition. Moses' ethnic undecidability thus begins to fracture an organic nationalist consciousness and profoundly questions the terms on which the Exodus—the paradigmatic journey of liberation—can be appropriated.[52]

Donaldson puts this very aptly, and I find it difficult to comment further without repeating well worn phrases about the undecidable ethnicity of the postmodern subject. But my point is that Hurston, in her awareness of the constructedness of racial difference, has anticipated this critical discussion by two generations. Her work is true to the liberating impulse of traditional African-American biblical interpretation. It is also remarkably prescient of contemporary interest in 'hybrid, diaspora, and borderland' identities that undermine the solidity of racist categories.[53] Both Hurston's tenacious black subjectivity and her displacement of fixed racial identity are powerful ways of resisting white domination.

Miriam's Story: Troubling Intersections of Class and Gender

Hurston's novel presents Moses as a revolutionary. 'The man is a radical', the Egyptians charge, 'he would have the common people talking about equality' (p. 475). As an Egyptian prince, Moses prefers the company of a lowly stableman, Mentu (who teaches Moses about

51. Hurston, *Moses*, p. 369.
52. 'Rereading Moses/Rewriting Exodus', p. 108.
53. Kawash, *Dislocating the Color Line*, p. 2.

creation in terms that happen to correspond to Genesis ch. 1; see *Moses*, p. 374). Leaving Egypt, Moses says quietly, 'I don't want to be anybody's boss. In fact, that is the very thing I want to do away with' (p. 402). Crossing the Red Sea, Moses envisions 'a nation he had never heard of where there would be more equality of opportunity and less difference between top and bottom' (p. 407). Moses' male superiority, however, remains secure, and gender-critical readers find it difficult to take Moses' naive egalitarianism seriously.[54]

Hurston depicts with bitter clarity the experience of women in a patriarchal order, above all in the character of Miriam. As an adult, Moses' sister is a rough-hewn former slave and prophet woman. Here Miriam experiences the arrival of Moses' pampered wife, Zipporah:

> Miriam came up to look and see because the whole nation of women was talking about nothing else, and she couldn't stay away. They had no more interest in prophecy and politics. They were still interested in the earrings of Mrs. Moses and her sandals, and the way she walked and her fine-twined colored linens. What she was doing was the way they all wanted to do. Anyhow they could all dream about it and talk, even if they couldn't be like that. Miriam stood off at a short distance from the elaborate tent being put up for the exclusive use of Mrs. Moses and her saliva turned to venom in her mouth. She went up closer to finger the royal linen that Moses had brought out of Egypt for his wife. Then, as before, she looked down at her rough clothing and work-twisted feet and hands and she became aware of class. This woman of Moses' had been oiled with something from birth that she lacked and the futility of wishing for it made her more angry than ever.[55]

This passage testifies eloquently to the capacity of social class divisions to create worlds of difference among women. Yet the oppression of women in Hurston's narrative also cuts across class and ethnic boundaries. Even an Egyptian princess is regarded by her people as little more than 'a passageway for boy children' (p. 372).

Hurston's negotiation of gendered terrain in *Moses* is not entirely pessimistic. Although the story centers on male protagonists, 'quite literally', as Melanie Wright notes, 'Hurston's *Moses* begins with women's voices. The cries of Hebrew women in labour, rather than

---

54. E.g. Deborah McDowell: 'The "place" of women in this narrative of patriarchy's origins is to be followers, and the places in which they figure in the novel are perhaps its most troubling' ('Lines of Descent/Dissenting Lines', p. xi.). Feminists' ambivalence toward Hurston's *Moses* is addressed by M.J. Wright, ' "Sunk in Slavery... Snarled in Freedom": Recent Feminist Analysis of Exodus–Deuteronomy and Zora Neale Hurston's *Moses, Man of the Mountain'*, *Biblicon* 2 (1997), pp. 39-49.

55. Hurston, *Moses*, pp. 537-38.

the words of Egypt's new ruler in Exod. 1.9, open this re-presentation
of the Bible'.[56] Indeed, one might infer that by rewriting Exodus,
Hurston gives herself voice as a new Moses.[57] The novel displays
strong women who struggle against terrible circumstances: Jochebed
defies the command to kill her baby as Pharaoh's soldiers approach;
Zipporah meets raiders on her household dressed up like a man and
ready to fight; Miriam is remembered for galvanizing the people's
resolve, 'her dust weighed as much as all Israel' (pp. 352, 424, 574).
There are intimations of woman-centered religious experience in Hurston's reading of Exodus. For example, rather than emphasizing God
as the Divine Warrior, the awesome and violent 'He' of the biblical
Exodus (e.g. Exod. 15.3), Hurston focuses on the holy mountain as a
living, maternal presence with 'heavy hips' (p. 549). Moses supposes
that he is made of the mountain's substance:

> There was the mountain to see and feel. It was easy for Moses to con-
> ceive that the dust he was made from came off that mountain there...
> The mountain hovered over him and called him as a mother would. He
> must go up and embrace his mother.[58]

The question of women's voices, however, is left painfully unre-
solved in Hurston's narrative. The cries of the Hebrew women at the
beginning of the novel, shuddering 'with terror at the indifference of
their wombs to Egyptian law', are stifled. 'They must cry,' Hurston
narrates, 'but they could not cry out loud. They pressed their teeth
together. A night might force upon them a thousand years of feelings'
(p. 341). When Jochebed's time comes, she flails against her husband's
hand clamped over her face like a vice, fighting in vain 'for her breath
and for the boon of shrieking out her agony and suffering'. The midwife exclaims, 'Ah, it is awful when a woman cannot even cry out in
childbirth' (p. 348).

Moses' silencing of Miriam (cf. Num. 12) is a grim scene in the novel.
Punished for challenging Moses' authority, Miriam spends the rest of
her days a broken and shunned woman, 'very silent' except for occasionally muttering to passers-by: 'He lifted his right hand. I saw him
do it' (p. 558). Years later she laments:

---

56. ' "Sunk in Slavery... Snarled in Freedom" ', p. 41.

57. A 'signifying' take, in other words, on the tradition of Mosaic Pentateuchal
authorship. Cf. Lowe, *Jump at the Sun*, p. 212.

58. Hurston, *Moses*, p. 422; compare the scene of Moses' birth: 'Then suddenly
Jochebed clenched her fists and groaned like the earth birthing mountains' (p. 12).
On goddess motifs in Hurston's *Moses*, cf. Donaldson, 'Rereading Moses/Rewrit-
ing Exodus', pp. 110-113.

I been through living for years. I just ain't dead yet…ever since I spent that week outside the camp…you beat me and then you bottled me up inside of my own body and you been keeping me in jail inside myself ever since. Turn me loose, Moses, so I can go on and die.[59]

Melanie Wright emphasizes Miriam's tragic character as a woman who is 'progressively silenced'. She observes that 'Hurston's text charts the career of a woman who loses her voice, or rather has it ripped from her by a male-centred, male-dominated society'.[60] Wright defends Hurston against the charge of creating in *Moses, Man of the Mountain* a text that marginalizes women's voices. She suggests rather that Hurston's narrative exposes this suppression of female voice to critique.[61] It has been surmised that Miriam's story is in important ways Zora's story. Like Miriam, Hurston spoke with a disruptive intensity, not welcome to her male contemporaries. Hurston never gained full acceptance by the male literary establishment of the Harlem Renaissance and its aftermath.[62] Her vindication as an artist came only after her death. I suspect that the pathos of Miriam's character springs in part from Hurston's self-identification with Miriam.

Conclusion: Hurston's Legacy

Henry Louis Gates, Jr cautions against sentimentalizing Zora Neale Hurston's 'disastrous final decade'.[63] Perhaps I am guilty of this already, but the facts of Hurston's last years are sobering. Today no account of American literature would deny Zora Neale Hurston an important place, but in 1960 she died in obscurity, an impoverished resident of the St Lucie County, Florida, Welfare Home.[64] She was buried in a segregated cemetery, in a grave that would remain unmarked until 1973, when Alice Walker placed a monument in the presumed vicinity of her resting place.[65] As Alice Walker has put it,

59. Huston, *Moses*, p. 572.

60. Wright, ' "Sunk in Slavery… Snarled in Freedom" ', p. 46.

61. Wright, ' "Sunk in Slavery… Snarled in Freedom" ', p. 46.

62. See, e.g., the reviews of Hurston's *Their Eyes Were Watching God* by Richard Wright (1937) and Alain Locke (1938), reprinted in Gates, Jr and Appiah (eds.), pp. 16-18.

63. 'Zora Neale Hurston: "A Negro Way of Saying" ', Afterword to Hurston, *Moses, Man of the Mountain* (New York: HarperCollins, 1991), p. 298.

64. Hemenway, *Zora Neale Hurston*, pp. 347-48.

65. A. Walker, 'In Search of Zora Neale Hurston', *Ms.* 3, 9 (March 1975), pp. 74-89; reprinted as 'Looking for Zora', in Walker, *In Search of Our Mothers' Gardens*, pp. 93-116.

Hurston was manifestly decades 'ahead of her time'. *Moses, Man of the Mountain* is an important resource for Womanist and feminist readings of the Bible. This novel along with the rest of Hurston's writings illuminates critical reflection on questions of difference and inclusion, domination and resistance.

OEDIPUS WRECKS: MOSES AND GOD'S ROD*

Ilona Rashkow

A significant link between psychoanalytic literary theory and biblical scholarship lies in the privilege both accord the language of images and symbols. One image that seems to connect the two disciplines is God's rod, first mentioned in Exod. 4.1-5 and later in 7.8-12 as an object that changes its form into a serpent and then back again into a rod. Since the language of images and symbols is equally important in mythology,[1] a discipline that bridges psychoanalytic literary theory and biblical scholarship, I would like to return *to* Egypt instead of *leaving* it as Moses did, and read the Egyptian myth of Isis and Osiris as a lens through which I view the symbolism, and hence, significance, of Moses and God's rod.[2] First, however, I would like to clarify some presuppositions, primarily in terms of 'who' or 'what' I mean by 'Moses' and in what sense is the text 'historical'.

Narratives are concerned with temporal events and incidents as well as characters and their personalities. Aristotle stressed the centrality of action and incident and, until fairly recently, literary criticism has tended to emphasize the importance of plot over character. Within the last several years, however, 'characterization' has become a focus of critical inquiry. As Henry James asks, 'What is [narrative] incident but the illustration of character?' Indeed, in James's view, the very purpose of literary narrative is to provide and elucidate the *varieties* of human characters and their eccentricities.[3] But who 'is' the literary character? Is the literary character a 'real' or 'historical' being?

---

* An earlier version of this paper was read at the 1993 Society of Biblical Literature Annual Conference.

1. As Freud wrote in 1926, 'mythology may give you the courage to believe in psychoanalysis' ('The Question of Lay Analysis', SE XII [1926], pp. 183-250, 211).

2. Of course, I am not the first to return Moses to Egypt. See, for example, Freud's *Moses and Monotheism* (SE XXIII [1939]) for a different reading of the Moses/Egyptian connection.

3. For a more in-depth analysis of the import of character for James see his

My premise is that literary characters are both more and less than real persons (contra Edmond Cross, for example, who rejects 'the referential illusion that would make a character something other than a product of writing and...would...presuppose the hypostatization of a real person').[4] Literary characters (and Moses is no exception) resemble 'real people' in that they represent human action and motivation. At the same time, literary characters are 'textual'. Pertinent information about a character is narratively presented and/or withheld in order to further the action and a character's behavior is determined by the writer's manipulation rather than divine, natural or social causes. From this perspective, Moses is part of the storyline and nothing else.

Back to Isis and Osiris. Briefly summarized,[5] Osiris, the great-grand-son of Re, grandson of Shu, and first son of Geb and Nut, succeeding his father as king in Egypt, married his sister, Isis. Osiris, widely regarded as a just and wise king, organized the agricultural, religious and secular life of his people, and assisted by Isis, acquired additional territory through many peaceful foreign conquests. This happy state of affairs was soon destroyed, however, by Seth, the younger brother of Osiris who, jealous of Osiris's power and prestige, wanted the throne and accolades for himself. When Osiris returned to Egypt from travels abroad, Seth invited him to a banquet at which 72 accomplices were also present. During the festivities, a beautifully decorated casket specifically built to the measurements of Osiris was brought into the hall. Seth promised that the much-admired casket would be given to the person who fit inside it perfectly. Of course, when it was Osiris's turn to try it out for size, it was...just right! Seizing the opportunity to usurp his brother's position, Seth and his followers closed the lid,

'Preface to *The Portrait of a Lady*, in *The Art of the Novel* (ed. R. Blackmur; New York: Charles Scribner's Sons, 1934).

4.   E. Cross, *Theory and Practice of Sociocriticism* (Minneapolis: University of Minnesota Press, 1988), p. 107. See also Robert Alter, who takes Harold Bloom to task for anthropomorphizing the biblical deity (*The World of Biblical Literature* [New York: Basic Books, 1992], p. 22).

5.   Unfortunately, no complete account of the myth of Isis and Osiris has been preserved in an Egyptian text, although several references and additional and varying details are found in Egyptian religious writings and monumental inscriptions. The only extant text of the whole legend is Plutarch's *De Iside et Osiride*, a late form of the myth with several Greek influences. However, Plutarch does provide a very useful story outline. In depicting this myth I have relied on J.G. Griffiths, *The Origins of Osiris and his Cult* (Leiden: E.J. Brill, 1980); R.B. Parkinson, *Voices from Ancient Egypt: An Anthology of Middle Kingdom Writings* (London: British Museum Press, 1991); and Judith Ochshorn, *The Book of the Goddesses: Past and Present* (New York: Crossroad, 1988).

fastened it securely, and threw the casket into the River Nile in the hope that it would be carried out to the Mediterranean Sea and lost forever. Unfortunately for Seth, the casket washed ashore near the city of Byblos on the Syrian coast, close to the base of a young tamarisk tree, which quickly grew to enclose the casket inside its trunk. The king of Byblos noticed the tree, ordered it to be cut down, and had it made into a column to support the hall roof in his palace.

Meanwhile, back in Egypt, Isis had heard what Seth had done to Osiris and in great distress she set out to find her husband/brother. Eventually she came to Byblos, succeeded in having the palace column removed, retrieved the casket, and took it back to Egypt where she hid it in the marshes of the Delta. Although Osiris was dead, Isis at least had the body of her late husband/brother.

One night, Isis left the casket unattended and Seth discovered it. Determined to destroy his brother's body permanently, he cut it up into 14 pieces and distributed them over all of Egypt. When Isis became aware of this outrage, she travelled throughout the country searching for the various body parts, assisted by her sister Nephthys (who also happened to be the wife of Seth). Gradually, they found 13 of the 14 pieces, reassembled them and reanimated them. The only part of Osiris's body she could not find was his penis that had been eaten by a Nile fish. To replace this irretrievably lost member, Isis created a simulacrum—the Phallus. The resurrected Osiris had no further part to play on earth. Thus, he became the ruler of the dead and Isis superseded Osiris as the fertility deity in Egypt. The simulacrum of Osiris's penis was now an object of veneration, and in honor of this Phallus, according to Plutarch 'the Egyptians even at the present day celebrate a fertility festival'.[6] Herodotus graphically describes the celebration:

> [T]he Egyptians...have...eighteen-inch-high images, controlled by strings, which the women carry round the villages; these images have a penis that nods and in size is not much less than all the rest of the body. Ahead there goes a flute-player, and the women follow, singing in honor of Osiris. Now why the penis is so much bigger and is the only movable thing in the body—about this there is a sacred story told.[7]

6. 'Of the parts of Osiris's body the only one which Isis did not find was the male member...but Isis made a replica (*mimema*) of the member to take its place, and constructed the Phallus, in honor of which the Egyptians even at the present day celebrate a festival' (*Moralia*, V [trans. Frank Cole Babbit; Cambridge, MA: Harvard University Press, 1936], p. 47).

7. Herodotus, *The Histories: Book 2* (trans. David Grene; Chicago: University of Chicago Press, 1987), p. 152.

Neither Plutarch nor Herodotus says anything further about the excessive dimensions of the Phallus or its movement. Indeed, Herodotus seems bound to silence. Apparently, it is a secret that had to be guarded—religiously. Indeed, Isis is depicted time and again in Egyptian monumental art hovering over the dead, penis-less body of her late husband/brother while holding a large simulacrum, and the 'religious' aspects of this cult apparently included hymns of praise dedicated to Isis as the new fertility goddess.[8] In more modern times, the religious practices of this cult so astonished Voltaire that he used the Phallus as an illustration of relativism:

> The Egyptians were so far from attaching any disgrace to what we are desirous as much as possible to conceal and avoid the mention of, that they bore in procession a large and characteristic image, called Phallus, in order to thank the gods for making the human frame so instrumental in the perpetuation of the human species.[9]

A long and tedious commentary would be necessary to give all of the details of this myth's wealth. In political terms, for example, the myth has been described as preserving dim historical elements of a time during the Predynastic Period when Egypt was divided into the two kingdoms of Upper and Lower Egypt, each with its own ruler. According to Parkinson, Osiris represents an early king whose death led to war between the two kingdoms. In agricultural terms, the death and resurrection of Osiris as a very early nature god apparently were celebrated each year in ceremonies at the time of the Nile flood when the crop was sown and when the harvest was gathered.[10] In ritual terms, the old agricultural ceremonies were joined with the cult of the dead to form the official Osirian rites and festivals, performed at the places where parts of the body of Osiris were reputed to be found, such as Athribis (heart), Busiris (backbone), Memphis (head) and so on. The festivals included 'mysteries', dramatic performances of episodes relating to the life, death and resurrection of Osiris, and often involved the planting of seed in Osiris-shaped molds to germinate and grow by the end of the festival.[11] But what is particularly striking

8.   See Lichtheim for a compilation of hymns dedicated to the cults of Isis and Osiris and Downing for examples of Egyptian art devoted to the enormous dimensions of the wooden Phallus.

9.   Voltaire, 'Ezekiel', *Philosophical Dictionary*, IV (trans. William F. Fleming; Akron: Werner, 1906), p. 305-11.

10.   Nahum M. Sarna, *Exodus* (JPS Torah Commentary; Philadelphia: Jewish Publication Society of America, 1991), p. 39.

11.   Griffiths, *The Origins of Osiris and his Cult*, p. 47.

from a psychoanalytic literary perspective is that the myth of Isis and Osiris interprets the dramatic relationship between the castrated 'real penis' of Osiris, the one-time fertility *god*, and the oversized 'Phallus'—now a fertility symbol—carried by the female devotees of the new fertility *goddess*.

What is the relationship between the spectacular simulacrum of the displayed, fully erect, sacred Phallus of Osiris carried in procession during religious ceremonies and God's rod? While 'Phallus' is interchangeable with 'penis' in ordinary usage, in psychoanalytic literary theory 'Phallus' does not denote the anatomical organ; rather, Lacan associates 'Phallus' with the concept of 'power'. The Phallus is emblematic of that which we want but cannot or do not have (that is, what we desire but lack), irrespective of which sex we happen to be. Rose, for example, attributes a sexual neutrality to the Phallus by characterizing it as 'a term which, having no value itself…can represent that to which value accrues'.[12] Similarly, Ragland-Sullivan asserts that 'the phallic signifier does not denote any sexual gender [or] superiority'.[13] For the cult of Osiris, the Phallus comes 'in place of' Osiris's penis. It is a fabrication, a constructed model, an artifact that simulates what is missing, and simultaneously, renders it sacred and larger than life to make it a goddess cult fertility object. Indeed, Lacan uses this very myth when he distinguishes the penis as *organ* and the Phallus as 'that simulacrum that it was in Ancient times'.[14] I read the Exodus narrative in a similar way: like Osiris's simulacrum, God's rod represents the ultimate power of a sacred Phallus.

When God first identifies himself to Moses, it is as 'the God of your *fathers*, the God of Abraham, the God of Isaac, and the God of Jacob', reminding Moses (who had been reared by Pharaoh's daughter) of the covenant made with the patriarchs (his biological father's ancestors)—a covenant that in no way includes the fertility goddess, Isis! Moses, perhaps remembering the parades of women carrying the immense Phallus so graphically described by Herodotus or perhaps anticipating skepticism by his fellow Israelites still in Egypt (who have been witnessing these fertility rites of Isis for 430 years), says in effect,

12. Jacquelin Rose, 'Introduction', in Jacques Lacan, *Feminine Sexuality* (trans. and ed. Juliet Mitchell and Jacqueline Rose; New York: W.W. Norton, 1982), pp. 27-57, 43.

13. Ellie Ragland-Sullivan, *Jacques Lacan and the Philosophy of Psychoanalysis* (Urbana: University of Illinois Press, 1986), p. 271.

14. Jacques Lacan, *The Four Fundamental Concepts of Psycho-Analysis* (trans. Alan Sheridan; London: Tavistock, 1977), p. 690.

'OK. I'll tell them "the God of your *fathers* has sent me", but what good will that do? They're going to need proof'. Thereupon, God gives Moses instructions. First, Moses is to tell all the '*sons* of Israel' that 'the Lord God of your *fathers*, the God of Abraham, the God of Isaac, and the God of Jacob has sent me'. This simple statement establishes opposition between 'the *sons* of Israel' and the *women* of the Egyptian villages, women who 'religiously' parade with an oversized fertility symbol and worship a *female* fertility deity. God reinforces this schism linguistically by saying 'this is my memorial (זכרי)', a word etymologically related to the word for—male (זכר). Next, Moses is told to gather the elders of Israel and using the same formulaic language ('the God of your *fathers*, the God of Abraham, of Isaac, and of Jacob') remind *them* of the covenant, a covenant made only with the *male* members of the community. The centerpiece of this covenant is God's promise that Abraham will have vast numbers of descendants, but only because of the intervention of the Israelite deity:

> I shall establish my covenant between me and you, and *I* shall make you exceedingly numerous...this is my covenant with you: You shall be the father of a multitude of nations... *I* shall make you the father of a multitude of nations. *I* shall make you exceedingly fertile, and make nations of you; and kings shall come forth from you (Gen. 17.2, 4-6; emphasis added).

By these two acts, Moses subliminally associates *God* (the Israelite *male* deity) with Abraham's fertility, thus diminishing the role of Isis (the Egyptian *female* fertility deity) in procreation. Moses, however, is still not completely convinced. As a result, God draws upon the authority of his 'rod'.

In the Hebrew Bible there are four words that are commonly translated as 'rod', all of which refer to an elongated object. While the distinctions in English are not particularly pronounced, in Hebrew the words are used for quite different purposes. The מקל, for example, is a 'rod' in the sense of a 'walking stick' or 'hand-staff'; the שבט is a 'rod' used for punishing; and the חטר is generally used to denote a 'twig'. A מטה, the term used in reference to God's rod, denotes a leader's staff and carries the Lacanian weight of power in both positive and negative contexts. (In Ps. 110.2, for example, the psalmist sings that 'Yhwh will send your strong rod [מטה עזך] out of Zion', while Ezekiel uses the term negatively: 'violence has risen to a wicked rod [למטה רשע, Ezek. 7.11]). Indeed, the only place where מטה is used to refer to a shepherd's 'rod' is here in the Exodus narrative, where the deity proves his might to Moses (the hesitating future leader) by changing his מטה into a—*snake* (נחש)! Snakes and rods, two time-honored phallic symbols, represent both Freudian sexual symbolism (the two phases of the male organ in its active and quiescent states) and Lacanian phallic/power symbolism. By juxtaposing a snake and his rod, God establishes *his* מטה as *the* signifier of ultimate authority, a simulacrum of even greater proportions than those the devotees of Isis carried, a signification that continues throughout the confrontation with Pharaoh.[15] That is, like Sarna, I see the interactions between God, Moses, Pharaoh and the magicians as attempts to discredit Egyptian polytheism in general, and worship of the Egyptian fertility goddess Isis, in particular.[16]

When Moses returns to Egypt he presents himself before Pharaoh, but wields God's rod, and this time it turns into a—*serpent* (תנין)! Pharaoh's magicians, wielding their *own* rods, apparently possess the same power. Thus, at first it seems that the emissaries of the Egyptian fertility goddess[17] carry phallic symbols as potent as God's rod: both sides can transform their elongated objects into *serpents*. The change in reptile from נחש to תנין, snake to serpent, however, is significant from the perspective of traditional biblical scholarship *and* psychoanalytic literary theory since both disciplines rely on the same strategy: being open to the sudden switches and rearrangements that reveal alternate messages and expose the dynamic play of meaning behind what may seem to be a simple statement. In the case of specific word choice, repetitions *and* shifts represent the basis for a wealth of scholarly material among biblical scholars and psychoanalytic literary critics. The study of lexical similarities and differences is a mainstay, since words can mean more than they seem to mean and do more than they seem to do. Among biblical scholars, Berlin, for example, explores how 'lexical cohesion' (the ways in which words are linguistically connected within a sequence) plays a role in interpretation, and how awareness of this relationship can lead to better readings.[18] In a very different kind of criticism, Bloom examines 'poetic crossings', the ways in which a text can destroy its own integrity if examined within the

---

15. Danna Nolan Fewell has reminded me that מטה also includes the meaning 'tribe', lending further weight to its procreative connotation: God's 'rod' produces the 'tribes' of Israel.

16. Sarna, *Exodus*, pp. 38-39.

17. The Hebrew חרטמים derives from an Egyptian title meaning 'chief priest' (Sarna, *Exodus*, p. 37); since the cults of Osiris and Isis were the most popular, it is likely that these 'magicians' were part of the cult of Isis and Osiris.

18. Adele Berlin, 'Lexical Cohesion and Biblical Interpretation', *Hebrew Studies* 30 (1989), pp. 29-40.

framework of lexical similarities and differences.[19] This particular change in word choice (from נחש to תנין—snake to serpent) has been commented upon by biblical scholars. Cassuto, for example, notes the change in reptile and attributes it to geographical factors: 'in place of the snake (נחש), which is more suited to the desert, where the sign was given to Moses, we have here a תנין (serpent)'.[20] Sarna, in a more literary vein, notes the 'special relevance to Pharaoh, who is addressed as follows in Ezek. 29.3 "Thus says the Lord God: I am going to deal with you, O Pharaoh, king of Egypt, Mighty Serpent (התנין הגדול)"'.[21]

I prefer to examine the change from snake to serpent from the perspective of both traditional biblical exegesis *and* psychoanalytic literary theory. In biblical Hebrew, נחש ('snake') derives from the verb 'to hiss'. It is used *literally* to signify the actual animal, and *figuratively* for enemies or oppressors (see, for example, Jer. 8.17; Isa. 14.29). תנין (or תנים, Ezek. 29.3) ('serpent') is an *intensive* noun which derives from the root תנן, 'to elongate'. It is used in more dramatic and dangerous circumstances, for example, a *'venomous* serpent', *'devouring* dragon', 'sea- (or river-) *monster'* (see, for example, Deut. 32.33; Jer. 51.34; Gen. 1.21). When תנין is used in the figurative sense, it refers to enemies, and again, the metaphoric usage is intensified (that is, it refers to *particularly* dangerous enemies such as the Egyptians [Job 74.13] or more commonly, the personification of chaos [Isa. 27.1; 51.9]. Here, in the Exodus narrative, Moses is first introduced to God's power by a נחש, a 'hiss'. When Moses does the wand-into-serpent trick before Pharaoh, God's rod becomes the more dramatic תנין ('serpent'), intensifying the strength of his authority in the eyes of Moses who, faced with the magicians of Isis, may still need encouragement. When the magicians of the fertility goddess Isis perform the same act, it appears that God's rod, in the hand of Moses, is no greater than that of Isis in the hands of her magicians. The more God's rod is wielded, however, the greater the significance of תנין and its derivation from the root 'to elongate'. As God's rod becomes longer, it becomes more potent, more able to wreak destruction upon the Egyptians. Finally, God's rod swallows up the sorcerers' rods. Most importantly, since by metathesis בלע ('swallow') suggests בעל ('possess'), by 'swallowing' the rods of Pharaoh's magicians, God's rod now 'possesses' the sym-

19. Harold Bloom, 'Poetic Crossing: Rhetoric and Psychology', *The Georgia Review* 30 (1976), pp. 495-526.

20. Umberto Cassuto, *A Commentary on the Book of Exodus* (trans. Israel Abrahams; Jerusalem: Magnes Press, 1983 [1967]), p. 95.

21. Sarna, *Exodus*, p. 21.

bolic procreative power and authority of Isis. At this point God's rod, *the* most elongated, and thus ultimate Lacanian Phallus, becomes the simulacrum that firmly identifies *this* deity as *the most* powerful. In the Lacanian sense, the symbolic and functional value of God's rod highlights God's desire—and ability—to vanquish Pharaoh's magicians, and stands for the ultimate symbolic authority *it* carries and that Pharaoh and the magicians of Isis lack. Due to God's 'elongated' rod, Pharaoh and his magicians symbolically have been castrated. Equally significant, the fertility goddess Isis has been dethroned. The Israelites' fertility deity, God, is one and he is Male. Parenthetically, it should be noted that metathesis allows a more Freudian interpretation as well—בלע also suggests בעילה ('sexual intercourse'). Perhaps it is in this context that Sarna describes the book of Exodus as 'the greatest *seminal* text of biblical literature'.[22]

As the myth of Isis and Osiris highlights, although the Phallus *is* a symbol and not an organ, it undeniably derives a part of its signifying attributes from what the real penis can evoke. Indeed, Freud proposed that symbolization works by pictorial analogy. Long, thin objects regularly represent the Phallus, and concave objects, vessels and containers represent the vagina.[23] As a result, it may not always be easy or even productive to differentiate sharply between penis and Phallus. Indeed, although psychoanalytic literary theory has benefited enormously from Lacan's distinction between the two, the metaphors of veiling and unveiling deployed by Lacan himself emphasize the difficulty of differentiating between them.[24] As Lacan writes, the Phallus, 'by virtue of its turgidity...is the image of the vital flow as it is transmitted in generation', emphasizing its irreducible anchorage in the function of reproduction.[25] Thus, Silverman notes that 'to veil the Phallus in this way is to permit it to function as a privileged signifier, as Lacan himself acknowledges. It is also to conceal the part that gender plays within many important Lacanian texts'.[26] In the Exodus narrative, the association of penis and Phallus is particularly strong. As if to highlight this relationship, the narrator reports an otherwise

---

22. Sarna, *Exodus*, p. xii; emphasis added.

23. Both Freud and his follower Ernest Jones insisted that although there are vast numbers of symbols, the objects or ideas symbolized are limited in number. Psychoanalytic symbols are restricted to the body and its functions (particular the sexual ones), family members, birth, and death.

24. Lacan, *Psycho-Analysis*, pp. 282-92.

25. Lacan, *Psycho-Analysis*, p. 287.

26. Kaja Silverman, 'The Lacanian Phallus', *Differences* 4.1 (1992), pp. 84-115.

irrelevant episode: on the trip back to Egypt Zipporah, Moses's wife, *circumcises* their first-born son while Moses carries—the rod of God![27]

How do snakes, serpents, penis, Phallus, and Isis relate to 'Oedipus Wrecks: Moses and God's Rod'? When Moses threatened Pharaoh with the eighth plague, locusts, he warned that it would be 'something that neither your *fathers* nor *fathers' fathers* have seen'. Later, in the desert, God explains to Moses that the purpose for the entire conflict with Pharaoh is 'that you may recount in the hearing of your *sons* and of your *sons' sons* how I made a mockery of the Egyptians and how I displayed my—*signs* among them'. I see these two simple statements linking the snakes, serpents, penis, Phallus and Isis to form a construct that locks God and Moses into a classic, Oedipal conflict. Let me explain.

According to Freud's famous Oedipal theory, the male child first loves his mother and his attachment to her becomes charged with sexual overtones. In the world of the son's unconscious fantasy, Mother is the object of incestuous desire. At this stage, the son's ego identity focuses on the active, 'masculine' genital organ—the penis. Father, who also possesses a penis, becomes a model. Simultaneously, however, the boy views his father as a rival for his mother's love, an adversary who must be destroyed or removed for gratification to be achieved. But the boy recognizes that Father is the *legitimate* owner of Mother, and as a result, the son views his desire as a transgression that produces anxiety, guilt and renunciation. Fearing retaliation (specifically, castration) by his father for his incestuous wishes, the boy experiences a conflict: love for his mother and fear of his father's power. In effect, Father's penis, the anatomical organ, becomes Father's Phallus—the symbol of Father's power. The only way the male child can keep his penis and masculine identity is by transcending the familial Oedipal triangle, and replacing it with the father-dominated superego, a process that for Freud is 'designed to make the individual

27. Ilana Pardes also sees interesting (but different) echoes of the Isis and Osiris myth in this incident with Zipporah, viewing the brief passage as an example of monotheistic censorship and a 'repressed cultural past'. According to Pardes, the well-known story of Osiris and Isis is retold in the circumcision scene, and Isis (as a character) is 'wrenched apart as her role of midwife-mother-sister-wife is divided among Shifrah, Puah, Yocheved, Miriam, Pharaoh's daughter, and Zipporah' (*Countertraditions in the Bible: A Feminist Approach* [Cambridge, MA: Harvard University Press, 1992], p. 93).

find a place in the cultural community'.[28] As Freud wrote, 'the father is the oldest, first, and...only authority'.[29]

According to Freud the Oedipal conflict, although universal in structure, undergoes transformations and is subject to cross-cultural variability. As Spiro notes, this is particularly true in societies in which the conflict is not successfully resolved, and thus necessitates constant repression.[30] With Freud and Lacan as the basis, I read this narrative from a psychoanalytic literary perspective: God is the father-image, Moses is the son, and the entire panoply of Egyptian gods and goddesses (the fertility cult of Isis in particular) is a *composite* mother-image.

Moses (the male-child figure) first loves his 'mother' (Isis) and has the unconscious desires Freud describes. (It is important to remember that, for Freud, the 'reality' reference of the Oedipus story is to the inner psychic reality of latent desire.[31] That is, the 'events' of the story constitute unrecognized wishes; they are products of fantasy *rather* than actual reproductions of memory. In fact, in the historical formation of psychoanalysis, Freud replaced the 'fairy tale' of infantile parental seduction in which the reality reference of the story was to *actual*, external, objective events[32] with the Oedipus myth. Consistent with Freud's theory, the son's ego identity (in this narrative, Moses) focuses on his active, 'masculine' genital organ (remember Zipporah and the strange circumcision scene?). When Moses sees God's rod symbolically rendering the simulacrum wielded by Isis's magicians impotent, in effect he hears the father's voice, what Freud calls the 'superego' and what Lacan calls *le Nom du Père*, 'the Name of the Father' (in French, *le Nom du Père* sounds like *le Non du Père*, 'the No of the Father', the latter being the verbal expression of the father's function as a disciplinarian). Thus, as in Freud's paradigm, Moses, fearing retaliation for his wishes, experiences a conflict: love for his mother (polytheism in general and Isis in particular) and fear of his father's power (if Osiris's *oversized* Phallus can be destroyed, what

28. Sigmund Freud, 'Female Sexuality', SE XXI (1931), pp. 223-45 (229).

29. Sigmund Freud, 'The Interpretation of Dreams', SE IV (1990), pp. 1-338; SE V (1900), pp. 339-621; quotation from p. 293.

30. Melford E. Spiro, 'An Overview and a Suggested Reorientation', in Francis I.K. Hsu (ed.), *Context and Meaning in Cultural Anthropology* (Homewood: Dorsey Press, 1961), pp. 486-87.

31. Sigmund Freud, 'On the History of the Psycho-Analytic Movement', SE XIV (1914), pp. 3-68 (16-18).

32. Sigmund Freud, 'The Aetiology of the Neuroses', SE III (1896), pp. 189-224 (203).

about Moses's penis?). Consequently, Moses sublimates his desire for the Egyptian goddess/Mother whose fertility rites he had observed for most of his life, identifies with his father-image, Israel's *male* deity, and renounces his affinity with and worship of Isis. By accepting Yhwh as *the* supreme Law—the will of the Father—Moses and his offspring, the 'sons of Israel', become a 'kingdom of priests' (Exod. 19.6). By reminding Moses of the covenant made with the *fathers*, the power of God's rod is thereby linked to the male organ, male sexuality replaces and sublimates the procreative power of Isis, and for Moses and the 'sons of Israel' the penis, and not the simulacrum of Osiris, is the focus of the holy covenant.

Once in the wilderness, however, God reminds Moses that this link with power, the penis, is to be circumcised. In fact, only those who *are* circumcised can commemorate their deliverance from Egypt. While biblical scholars have discussed the political and religious implications of this covenant,[33] they have not paid much attention to the 'token' that seals the arrangement. Why the penis? Certainly, if the purpose was to distinguish this band of wanderers from all other people, a more obvious part of the body might have been chosen, for example piercing the ear or the nose. Indeed, there are some interesting resonances in the terms of a relationship that stipulates that those who do not 'cut' will be 'cut off'. As Sarna notes:

> This punishment…is peculiar to ritual texts and is largely confined to offenses of a… sexual nature. [T]he impersonal, passive form of the verb is used…so that…the executive authority is uncertain. In Lev. 20.3 the active first person is used with God as the subject of the verb: 'I shall set my face against that man and will cut him off from among his people'. This reasonably presupposes that כרת is not a penalty enforced by the courts but a punishment left to divine execution… Certainly the general idea is that one who deliberately excludes himself from the religious community of Israel cannot be a beneficiary of the covenantal blessings and therefore dooms himself and his line to extinction.[34]

Significant for the purposes of this paper, Freud sees circumcision as the 'symbolic substitute' for castration, for what is no longer there, since the circumcised penis both asserts the possible threat of castration (the foreskin has been removed) and denies it (the head of the

---

33. See, e.g., Robert Graves and Raphael Patai, *Hebrew Myths: The Book of Genesis* (New York: Greenwich House, 1983), p. 240; Robin Fox, *Kinship and Marriage* (London: n. pub., 1967), pp. 557-96; Nahum M. Sarna, *Understanding Genesis* (New York: McGraw–Hill, 1966); Roland de Vaux, *Ancient Israel: Its Life and Institutions* (New York: McGraw–Hill, 1961), pp. 46-48.

34. Sarna, *Exodus*, p. 58.

penis is prominent as in an erection).[35] Thus, the sexual symbolism in the relationship between Moses and God is powerful in its reverberations. The original covenant was with *males* only, and the essence of the arrangement was the multiplication of *men*. Offspring are possible, however, only with the assistance of *this* male god ('*I* shall make you exceedingly numerous... *I* shall make you the father of a multitude of nations... *I* shall make you exceedingly fertile, and make nations of you').[36] (Of course, not only psychoanalytic literary theorists have reached this conclusion. Indeed, relying heavily on ethnographic literature, H. Eilberg-Schwartz argues that 'the practice of circumcision, despite its role in symbolizing the covenant...nonetheless symbolized the fertility of the initiate...and ability to perpetuate a lineage of *male* descendants').[37]

Repeating the terms of the covenant to Moses has two results: first, God implicitly erases the female fertility rites of Isis's followers. Since the covenant of circumcision signifies that procreativity now lodges in the relationship between God and human *males*, Isis, the Egyptian fertility goddess/Mother, is displaced by the fertility God/Father. Male sexuality forms the nucleus of filiation, a common bonding (Eilberg-Schwartz), and the Israelite penis, rather than the Egyptian god Osiris's simulacrum, is once again the focus of the holy covenant. The male organ is linked with power (both in the sense of Eilberg-Schwartz's comparative fertility thesis and mine) and goddess-Mother-worship is re-channeled.

Since the covenant endows life-engendering to the male, and then extends this ability from father to son, by implication Moses would *seem* to possess both God's procreative powers, as well as the authority to wield God's rod, a paradigmatic representation of the Freudian male-child's Oedipus construct. The second consequence of reminding Moses of the terms of the covenant, however, is that God immediately establishes the vulnerability of the human anatomical organ, the penis. Although, once again, God promises to bless Israel's 'seed', Moses must depend upon *this deity* for fertility. Certainly, no other

35. Sigmund Freud, *Introductory Lectures on Psycho-Analysis*, SE XV, pp. 15-239; SE XVI, pp. 243-463; quotation from p. 165; *idem*, 'Terminable and Interminable', SE XXIII (1937), pp. 216-53.

36. See Ilona Rashkow, *The Phallacy of Genesis: A Feminist-Psychoanalytical Approach* (Louisville, KY: Westminster/John Knox Press, 1993) for an elaboration, particularly with reference to Genesis narratives.

37. Howard Eilberg-Schwartz, *The Savage in Judaism: An Anthropology of Israelite Religion and Ancient Judaism* (Bloomington: Indiana University Press, 1990), p. 142; emphasis added.

part of the body would emphasize as effectively the connection between male reproductive capacity and the deity's ultimate potency.
The lure for Moses is affiliation with the father/God and the power
inherent in his rod, the superiority of masculine identification and
masculine prerogatives over the feminine influence of Isis. (Freud, as
one recalls, writes that 'whosoever accepted this symbol [circumci-
sion] showed by so doing that he was ready to submit to the father's
will, although it was at the cost of a painful sacrifice'.)[38] As in Freud's
Oedipal construct, however, there is the potential threat of castration
and struggle is inevitable. Oedipus wrecks!

Curiously, the Freudian account of the Oedipus story reveals a
peculiarly selective reading of Sophocles's text: Laius, who is rife with
anxieties, is absolved by Freud of his crime, and his sins and fears
have been displaced by the guilt of his son, Oedipus. In the biblical
narrative, the relationship between Moses and God exposes similar
displacements. Circumcision, seen as a partial castration, is the price
God-as-father exacts from Moses-as-son to be in a somewhat, but not
quite, analogous paternal position vis-à-vis the 'sons of Israel'. That is,
only the deity has a thoroughly intact organ, and thus, only the deity
can provide offspring.

Further, circumcision symbolically feminizes. As the midrash asks
concerning God's actions in Egypt: 'Why is it written, "And the Lord
will pass over the door" [Exod. 12.23]?... Read it [door] literally as
"opening!"...the opening of the body. And what is the opening of the
body? That is the circumcision' (*Zohar* 2.36a). In Freudian analysis, of
course, the 'door/gate' is a symbol of the female genital orifice.[39]
From a psychoanalytic perspective, by reminding Moses that he and
his offspring the 'sons of Israel' are to be circumcised, God displaces
his own anxieties and views Moses as well as the 'sons of Israel' as
female. Hence, there is no threat to his power.[40]

From this perspective, Moses' relationship to God's rod reads almost
like a Freudian case study! Moses-as-son emulates the father; in place
of the women of Egypt dedicating their sexuality to the goddess Isis
by engaging in a ritual parade while carrying Osiris's oversized
phallic simulacrum, Moses will now celebrate the fertility (and viril-

---

38. Freud, *Moses and Monotheism*, p. 156.

39. Freud, *Introduction Lectures*, p. 156.

40. Contra D. Boyarin, who posits that 'circumcision is a male erasure of the
female role in procreation' (' "This We Know to be the Carnal Israel": Circumcision and the Erotic Life of God and Israel', *Critical Inquiry* 18 [1992], pp. 474-505
(476).

ity) of a *male* deity and *male* procreativity. Implied within this construct, however, is a warning by the father/God: 'if you worship women, and specifically, Egyptian goddesses (that is, if you continue to desire Mama/Isis), I'll finish the job started by circumcision, and *fully* castrate you to *make* you a woman'. This implied threat symbolically insures that the son can never be as powerful as the Father.

As many commentators have noted, the stories about Moses in Exodus through Deuteronomy are not really about the *man*, but rather the God who stands behind the man. Despite Moses' seeming power, he does nothing except in response to the deity's commands. Indeed, Schnutenhaus describes Moses as a 'Jahvemarionette'.[41] In Lacanian terms Moses may possess the penis, but never the Phallus, the ultimate symbol of paternal authority and the privilege it signifies.

The relationship of Moses and God's rod lasts beyond Egypt.[42] In Num. 21.4-9, for example, 'venomous snakes' attack the Israelites because of their rebellion against both God and Moses, their bites causing the death of many of the people. The remaining population confesses their sins and Moses, interceding for them, receives instruction for the remedy: a bronze *snake* on a *pole* that will reverse the fatal quality of the bites. Those stricken need only see this double phallic symbol in order to survive the fate inflicted by the snakes. Although there is no explicit connection between God's rod and the bronze snake in Exodus *and* Numbers, serpents, rods and God's power merge. As in the myth of Isis and Osiris, a sacred Phallus has been invested with power.

The fundamental themes of the Oedipal conflict—desire, the meaning of the father figure, law and guilt—characterize the relationship of Moses and God's rod. Isis has been displaced by God's rod; the Egyptian sacralization of *female* sexuality has been displaced by Israelite *male* sexuality; and Egyptian women carrying 18-inch-high images with 18-inch-long nodding Phalluses have been displaced by the *circumcised* penises of the Israelites, *the* manifest symbol of the relationship of Moses and God's rod. That is, Moses may wield God's rod, but never its power. For Freud, Oedipus wrecks. So too for Moses.

41. Quoted in George Coats, *Moses: Heroic Man of God*.

42. Rabbinic legends relate the history of God's מטה (how it was handed down from Adam, generation by generation, until it came into the possession of Moses), and tell of the Tetragrammaton which was inscribed thereon, the mnemonics of the Ten Plagues which were also engraved on it, and other similar details (*Exod. R.* 8.2).

Works Cited

Individual works from the SE cited in the text are listed chronologically in the Bibliography, by the year of the first German edition. Different works published by Freud in the same year are distinguished by the lower-case letters assigned by Strachey in his complete listing of Freud's publications (SE XXIV: 47-82).

DIVINE PUPPETEER: YAHWEH OF EXODUS

Cheryl Kirk-Duggan

In pain,
We cried.
You heard:
Did You listen?
In your time, You did.
At what cost?[1]

In the last decade, many church liturgies have adopted a call and response oratory where the leader proclaims: 'God is Good' and the congregation responds: 'All the Time'. This portion of their liturgy reflects a theology of absolute divine benevolence. A review of the received Exodus text questions the wisdom of canonizing absolute magnificent benevolence. Prevalent violence and the use of women as bookends to the story of Exodus 1–15 call into question historical reality, literary license, humor, irony, paradox and reader response.

The dramatization of Cecil B. DeMille's *The Ten Commandments*[2] featuring Charlton Heston as the protagonist resounds, particularly in the USA, whenever one thinks about the text and the salvific-deliverance movement of the Exodus and recent civil and gender rights movements. That Heston was the former head of the Screen Actors' Guild and is the current head of the National Rifle Association makes the popular culture access to this story a bittersweet reality. Heston's

---

1.   All of the poetry included in this paper is written for this essay by the author.

2.   In 1956, DeMille directed, narrated and produced the remake of his 1923 silent, color epic, *The Ten Commandments*, with Paramount. His production of this biblical story reached a scale never before achieved by any filmmaker, and it grossed over $80 million. *The Movie Guide* notes this moving production where 'Heston's stalwart prophet really does look like Michelangelo's Moses' and 'DeMille's vision remains a powerful one, a testament to his inestimable talent as the master of epic vulgarity and self-justified righteousness'. (James Monaco *et al.*, *The Movie Guide: A Comprehensive, Alphabetical Listing of the Most Important Films Ever Made* [New York: Perigree, 1992], p. 941).

persona, so closely tied to this story, requires a critical reading that
sees hints of cinematographic romanticism and grandeur along with
more accepted yet heinous genocide. Almost two decades prior to
DeMille's gigantic production with a cast of thousands and powerful
cinematic brilliance, novelist Zora Neale Hurston tackled the story of
Moses.

Hurston uses allegory and satire, framed by folklore, to retell the
story of Moses in a twentieth-century prose form when she recounts
the experience of African-Americans within an Exodus motif: Goshen
Jews become African-Americans; every Egyptian becomes a European
American. Hurston critiques divisions in the Black bourgeois and
assails the leadership of Aaron and Miriam, not Moses. In her reading
of Exodus and the myths of Moses circulating in African-American
folklore, legend and song, Hurston moves Moses from an Egyptian
Prince to a religio-social activist. Hurston weaves the life of Moses to
where she builds self-identity and communal awareness in a context
of satire, humor, psychological and philosophical insights in a powerful, complex, persuasive novel.[3] Using music 'as a tool of narration',
with 'pioneering technology' DreamWorks productions brought *Prince
of Egypt*, a redacted version of Exodus 1–15, to the movie screen in
1998. This drama involved over 350 artists, animators and technicians
from 35 different countries. Devoting four years together to bring this
film to the screen, this different reading and representation of Exodus
creates powerful new scenarios, worthy of reflection. The women are
central to the action throughout the drama: Miriam and Zipporah are
consistent major players. The divine egos of Pharaoh and Yahweh and
the brother relationship between Ramses and Moses shape all the
events that unfold, with a healthy dose of divine and human compe-
tition. Early on, we see sibling rivalry between Ramses and Moses;
Moses always gets Ramses in and then out of trouble. Echoes of the
prodigal son parable emerge when Moses, the runaway, returns to
Egypt to deliver Yahweh's edict for the freedom of Israel, with a twist.
The brother, Ramses, has now become the Egyptian god, the Pharaoh,
by virtue of his office. A bit of humor and irony surfaces in the introduction of two new non-Biblical characters, magician/priests Hotep
and Huy. Yahweh outdoes Pharaoh as music, animation and technology embody the honor and glorification of divine violence. On a
poignant note, *Prince of Egypt* portrays an Exodus story where Hebrew

---

3.   Blyden Jackson, 'Introduction', in Zora Neale Hurston, *Moses, Man of the
Mountain* (Chicago: University of Chicago Press, 1984 [1939]), pp. xvi-xviii.

children and adults experience new life, and the Egyptian children and soldiers die.[4]

My reading of Exodus reveals a Yahweh that is benevolent to some of the Israelites some of the time, but who punishes and manipulates other Israelites at other times, and punishes and manipulates most of the Canaanites and Egyptians most of the time. The 'I-Am'-ness motif that pervades the Exodus text speaks of that divine jealousy which organizes the first four edicts of the Decalog: (1) I am the Lord, thy God…, (2) Thou shalt not have strange Gods before Me…, (3) Honor thy Father and thy Mother…, and (4) Keep Holy the Sabbath… The brokering of power and the tensions within the triangular relationship between Yahweh (Adonai), Moses and Pharaoh challenge the notion of divine benevolence, and question the realms of divine and human psychology, politics, and posture.

A question of domestic rivalry emerges in the sibling triangle of Moses, Aaron and Miriam. One must also consider the role and place, in the Exodus text, of Moses' mother, Pharaoh's daughter, Moses' sister Miriam, and the consanguinity of these women with Moses, particularly since there is not one positive mother–daughter story or model in the entire Hebrew Bible. The patriarchal male-centered God of the Israelites is the covenant God of Abram and Sarah, of Isaac and Rebecca, and of Jacob, Leah and Rachel.

This essay explores the dynamics of divine power, ego and attitude, and their impact on human community in Exodus 1–15. After a brief overview of Womanist biblical theology, the investigation pursues: (1) a contextual and thematic characterization of Exodus; (2) the role of women in the preservation of Moses; (3) the relationship between God and Moses; and (4) the psychological and political puissance between Pharaoh and God.

Womanist Biblical Theology[5]

Listening for colors of purple;
Imaginative words,
Crying for those
Perennially living in the wilderness.

---

4. The animated epic took shape before Jeffrey Katzenberg, Steven Spielberg and David Geffen formed DreamWorks in 1994. See:

http://movieweb.com/movie/princeofegypt/princegy.txt
http://movieweb.com/movie/princeofegypt/index.html

5. I first developed this definition of Womanist biblical theory and put it forward in my presentations for the Mordecai Johnson Lecture Series, Colgate

> Hush, we need to hear them.
> Them are they and they are us:
> Seeking an oasis
> Amid depression and shame.
> Aware that there's another message here.

Womanist theory calls for one to live in the present, to be aware of history, to engage in radical listening, to see, to know and to make a difference. This interdisciplinary, spiritual field of study and way of thinking takes the oppressive experience of race/sex/class seriously. 'Womanist', derived by Alice Walker[6] from the term 'womanish', refers to women of African descent who are audacious, outrageous, in charge, and responsible. A Womanist emancipatory theory embraces mutuality and community, honors the *Imago Dei* in all persons, and uses the modes of cultural production of African-American women as resource material. Womanist thought, as theory and praxis, appreciates the importance of prayer and having ongoing intellectual and spiritual dialogue to prepare individuals to experience their own healthy, fulfilling reality. *Womanist* theology,[7] the study or discipline of God-talk that emerges out of the rich yet oppressive experience of African-American women, analyzes human behavior in concert with the divine, seeing the misuse of power and the politics of language.

The body of knowledge and research of Womanist thought includes, but is not limited to, issues in theology (identity, sacrality, spirituality); Bible and/or other sacred texts (authority, characters, rituals, history); ethics (value, visibility, integrity); and context (culture, aesthetics, ecology, community). Womanist theory is a tool to name, expose, question and help transform the oppression women, particularly those affected by race and class domination, face daily. Womanists champion the struggle for freedom: a gift and a right given by God. God is personal, not an abstract, philosophical construct. Since God spoke the world into being, many Womanists take language usage

Rochester Seminary, March, 1999. Subsequently I refined the concepts for my essay, 'Hot Buttered Soulful Tunes & Cold Icy Passionate Truths: The Hermeneutics of Biblical Interpolation in Rhythm & Blues', presented April 1999, for the African Americans and the Bible Project Conference, Union Theological Seminary, in Vincent L. Wimbush (ed.), *African Americans and the Bible: Sacred Text and Social Texture* (New York: Continuum), forthcoming 2000.

6.   Alice Walker, *In Search of our Mother's Gardens: Womanist Prose* (San Diego: Harcourt Brace Jovanovich, 1983), p. xi.

7.   Diana L. Hayes, 'And When We Speak: To Be Black, Catholic, and Womanist', in Diana L Hayes and Cyprian Davis, *Taking Down Our Harps* (Maryknoll, NY: Orbis Books, 1998), pp. 102-19.

seriously between the divine and the human, and within human society, the *Imago Dei* incarnated. The politics of language, where words and expressions inspire or subjugate, are vital to analysis, particularly that of biblical texts. A Womanist biblical theology, or reading and interpretation of biblical texts, needs a hermeneutics of tempered cynicism, creativity, courage, commitment, candor, curiosity, and the comedic.

Tempered cynicism or suspicion presses one to question, with a sensitivity that knows the joy of the impossible, the hope of the embedded faith, together with a scholarship that helps one appreciate the complexities of such work. Creativity provides a context where standard interpretations and traditions do not impede exploring texts in new ways. Courage provides the cushion for moments when the analysis leads to more of the same or mystery. Commitment to the hearing and just, appropriate living of these texts undergirds the process of discovery, from a Womanist perspective, which is never irrelevant to the lives of people. Candor provides the impetus to reveal the oppression within the texts and the communities that have incorporated such tenets to produce an oppressive faith. Curiosity presses one to keep searching the realm of the sacred towards an atmosphere of inclusivity, mercy, justice, and love. The comedic reminds us not to take ourselves so seriously that we fail to grow and to respect other ways of seeing, though we may disagree.

Womanist biblical scholarship, located in the academy and the church, signifies the fire and passion of Womanist scholars as they study, teach, write, interpret, preach and minister. Located in a cosmological setting where Black women intimately know the tridimensional oppressive experience of race/sex/class, Womanist biblicists commit to the gift of education as transformative power. More Womanist biblical scholars are wrestling with Scriptures as they deal with the madness and absurdity of oppression: calling for a ceasefire, for accountability, and for change. Womanist biblical scholars want us to report systemic and personal evil in our society, and move to transform that evil, be it apathy, abuse, or affliction. Such theology analyzes human individual and social behavior in concert with the divine toward seeing the ramifications of injustice. Such injustices produce a malaise due to racism, classism and sexism, other phobias, and the use of power. Womanist biblical theology sees, studies and wishes to exorcise oppressive evil, moving toward change, balance and promise. As a Womanist biblical scholar, I seek a biblical formulation that champions immediacy and inclusivity. Though some biblical texts are less than relevant, Exodus begs for creative readings in light of its

prominence in movements of liberation, despite the lethal violence
that pervades the text.

Contextual and Thematic Characterization

As a theological testament, the book of Exodus rehearses an intimate
connection between the divine and the oppressed of Israel. Although
we cannot document and validate the detailed historicity of Exodus,
most scholars agree that an Exodus event occurred, where the Israelites were in bondage and Moses helped to liberate them. The God of
the patriarchs and matriarchs, Yahweh, is the God of Exodus. The
received text is a cornucopia of stories witnessing the testimony of
generations of poets, cult officials, storytellers and legal minds. The
liberatory tapestry embraces women's protest via civil disobedience,
women who assure Moses' survival. The laborious liberation culminates as the Hebrew children cross the sea and tarry in the wilderness,
where they learn about core theological topics of justice, simplicity
and trust.[8]

The Exodus experience embodies justice in the liberation from slavery, which embraced the forging of a new historical, journeying people, transcending geographical and sociopolitical obstacles.[9] In the
Exodus text, two societies, with two divine–human relationships,
struggle for power and freedom. God's power intensifies and God
exacts judgment with the murder of the first-born. As God removes
Israel from any participation in vengeance, the reader becomes more
empathetic toward Egypt, while seeing Pharaoh in the role of an
isolated, obsessive, perhaps compulsive ruler. Throughout the narrative, the differentiation between groups within Israelite and Egyptian
society heightens.[10] We get to see humanity with its brilliance and its
blemishes.

The received text does not depict the Israelites as all good, nor the
Egyptians as all bad. Pharaoh is held apart from the Egyptian people
and his officers. That Pharaoh does not know Joseph, nor Joseph's
God, points toward a nationalistic and universalistic purpose of the

8.   Rita J. Burns, 'The Book of Exodus', in Bas van Iersel and A. Weiler (eds.),
Exodus: A Lasting Paradigm (Edinburgh: T. & T. Clark, 1987), pp. 11-21 (11-17).
9.   John Newton, 'Analysis of Programmatic Texts of Exodus Movements', in
Bas van Iersel and A. Weiler (ed.), *Exodus: A Lasting Paradigm* (Edinburgh: T. & T.
Clark, 1987), pp. 56-62 (56-57).
10.   Jonathan Magonet, 'The Attitude Towards Egypt in the Book of Exodus', in
Wim Beuken, Sean Freyne and Anton Weiler (eds.), *Truth and Its Victims* (Edin-
burgh: T. & T. Clark, 1988), pp. 11-20 (16-18).

Exodus, and toward the intent that the Egyptians and Pharaoh will come to know God. The increasing numbers and the social location of the Israelites make them prime candidates for being scapegoated to assure the power of the dominant culture. The scapegoat mechanism is effective through various tiers of subjugation. The request for execution at birth by midwives, disenfranchisement in a manner where the Israelites will not lay blame at the feet of the Egyptians, and the use of Israelite foment over Israelite slaves—use of race and class alienation by effective methods—are geared to divide and conquer. Pharaoh attempts to cause a rift between Moses and the Israelites by giving the latter more work, while blaming the former. Ironically, the same mechanism returns to haunt Pharaoh, himself.[11]

One can read the Exodus experience as the disregard or rejection of any power or construction, regardless of the origins—benevolent or oppressive. The interconnectedness of culture in the ancient Near East meant that any political structure had divine origins. If one opposed a particular cosmic order, one also opposed the related responsible divine powers, creating both 'religious rebellion as well as social revolt …in favor of an egalitarian confederation'.[12] From a biblical, theological hermeneutical perspective, Exodus recalls divine deliverance from Egyptian bondage and reminds Israel of her chosenness, her roots, and her responsibilities. From a feminist perspective, Diane Bergant notes that one can use the Exodus-symbol as a hermeneutical approach. Such an approach takes into account that the subjugation of women through confinement and restriction establishes the issue, that revelation discloses reality, and that biblical stories and traditions give witness to revelation, but is not inherently revelation itself.[13]

I read the text as an inquirer, and observer, a cynic whose mind remains boggled by the audacity of the Divine intentionally hardening the heart of Pharaoh and later the Egyptians. I am particularly amazed at how the liberation tradition of Exodus, which has been so important, virtually ends the book at Exodus 15. My reading applauds prior in-depth readings of great theological, archaeological, literary, ethical and artistic insights, ever listening to see what my experience brings to the text, as a teacher-learner-preacher-performer. Elements of courage and commitment prompt a reading that may go against the grain, may even seem heretical to some. Candor allows me to expose the

11. Magonet, 'The Attitude Towards Egypt', pp. 12-14.

12. Dianne Bergant, 'Exodus as a Paradigm in Feminist Theology', in Iersel and Weiler (eds.), *Exodus*, pp. 100-106 (101).

13. Bergant, 'Exodus as a Paradigm', pp. 101, 104, 105.

ingenuity of the women, rehearsed in many other settings, alongside the tremendous amount of divine violence, which is often explored, but usually quickly justified as caring activity on behalf of the Israelites. But if this same God created everyone, and they had not yet experienced this particular revelation, how in the world can the death of all those Egyptians be reconciled? My curiosity has been bubbling over about this text for years since Hebrew study and exegesis courses at seminary. Finally I get to push the curiosity to also view the text from the side of the Egyptians. The comedic makes this work joyful, amid my location in the academy and the church, called to be, in the words of Alice Walker, 'audacious, outrageous, in charge, responsible'.[14]

Moses and the Women

We birthed, caught, nursed,
Protected, watched
Adopted you.
We married, got impregnated, protected you, again.
They acquiesced our voices for us:
Voices that you
And your God engage, yet overpower.
You are/were
Because we were/are
And then, before, during and after
There's God.

The women of Exodus were conscientious objectors who often engaged in typical female tasks, in a context of spiritual subversion. In the mores of gender and class they participated in a righteous revolution. Their praxis was radical, undermining the dominant culture, as women from the dominant and oppressed culture joined ranks. They forged a sisterhood that related to the well-being and elevation of Moses, and refused to allow Pharaoh to dictate their actions. Consistently, Pharaoh seems to lack wisdom, becomes a comedic character, speaks with irony, and ultimately acquiesces his power to the women in the Exodus prologue. Time after time, Pharaoh loses ground as the midwives and others fear Yahweh, the God of Israel, and not Pharaoh, the god of Egypt.[15]

14. Walker, *In Search of our Mother's Gardens*, p. xi.
15. J. Cheryl Exum, ' "You Shall Let Every Daughter Live": A Study of Exodus 1.8–2.10', in Athalya Brenner (ed.), *A Feminist Companion to Exodus to Deuteronomy* (Sheffield: Sheffield Academic Press, 1994), pp. 37-61 (43, 48, 50) (reprinted from *Semeia* 28 [1983]: pp. 63-82).

Although the received text most often depicts daughters as objects, rather than subjects and protagonists, the Exodus 1–2 pericope presses the centrality of Moses, amid the parallel construct of 12 daughters to the 12 sons and tribes of Jacob. This 12 includes: Pharaoh's daughter, midwives Shifrah and Puah; Moses' mother, the daughter of Levi (Jochebed), Moses' sister (Miriam), and the seven daughters of Reuel (Jethro), the priest of Midian. Unlike the motherly or sisterly concern of previous 'daughters', the priestly daughters meet Moses as an adult, whom they bring to their father's house, as an Egyptian man who marries one of the priest's daughters, Zipporah.[16] In view of the fact that women almost overrun the Exodus 1–2 text, it is curious that they are absent in subsequent chapters. Two tactics may be at work: (1) the primacy of infants, particularly baby Moses, and the rendering of honor to God, who uses the weak to overcome the strong, and who registers the role and secondary status of women in deference to patriarchal motivations. (2) Patriarchy spins a powerful strategy by rewarding women for being complicit in their own subordination, being relegated to domesticity, and at the same time being accorded recognition as national s/heroes for saving male babies and for embracing Motherhood. Whatever the motivation, women's power is contained through diffusion, suppression, and in Miriam's case, punishment.[17] What we fail to learn about Moses' immediate female kinship in Exodus, we learn in Numbers 12, in the dispute over Moses' authority. Numbers 26, the report of the second census, 'documents' Moses' genealogy or family tree. The Exodus and Numbers texts allow a sociocultural picture of the man called Moses and the impact of women on his life.

As social productions, biblical texts have particular sociocultural settings, and take particular ideological stances, advocating for or critiquing particular characters. Exodus, told from the view of the Hebrews, tends to denigrate the Egyptians and outline the sociopolitical conditions and identities of Israel. One can quickly size up who has power and who does not. In addition to the fear of sheer numbers, and the military and political threat that more Hebrew boy children ultimately pose, a major ontological reality is that the text views Hebrews and Egyptians as different. Social order depends upon strict adherence to 'differences between people, differences that eventuate in stereo-

16. Jopie Siebert-Hommes, 'But if She Be a Daughter…She May Live! "Daughters" and "Sons" in Exodus 1–2', in Brenner (ed.), *Exodus to Deuteronomy*, pp. 62-74 (62-72).

17. J. Cheryl Exum, 'Second Thoughts about Secondary Characters: Women in Exodus 1.8–2.10', in Brenner (ed.), *Exodus to Deuteronomy*, pp. 75-87 (76-86).

types, differences that manifest themselves in power relations'.[18]
Three confrontations challenge the ethos of dominant culture. There
are threats to Pharaoh's leadership (an attack on Egyptian hegemony),
Pharaoh's authority, and Pharaoh's control over the Israelites' destiny. These threats question assumptions of Egyptian rule: power,
wisdom and authority. The social conflict in Exodus 1 presses one to
critique the use of power, the exploitation of human labor, and the
options the powerless have to refuse. Further, the narrator does not
challenge the concept of difference, but recasts them, sanctioning religious superiority as opposed to class or racial-ethnic pre-eminence.[19]
That the women who care for Moses, his mother, sister and Pharaoh's
daughter, apparently come from different races and classes, does not
inhibit their womanish support and nurture of Moses, even when,
apparently, God is missing in action from intervening into their lives.

While human characters, especially these women, are about creating
and preserving life, God is absent in Exodus 1–2, and is only mentioned once prior to Exod. 2.23-25, which starkly contrasts with the
remainder of the book where Yahweh predominates the action.
Scholars like Donald Gowan argue that God's absence or hiddenness
is deliberate. Like other episodes in the Hebrew Bible, we do not
know what God is doing at these moments and the editor provides no
commentary. Yet, God is not silent forever and the editor rehearses
the times when God does act. In some historical and prophetic books,
the suffering and experience of divine abandonment occur because the
people abandoned God; God did not abandon them. Such is not the
case in Exodus 1–2. Interestingly, Exodus 1–2 has the sentiments of a
psalm of lament—a sense of God's absence in step with grave suffering. In the prophetic works, God's absence is often viewed as the
result of human sin. The Psalms do not rationalize God's absence, but
declare their bewilderment.[20] Samuel Balentine, in *The Hidden God*,
notes that God's absence and God's presence are integral to God's
nature.[21] God's apparent absence did not hinder the presence or
creative imagination of Jochebed.

18. Renita Weems, 'The Hebrew Women Are Not Like the Egyptian Women:
The Ideology of Race, Gender and Sexual Reproduction in Exodus 1', *Semeia* 59
(1992), pp. 25-34 (30).

19. Weems, 'Hebrew Women', pp. 26-33.

20. Donald E. Gowan, *Theology in Exodus: Biblical Theology in the Form of a Commentary* (Louisville, KY: Westminster/John Knox Press, 1994), pp. 2-7, 23.

21. Samuel Balentine, *The Hidden God: The Hiding of the Face of God in the Old
Testament* (Oxford: Oxford University Press, 1983), p. 172 (quoted in Gowan, *Theology in Exodus*, p. 13).

The texts tell us little about Jochebed. We learn her name in Num. 26.59. In Moses' birth narrative, she is unnamed. This narrative parallels birth legends of other heroes, like Sargon of Agade, who was saved at infancy by being put into a sealed basket and that basket then floated on a river. This was the ingenuity of the unnamed Levite woman who married a man from the house of Levi (Exod. 2.1). That her name means 'glory of Yahweh',[22] indicates that God's self-revelation of the divine name in Exodus 3 is not the first time that this name was revealed. This notion supports the argument of a different textual arrangement, that ch. 3 originally came before the material in chs. 1 and 2, posited by Randall Bailey and discussed later in this essay. We learn that Jochebed actually marries her nephew, Amram, as she is his aunt, 'his father's sister' (Exod. 6.20). Jochebed had to be a remarkable woman to hide Moses, knowing of the dictum to kill all Hebrew baby boys, and then to put him in the basket or ark, with the possibility of it overturning and Moses drowning. She was also astute enough to be waiting near the proscenium to enter the stage when summoned by her daughter. Her love, faith and courage to subvert a horrendous system paralleled the courage of women engaged in midwifery throughout Pharaoh's kingdom.

Shifrah and Puah, clever midwives who reflect the religious sensibilities of the wisdom circles, manage to dupe the allegedly shrewd Pharaoh. Much conversation has occurred around the nationality of the midwives, whether Egyptian or Hebrew. Their respect or fear of God made them loyal to Yahweh, not to Pharaoh, exercising their faith as opposed to trembling amid Pharaoh's tyrannical, asinine power. Scholars argue both cases, but the Masoretic Text accepts the midwives as Hebrew. Moses' unnamed sister (Miriam) and her unnamed mother (Jochebed) subvert the status quo when they can no longer keep the baby hidden. Miriam then maneuvers to have Jochebed wet nurse Moses and get paid in the process. Pharaoh's daughter also subverts the system and her father's rule by caring for and adopting Moses. Pharaoh's plans are thwarted by the women in his kingdom, including his own daughter, not armies or heads of state.[23] What were his daughter's motives? Did she previously want children of her own? Recognizing the child's ethnicity, was she shielding the child to double-cross her dad? Was she feeling guilty about her

22. Herbert Lockyer, *All the Women of the Bible* (Grand Rapids: Zondervan, 1988), p. 79.

23. Brevard S. Childs, *The Book of Exodus: A Critical, Theological Commentary* (OTL; Philadelphia: Westminster Press, 1974), pp. 13, 16, 18-19.

father's actions, and perhaps feeling great empathy with the Hebrew women? Like bookends, women open and close Exodus 1–15 as major players. Miriam's voice is also strategically heard at the end, as her song lends a revelatory voice to the celebration of redemption.[24] Or perhaps Moses was the outcome of a liaison between Pharaoh's daughter, a precursor of Cleopatra, and a Hebrew prince? Thus Moses was a lineal heir to Pharaoh.

Under Pharaoh's rule gender controls who lives and dies, as Hebrew girls get to live and Hebrew boys are supposed to die. As a girl, Miriam is also a daughter and a sister who remains unnamed until ch. 15. Her voice is silent in most of the text. Even in the setting of her song, and with her status as prophet and a collaborator in Moses' safe passage, the received text downplays her role. The editor limits Miriam's role, in that the editor derives Miriam's song from the song of Moses. Yet Miriam thrives and creates continuity for the story as she initiates Moses' safety on the water bank, and at the parting of the Reed Sea.[25] Can we learn anything else about Miriam?

Although many scholars recognize Miriam as the sister of Moses and Aaron, and as a prophetess, we first learn of her name in Exodus 15. Additional textual references occur in Num. 12.1-15; 20.1; 26.59; 1 Chron. 5.29; Deut. 24.8-9; Mic. 6.1-5. In working to develop a biblical portrait of Miriam, Rita Burns and others conclude that Miriam's title of prophetess is an anachronism, an improper placing of people, things or events in a time period. These scholars argue that Miriam did not engage in any true prophetic (ecstatic) activity. She probably served as a leading community figure, in a priestly function in a cult. Miriam seems to have been a cult official, a leader in the Kadesh wilderness tradition, one who mediated God's word. Burns also argues that we must see Miriam's sibling connection with Moses and Aaron as coming from a wilderness tradition of tremendous witness to Miriam's leadership in the community. The brother–sister designation implies that Miriam was a colleague of Moses and Aaron, and thus editors probably used kinship to clarify her authority in concert with the reputation of the two men.[26] Like Jochebed and Miriam Zippo-

---

24. J. Gerald Janzen, 'Song of Moses, Song of Miriam: Who Is Seconding Whom?', in Brenner (ed.), *Exodus to Deuteronomy*, pp. 187-99 (197).

25. Phyllis Trible, 'Bringing Miriam Out of the Shadows', in Brenner (ed.), *Exodus to Deuteronomy*, pp. 166-86 (166-73).

26. Rita J. Burns, *Has the Lord Indeed Spoken Only Through Moses? A Study of the Biblical Portrait of Miriam* (SBLDS, 84; Atlanta: Scholars Press, 1987), pp. 8, 47, 67, 124, 130.

rah, Moses' wife, also ended up caught in a web of intrigue over keeping Moses alive and well.

The scenario where Zipporah saves Moses is a problematic text (Exod. 4.24-26), rife with exegetical challenges. Most scholars agree that it is difficult to unearth the original meaning of the story. The text fails to reveal why Yahweh attacks Moses. Apparently circumcision as a rite was known to Israel and deemed important at an early date. All of that stated, Zipporah's act saved Moses' life.[27] The troubling factor about God wanting to kill Moses is both how that murder rankles with God's justice and mercy, as well as how an omnipotent God managed to fail. The ambiguity of the text does not help. The third person pronoun confuses us as to who is the perpetrator and who is the victim. Some scholars posit that God wanted to kill the child. Others argue over which child was the intended victim, Gershom or Eliezer. Some scholars argue that the problem is that Moses was not circumcised and that this agitated God. Ancient folk could not fathom that God would chose an uncircumcised male to be lawgiver and liberator of God's chosen. Other ancient sages argue this episode occurred because of Moses' lack of enthusiasm for the task. While much biblical theology focuses more on God's justice, benevolence, and mercy, one can not deny that biblically, God had murdered before, and would murder again. Despite all the rationale for cause and effect, the bottom line is that Zipporah confronted and defeated the Almighty.[28] Moses' relationship with Zipporah occurs at a time when Moses is a man on the run, a felon on the run, wrestling with issues of identity,[29] of race and class, an alien in a land away from what he previously called home.

God and Moses

Convicted and called,
By fiery bushes:
Mysterium tremendum fascinans
Slapped you speechless;
Set you up to see further than ever.
An Olympic decathlon
Was your journey

27. Childs, *The Book of Exodus*, pp. 98, 101, 103-104.

28. Jonathan Kirsch, *Moses: A Life* (New York: Ballantine Books, 1998), pp. 130-34.

29. Walter Brueggemann, 'Exodus', in Leander E. Keck (ed.), *The New Interpreters's Bible: Genesis to Leviticus* (Nashville: Abingdon Press, 1994) pp. 703-705.

> Till you walked through
> The Reed Sea.
> But then you didn't
> Get to get over.

Using the language of Rudolf Otto, one can experience the dimensions of God in Exodus as *mysterium* (analogous to wholly other, totally incomprehensible), *tremendum* (energy or urgency, awefulness, overpoweringness), and *fascinans* (fear shaped by indescribable attraction). When encountering this God, one experiences a unique, central force and presence which invokes deep emotional response. Such a response can shake one's very foundation in a holistic positive manner, which response then translates as 'analogies of love, grace, mercy, forgiveness, pity, and comfort to be applied to the Holy One, and bliss, rapture, peace and trust to the person involved in the numinous experience'.[30] The faith underpinning this numinous experience, put forth in the Hebrew Bible, emerges as revelation of the voice at Sinai accompanied by the nonrational divine word as *mysterium, tremendum*, and *fascinans*.[31]

Studying the Yahweh of Exodus pushes us to the names of God, and invites us to wonder about the particular questions regarding the meaning, memory of, and the means for testing prophetic call. T.C. Vriezen and Brevard Childs concur that the 'I Am Who I Am' formula means that God is really present. A key significance of God's name is its connection with the God of the patriarchs and matriarchs. The naming of God transcends simple identification to the revelation of God's authority and power, reveals God's character, and confirms and restates God's covenantal promise of land to Abraham. The revelation to Moses and to Abraham is different, in that Moses does learn God's name: a guarantee of the validity of God's promises. God's name cues the future relationship with Israel and engenders and invites trust in the one who self-discloses a promised inheritance.[32] This God of trust ropes Moses in to lead a freedom and deliverance expedition.

Moses did not volunteer himself to lead the liberation movement. Indeed, the editor invokes a call narrative to demonstrate that this

---

30. Gowan, *Theology in Exodus*, p. 35.

31. Gowan, *Theology in Exodus*, pp. 32-35, 40. See also Rudolf Otto, *The Idea of the Holy: An Inquiry into the Non-rational Factor in the Idea of the Divine and Its Relation to the Rational* (repr., trans. John W. Harvey; New York: Oxford University Press, 1958 [1917]).

32. Childs, *The Book of Exodus*, pp. 68-70, 88, 89, 113-15.

activity was not that of a social activist. In Exod. 3.1-12, this process is a call by God, which includes: divine confrontation; divine introduction; divine commission; Moses' objections; divine reassurance; and a divine revelation or sign.[33] With several traditions coming together, Exod. 3 portrays the divine and human initiatives framed by a theophany and call experience. In concert with divine initiative, Moses' call implies he has initiative and will, and is not a puppet. Though Moses is reticent and fearful, God assures him that Pharaoh's heart will be hardened, the children of Israel will believe, and liberatory deliverance will occur. When Moses returns to Egypt, within this context he returns as a messenger of deliverance, not as a prodigal or adopted son, nor a political fugitive. When Moses protests the ongoing, intensified suffering of the children of Israel, God simply declares what is to come (5.22–6.1).[34]

The God of Exodus 3–4 is a God of promise. When Moses shies away from his call, the divine notes, 'I will be with you' (Exod. 3.12a), a first response to others like Jeremiah when they first objected to being commissioned to awesome, difficult, prophetic work. Moses' call comes as God hears, sees, and knows the suffering of Israel and recalls the covenant made with Jacob; then God calls Moses to tell Pharaoh, to 'Let my people go', This call story genre occurs frequently when God calls people to the impossible and their response is to object. God's promise that 'I will be with you', unfolds in the same scene where God self-reveals, as the text utters God's name, indicating the most profound knowledge a human being can have of God. The naming of God introduces a profound revelation in history, the One active, involved in change, as the Designated Intervener. That God reveals God's name makes the invisible visible and available for intimate connections. The God who will be with, and who self-reveals, is an oath taker, an ancestral God, who makes covenantal promises.[35] One begins to wonder if inherent to a divine call is a need to be reticent. Is the hesitancy out of respect for the divine? Do those receiving a prophetic call feel unworthy or over their head? Is the hesitancy a kind of ritual dance between parties of different status, until a suitable time period has passed to make the relationship permissible; and if so, permissible to whom? Is the appropriate amount of hesitancy a way the writers construed to honor the first four commandments given later at Sinai (Horeb)?

33. Burns, 'The Book of Exodus', pp. 15, 21.
34. Childs, *The Book of Exodus*, pp. 72-73, 77, 87, 101, 102, 106-107.
35. Gowan, *Theology in Exodus*, pp. 54, 55, 61, 77, 83, 87, 90, 97-100, 102, 125-26.

Our contemporary profile of Moses embodies several thousand years of story, theology, politics, music, art and propaganda, which has taken a corporeal man and immortalized him into mythic proportions of an idealized saint. Moses has held the fascination of many, from Philo of Alexandria, who saw Moses as the height of humanity, to supporters of the French Revolution, and fascist Nazi propagandists who used Moses' image on concentration camp currency at Terezin. While storytellers have redacted, reshaped and embellished Moses, the Bible sheds other light on the monotheist law-giver. His portrayal spans the gamut from that of a Las Vegas magician, to a burlesque star, to a priest of blood sacrifice. This sometimes liberator and deliverer also get depicted as 'an autocrat and an authoritarian' who can be ruthless and punitive, bent on enforcing his revealed experience of truth. The biblical portrait of Moses is a mosaic (pun intended), a montage of biographical relics, much of which rests in uncertainty. The Moses we have come to know, then, may be an ancient, priestly symbolic figure or a protagonist in an epic historical novel. Moses may result from the compiled musings of storytellers intent on forging a nation of Israel or, as Childs notes, from the conventions of an early pre-monarchial 'religious institution of covenant renewal' or Mosaic office.[36]

The advent of modern technology has made it almost impossible for persons in office to act with indiscretion and not be discovered. In an empathetic moment of inquiry, Moses ended up with an indiscretion and a secret. When inquiring about the Israelite's plight, Moses tries to mediate a dispute between an Egyptian and a Hebrew, and then ends up killing the Egyptian. Moses has to flee. Because he initially had no authority, he had to act in secret. As he flees to Midian, Moses realizes he is a foreigner, a sojourner in an alien country, a stranger in a strange land. When Moses realizes that his attempt at justice has resulted in creating an enemy among a couple of Hebrews, he is in quite a vulnerable position, a political fugitive.[37] This raises a critical question that the text does not answer: Does Moses ever feel that he belongs? As he lives in the palace of Pharaoh, when does he develop empathy for the Hebrews? Because of his hesitancy to take on the role of prophetic leader, does he ever really feel at home in that role? Interestingly, the text does not condemn or castigate Moses for the murder he commits. The text raises multiple questions amid numerous ambiguities about the role of violence in attaining justice,

36. Kirsch, *Moses*, pp. 3-4, 7-8, 11, 15, 21.
37. Childs, *The Book of Exodus*, pp. 30-32, 44-46.

as well as questions about the nature of the relationship between God and Moses.

A tremendous amount of tension exists between God and Moses. God not only stalks Moses, but spends a tremendous amount of time trying to convince him of his call. Years later:

> God's homicidal rage welled up again... [when after] Moses spent the last forty years of his life doing exactly what God asked him to do, and...the Israelites were ultimately transformed...almost in a fit of pique, God decided that Moses would not join the rest of the Israelites in crossing the Jordan River into the land of Canaan after all.[38]

Moses does not automatically fold to God's pressure, and is willing to challenge and debate with God. Moses is not a puppet or yes-man. Moses' bittersweet story ends in heartbreak, for ultimately he fails at his lifelong mission, because the same God who recruited Moses decided to take the reward, the honor, away from Moses at the last moment. Among the majesty and miracles, and despite the tragedy that shaped the relationship between God and Moses, the former continues to have a memory within the biblical text and tradition of epic proportions.[39]

Several different Moseses emerge when viewing his depictions through the lens of social science. His leadership, comprehensive yet flawed, spans key types of political rule: (1) Egyptian slavery; (2) anarchy at the foot of the mountain; (3) equity in the desert; to (4) his final attempts at institutionalized hierarchy. The power source for the first two is external, for the latter two, internal. Moses' leadership, shaped by various political regimes, is a complex storied structure, upon which future generations build by learning to question new experiences as they remember their history. As Moses learns a great deal from failure and error, the Mosaic tradition sees failure as a challenge to wisdom and attaining knowledge as opposed to being a reason for depression or misery in defeat.[40] Moses is not a poster boy for a modern Fortune 500 company—he hesitates about leading; whines about difficulty and disappointment. Much more than success and working 80-hour weeks disrupts Moses' career. Yet, theologically, he succeeds as he acts morally and is obedient to God. Like a nursing father carries a sucking child, Moses, who helps liberate and delivers his people 'from the womb of bondage...is the moral midwife of

---

38. Kirsch, *Moses*, p. 12.

39. Kirsch, *Moses*, pp. 12-13, 14, 118.

40. Aaron Wildavsky, *The Nursing Father: Moses as a Political Leader* (University of Alabama Press, 1984), pp. 1, 5-9, 21-24, 57.

Israel'.[41] Another side of Moses emerges when we shift from analyzing the theological, political, leadership angle to see a brief sketch of the psychological profile.

As a prophetic voice called by God, Moses functions as a superego; since he is also human he symbolizes a superego in the state of becoming. Freud, in his _Moses and Monotheism_, viewed Moses' rescue story as mythological, where Moses is Egyptian. Further, in the biblical text, there is a reversal of Hebrew humble beginnings to Egyptian privileged prince. Moses' infancy parallels the stories of heroes' births, which include adoption, depicting a common children's fantasy or daydream. One can see the biblical story as a condensation of a myth that includes the hero's birth, later boyhood fantasy; or family romance, projected back in time; and one can also see the story as factual. Often biblical birth story circumstances foreshadow one's personality or life's mission. Moses' life symbolizes the life of Israel, and like Israel, Moses inherits the spiritual patriarchs and matriarchs. One could also imagine that Moses' fantasy of being liberated from his family or group might be related to feelings of guilt. Notably, one of his first adult acts is to identify with his own people when, in defense of a Hebrew, Moses murders an Egyptian. In Exodus 1 and 2 one can see psychological biography and historical truth.[42]

Taking literary traditions gravely, Randall Bailey argues that Exod. 2.1-10 is a late addition and that 3.1–4.10 does not follow from the earlier chapters. Exodus 3 introduces the key figure and his father-in-law, implying the reader does not know of the relationship. Bailey also shows the information that backs up Moses having an African heritage, and how traditions undermine this hypothesis and establish Moses as Hebrew. Of particular import is his understanding of Moses' mother. From the perspective of the narrator, Jochebed marries, gets pregnant, pronounces her son good, makes sure her son is protected—hidden and then placed in an ark, which parallels the Noah story—then gets her daughter to watch over Moses, and Jochebed is paid to nurse her own child. Again, the women subvert Pharaoh; they protect Moses. Not only is it a cognitive impossibility to fashion Moses as Egyptian, but the liberation stories appear to have focused on class and national struggles.[43] When ch. 14 ends, Moses is esteemed, as the

41. Wildavsky, _The Nursing Father_, p. 58.

42. Dorothy F. Zeligs, _Moses: A Psychodynamic Study_ (New York: Human Sciences Press, 1986), pp. 23, 26, 28-29, 31, 33-36, 40.

43. Randall Bailey, 'Is That Any Name for a Nice Hebrew Boy?', Exodus 2:1-10: The De-Africanization of an Israelite Hero', in Randall Bailey and Jacquelyn Grant

people believe in Yahweh and Moses; but when the curtain opens on ch. 15, Moses is absorbed into the community. Even though Moses and Yahweh are both accorded honor for helping to deliver Israel from Egypt elsewhere (3.8, 10; 32.1, 11) only Yahweh is held in esteem, the object of worship (15.1).[44] The bottom line is that a Hebrew can have other gods, but a Hebrew cannot have other gods before Yahweh. The shift in ch. 15 affords the editors an ability to assure that while Moses is the prototype of prophet and priest, there is ultimately no need to idolize him, or be confused over who is mastering minding the action. Is Moses then a puppet and God a divine puppeteer? Is Pharaoh a puppet, too?

Pharaoh and God

A pawn
In a chess game of life.
Is there a Pharaoh in all of us?
Questions without answers.
Do you know
Whom you are praying to?

In many respects, Pharaoh is at the wrong place at the wrong time. In reading the first two chapters of Exodus, feelings of outrage emerge and the reader gets pushed toward a tragedy-comedy sense of retributive justice, revenge and incredulity. We want Pharaoh to be not greedy and to leave the Israelites alone. How dare he not be privy to the great history of Jacob's boys? After all, Joseph bailed the Egyptians out of trouble; these are God's chosen people! Incredulity stands on two accounts. Even before God changes Abram's and Sarai's names to Abraham and Sarah, God tells Abram as he sleeps that Abram's descendants will be slaves, they will be strangers in a strange land, for four hundred years; yet, God will rescue them and judge their oppressors (Gen. 15.13-16). On one hand, the Exodus deliverance competes with the Genesis foretelling. We already knew this scourge of slavery would happen, and it does. Some scholars note that the four hundred years is an insertion to explain the delay on the land acquisition promised in Gen. 12.1-3, and restated in covenantal terms in Genesis 15. This scenario begs the question of why the delay and why the need for the Hebrews to be enslaved. What is at stake for God, that

(eds.), *The Recovery of Black Presence: An Interdisciplinary Exploration* (Nashville: Abingdon Press, 1995), pp. 25-36 (26-36).

44. Janzen, 'Song of Moses, Song of Miriam', pp. 187-99, 189.

God's chosen will be oppressed, notably so that God can rescue them. Is this a case of a divine ego run amuck, of a divine ego needing to be in control, regardless of the cost? Or is this a case of omniscience, where God understands human nature and knows the Hebrews will be fertile, which will be problematic for those in the dominant culture? The second amazing occurrence is the Hebrew population explosion.

The Hebrew women kept having babies and the infants managed to live, without modern medicine and technology. As late as the early twentieth century, women often died in childbirth. If their babies survived the birth process, they often died from early childhood disease. The institution of slavery required lots of hands, so the multiplying of the children of Israel meant a steady supply of cheap labor. In societies with slave culture, it is not unusual for the slaves to outnumber their masters. An intriguing note is that Pharaoh assumed that, in case of war, the slaves would join with the enemy and fight against Egypt and then escape. This assessment shows more about Pharaoh than it does a slave mentality. Of course, some slaves would escape. Often in slave cultures, however, the slaves became accustomed to slavery and have been so oppressed and divided that it became difficult for them to galvanize enough trust among themselves to organize, band together, and successfully escape. As the curtain rises on chs. 3 and 4, there are 'two kings' engaged in a chess game; acknowledged public sovereignty and the children of Israel are the prize.

When God declares Israel to be 'my firstborn son', (4.22-23), this utterance affirms the unique relationship between God and Israel, and then God immediately follows with an actual threat to Pharaoh's Egyptian first-born. Part of what is at stake is the motif that Pharaoh does not know Yahweh. In calculated totalitarianism (Exod. 1) Pharaoh schemes to break the Hebrews, seeking to divide and conquer, sowing grave discontent. Prior to the unleashing of and during the plagues, the question still remains, Will Pharaoh ever discern the presence and power of Yahweh? To what lengths is Yahweh willing to go to get Pharaoh's acknowledgment of Yahweh's sovereignty? Why does God choose to harden Pharaoh's heart, even when the latter is ready to concede defeat? Childs suggests that ultimately the hardening is not psychological intrigue between Moses and Pharaoh or Pharaoh and God, but a theological edict of Yahweh's judgment on Egypt, and that Pharaoh refuses to listen.[45]

45. Childs, *The Book of Exodus*, pp. 102, 105-106, 151-53.

Some scholars read the hardening saga psychologically; others, like Childs, search for a philosophical or theological position. Working from the documentary hypothesis, some scholars note that the Yahwist has one focus; the Priestly writer (similarly Elohist) has another. With J, hardening is a reactive posture, coming after the plagues episode, and consequently the plagues do not achieve the intended response; whereas the signs do reveal Yahweh to Pharaoh. The removal of the plagues (8.6; 9.29) functions to stop the results of the plagues, for hardness is not an attitude or mindset, but a negative response to God's signs. For P, the hardening occurs to effect the plagues, so that Pharaoh's lack of discernment allows for God sending more signs; resulting in divine judgment. In J, hardening the heart precludes the signs from disclosing the knowledge of God. In P, hardening increases the signs as judgment. Biblical writers used the vocabulary of hardening to portray the resistance that stopped the signs from accomplishing their designated task. However, the polarization between hardening as Pharaoh's decision and as God's purview was never perceived to be a critical issue.[46]

The Hardening of Pharaoh's Heart (Exodus 1–15)

Specific Word Usage	Citations in Exodus
The Lord (God) said, 'I *will harden* his (Pharaoh's) *heart*' [Last cite: I will harden the hearts of the Egyptians]	4.21; 7.3; 14.4; (14.17)
The Lord said, 'I *have hardened his heart*, in order that…you may tell… how I have made fools of the Egyptians'	10.1
The Lord said, 'Pharaoh's *heart is hardened*'	7.14
But the *Lord hardened the heart* of Pharaoh [Last cite: that my wonders may be multiplied]	9.12; 10.20, 27; 11.10; (14.8)
Pharaoh's *heart remained hardened*.	7.22
Pharaoh (he) *hardened his (own) heart*.	8.15, 32; 9.34; 8.11, 28
Pharaoh's heart *was hardened*	7.13; 8.19; 9.7, 35

46. Childs, *The Book of Exodus*, pp. 170-74.

חָזַק, 'to be strong, prevail, harden, be courageous, be sore or severe; focus on the pressure exerted'	4.21; 7.13, 22; 8.19; 9.12, 35; 10.20, 27; 11.10; 14.4, 8, 17
כָּבֵד 'to be heavy, grievous, hard, focus on the weight of something bearing down'	8.15, 32; 9.34
כָּבֵד 'to be heavy'	7.14; 9.7; 10.1; 8.11, 28
קָשָׁה 'to be dense; focus on a overly heavy yoke, which is hard to bear; second, the rebellious resistance of an oxen to the yoke'	7.3

That the writers and redactors do not see the hardening device as an issue is fascinating. I found the scenario troubling. Initially, I thought I was misreading the text, and that there must be some mistake. Why would the God of Israel need to be in a duel or chess game with Pharaoh? On one level, the underlying issue seems to be one of territorial matters, power and control. From another view, if one names Yahweh as Creator and Lord, can this God ever have boundaries? If this God must follow the rules of 'thou shall not kill', even for the sake of justice, have we robbed God of divine freedom? Is the giver of the law always above the law? The fact that most commentators see all things done by God as good, even the hardening of Pharaoh's heart as an act toward deliverance, is most intriguing given that the specialized meaning of חָזַק with the heart as object, indicates that there is little good or positive in this action. A hardened heart, by definition, cannot be open to outside influences, 'for the entire person whose heart has grown "hard" shows himself [or herself] intractable, obdurate, hardened'.[47] By definition then, the issue cannot have ever been to change Pharaoh's mind, since he could not be open; the significant purpose for hardening Pharaoh's heart unfolds as a mechanism for making it clear that Yahweh is the sovereign, omnipotent, omnipresent God.

The repetitive nature of 'Pharaoh's hardened heart', in the active or passive sense, echoes the call and response motif of African rhetoric, on the continent or in the Diaspora. Here Pharaoh can symbolize all persons who resist God, until God judges them. The persistence of God hardening Pharaoh's heart seems to deny Pharaoh any freedom, a case of predestination, where Pharaoh seems to be a pawn in God's chess game, which the Exodus editors do not address. God either

47. 'חזק', *TDOT*, IV, p. 308.

hardens Pharaoh's heart, Pharaoh hardens his own heart, or his heart is hardened about 20 times. From a hermeneutical view, James Plastaras suggests that because Israel viewed the heart as the organ of will and thought, as opposed to feelings, the hardening of heart pertains to obstinate refusal to know and understand, and then to believe and obey. In this contest between gods (Yahweh and Pharaoh), Pharaoh is confident that he will remain triumphant. Exodus's editors present Pharaoh's determined unbelief as a case study and warning to Israel.[48] This scenario places Pharaoh in a no-win situation. After all, his office made him a god; how does one god recognize the power of another deity without subverting his own power and authority?

Although God is the protagonist and the progenitor of violence in the plagues, which include the murder of the Egyptian first-born, historically in English translations, God is never the subject or doer of the Hebrew term חמס, usually translated as 'violence'. This use of terminology is captivating, given that God warns that God will use force to liberate Israel. Some scholars contend that God's rationale for hardening Pharaoh's heart is to allow God to self-reveal through signs, 'events that are intended to convey information of some kind about God'.[49] In the hardening process, there is almost no terminology about suffering or oppression. The story does note that Pharaoh has no knowledge of Yahweh and does not intend to release the Israelites. The contest between Pharaoh and Yahweh, which embodies the hardening of heart, occurs so that Yahweh emerges as the singular existing, sovereign power. Along with the absence of terms of suffering and oppression goes the absence of terms related to human freedom and justice. Gowan argues that the prime directive for the hardening, and thus the plagues, is not liberating the Israelites, but to demonstrate that Yahweh alone is God. Brevard Childs cautions against theologizing this situation as an argument for determinism and free will. Gowan further suggests that the hardening or making Pharaoh's heart hard is not paradigmatic as to how God usually relates to humanity. The hardening is Israel's reading of God's sovereignty, redacted during the exile, when Israel was instituting monotheistic claims.[50]

This interpretation pushes one to explore God's motive given various scenarios: did the plagues and the sea adventure actually occur, making God totally responsible, with humans recounting the story? If

---

48. James Plastaras, *The God of Exodus: The Theology of the Exodus Narratives* (Milwaukee: Bruce Publishing, 1966), pp. 133-36.

49. Gowan, *Theology in Exodus*, p. 133.

50. Gowan, *Theology in Exodus*, p. 139.

so, why? If one posits that no evidence supports these events, but Israel did a re-reading of particular natural disasters, then either Israel needed to glorify violence or maybe God is a destroyer. If the story is all fiction, then it celebrates a human passion for violence and still leaves a mystery about God. René Girard sees the Hebrew Bible as a tedious, laborious journey out of a cosmology of violence, while Walter Stuermann[51] argues given that nature is a combination of order and chaos, then God's nature is that of Chaos–Order. Throughout the Hebrew Bible, however, God's mercy and wrath are coexistent. Ancient Near Eastern theologies commonly held that a deity would destroy its enemies. A nonviolent god was not a part of Near Eastern theologies nor Israel's cosmology or theology. Gowan argues that the purpose of the plagues is to know God. Some theologians place all destruction in the cauldron of the alleged Fall, or Original Sin. Ultimately in the Hebrew Bible the same God who punishes, who moves from chaos to creation to chaos, eschews mercy and grieves over human iniquity.[52]

The editors of Exodus 6 and 7 seems to posit that theologically the plagues will teach the Israelites and the Egyptians of the 'I Am' deity. Interestingly, beyond the Exodus text, the plague tradition is basically ignored or significantly reworked in biblical tradition; for example, for some it becomes a product of God's grace, rejected by Israel; or the plagues are dismissed in favor of other cosmic disasters; or they receive an apocalyptic interpretation.[53] God may harden Pharaoh's heart as a necessary means of accomplishing liberation, in concert with God's own glorification, as opposed to this act being judgment

51. Walter Stuermann, *The Divine Destroyer: A Theology of Good and Evil* (Philadelphia: Westminster Press, 1967), pp. 15-34, 115-40 (quoted in Gowan, *Theology and Exodus*, p. 147).

52. Gowan, *Theology in Exodus*, pp. 132-39, 147-49. See also René Girard, *Violence and the Sacred* (Baltimore: The Johns Hopkins University Press, 1977); *idem*, *The Scapegoat* (Baltimore: The Johns Hopkins University Press, 1986); Raymund Schwager, *Must There Be Scapegoats? Violence and Redemption in the Bible* (San Francisco: Harper & Row, 1987). Interestingly, Gowan argues that Girard's theory is intriguing regarding sacrifice, but not so suitable for biblical texts. Other scholars like Robert Hammerton-Kelly, Gill Baille and James Williams would disagree: Robert Hammerton-Kelly, *Violent Origins: Walter Burkett, René Girard, and Jonathan Z. Smith on Ritual Killing and Cultural Formation* (Stanford, CA: Stanford University Press, 1988); Gill Baille, *Violence Unveiled: Humanity at the Crossroads* (New York: Crossroad/Herder & Herder, 1997); James G. Williams, *The Bible, Violence, and The Sacred: Liberation from the Myth of Sanctioned Violence* (Valley Forge, PA: Trinity Press International, 1995).

53. Childs, *The Book of Exodus*, pp. 102, 118, 169.

or punishment or sin. The issue is not fairness, justice, just war captives, legal slavery, nor property rights. Here, 'you reap what you sow' theology means that God intends for Pharaoh and his minions to suffer because they made the Israelites suffer. That God's 'Lone Warrior' acts of destruction and death toward the Egyptians predominate in Exodus 5–15, raises questions of justice and theodicy. Just as God hardened Pharaoh's heart, could not God have softened or sweetened Pharaoh's heart? If these events did not occur, what then is foundational to Israel's faith?[54] So rankled by these texts, I sought out two friends, colleagues whose opinions I value, to get their take on the hardening process: Sandor Goodhart, Purdue University, Jewish studies and Girardian theorist, and Mignon Jacobs, Fuller Seminary, Hebrew Bible scholar and Womanist biblical hermeneutician.

Goodhart argues that René Girard would call the hardening episodes 'dehumanization', giving to the divinity what is really human responsibility. The dehumanization process here assumes the form of the text itself: we read the narrative as if 'the text' is telling us this is Moses' true situation, not his character. Nevertheless, this is still dehumanization (of violence and responsibility for violence), for that is expressed. Goodhart contends that the text embraces this dehumanization, because the dehumanization occurs both within the text and within the world in which the text continues to be read, namely our world, where we play the role of readers of that text. Readers of the text are as much potential idolaters as are the characters within the text. Notably, we are the most important audience since the characters are fictional, and we continue to have the potential for idolatrous or anti-idolatrous readings. For the rabbis the Torah is the blueprint of the world, so in a most concrete sense we read from within the text anyway.[55] Goodhart interprets 'God hardened Pharaoh's heart' or its variations to mean that human beings (Moses, or another) have studied the situation, seen their failure to achieve their end (Pharaoh's relinquishing of the Hebrews from Egypt), and attributed that failure to God, not themselves. That is, when we as humans fail, we can claim that God made it impossible for us to do it. The variations of the hardening statement merely reflect the many different contexts in which we find it useful to employ such displacements of responsibility.

Studying the Exodus text as a script, when questioned about God's character and Moses' character, Goodhart argues that we can learn

---

54. Gowan, *Theology in Exodus*, pp. 125-28.

55. Phone and email interview with Sandor Goodhart, Purdue University, June 1999.

nothing about God's character, because God is not a character; Moses and others in the text are, but God is not. God is a prophetic teacher. He suggests the text teaches that we need to read prophetically, without attributing anything to God. According to the rabbis, God has no attributes, although we mistakenly make attribution to God all the time. About Moses' character we learn that Moses does what all people do: namely he attributes to God what is really human responsibility.[56]

Mignon Jacobs suggests that the hardening of the heart occurs in the same category with other traditions that attribute the 'negative' aspects of human behavior to God. Several aspects of the hardening of the heart phenomenon come to mind. First, the various formulations signal underlying differences. That the formulations employ different Hebrew words may not be as significant as the traditions and ideologies that they reflect. These ideologies displace human behavior and they present characterizations of God, specifically God's involvement in human affairs. No doubt, the characterizations are always perceptions filtered through the particular ideological concerns of the perceiver. Second, this concept of the hardening of the heart is exclusive to Exodus. Attributing human behavior to divine influence is expressed differently in the other instances (for example, deception). As stated earlier, Jacobs notes the different scholarly tracks of interpretation: there are at least two juxtaposed traditions concerning the hardening of the heart, which assign a different interpretation to the relationship between the hardening of the heart and the plagues/ refusal to release Israel.[57]

The 'J Tradition', that the hardening of the heart follows the plagues, tends to emphasize the psychological aspect of the hardening: the person reacts to an event, stimulus, or whatever. That reaction so overpowers that the person cannot stop it, and the reaction plays itself out. The primary agent of the hardening may or may not be God. In this tradition, it seems that the plagues are brought about to show Pharaoh who God is. As the 'P Tradition' depicts the hardening of Pharaoh's heart as the cause of the plagues, the plagues are justified as the divine response to human behavior. This is where many place the concluding formula (e.g. Exod. 7.13, 22; 8.15). Even with the proposed answers of the J and P traditions, other unanswered questions remain concerning the agent of the hardening. For example, Exod.

56. Author email interview with Goodhart.
57. Email interview with Mignon Jacobs, Fuller Theological Seminary, 29 June 1999.

4.21 does not merely anticipate Pharaoh's reaction; it assumes that reaction on the basis that God will cause it. Elsewhere Pharaoh is said to harden his own heart (8.15; 9.34).[58]

Both Jacobs and Goodhart bring illuminating data to this most complex discussion about God hardening Pharaoh's heart. Jacobs reminds us of the integral place of differences within the texts, and ultimately, I think, within ourselves. Jacobs notes that the various traditions and ideologies that underlie the text may be significant. Though this cannot be fully mined here theologically, I wonder what the presence of different traditions and ideologies can teach us about the awesomeness of creation, the clearly different way human beings see and hear. This reality pushes us to ask what does it mean that our interpretations can be vastly different regarding the same data. Perhaps one key question pertains to the nature of our explicit and implicit agendas, particularly at the points of research, teaching and preaching. I am struck by what I see as both a theological and psychological reading of attribution by Goodhart. To attribute certain qualities to another can be complimentary or scapegoating, leading to a pathology. Attribution can accord worship or denial and oppression. If the editors attribute the hardening to God, because that is the practice of other ancient Near Eastern societies, then we may have a case of syncretism. If they attribute the hardening to God because of human desire to blame or to be like God, then we have a case of scapegoating and projection. The psychological ploy is a reversal of blame that allows us not to take responsibility; this may also ultimately allow God not to take responsibility for the genocide of Egypt's first-born.

Conclusions

Liberation?
Deliverance?
From what to where?
Ambiguity blurs
Memory, reality, history.
Of what was:
Giving us lots of responsibility
For what is.

My Womanist biblical theological hermeneutic of tempered cynicism, creativity, courage, commitment, candor, curiosity and the comedic gave me the room to navigate complex texts and permission

---

58. Author email interview with Jacobs.

to ask hard questions, whose answers range from textual irrelevance to intrigue to dissatisfaction. My social location of town and gown, of the academy and the pastorate, by definition riddle my readings with tension, with paradoxical interpretations that will fall on the ear of the scholar in one way, and may touch the ear of a believer in quite another. From a perspective of reader-response theory, I find the activity of God on behalf of Israel noble, blessed, liberative, and can understand why peoples from much later times use the Exodus as a metaphor for liberation. Simultaneously, I find the activity against the Egyptians and the Israelites reprehensible. If this text is a reading back onto the divine that which is accomplished by human beings, I take issue with those editors who decide that one's ethnicity and belief system, particularly the Egyptians other than Pharaoh, is sufficient cause to murder the first-born and to remove one's property. I also take issue with the enslavement being foretold and then played out. Whoever is to blame, this text glorifies violence and justifies violence as a tool of liberation.

In the cause of liberation, however, I see as subversives the women who embraced the ideology of women's lib long before late-twentieth-century feminists coined the term. Without the women, Moses could not have become the prophetic deliverer. As for Yahweh, the 'I Am' God has a big ego, wields lots of power, and will suffer no encroachment of that power. Yahweh does share the fame, though briefly, with Moses. Yet, Yahweh recruits, equips and later cuts Moses off, which seems to foretell some of the cutthroat hiring and downsizing policies of multinational corporations today. Pharaoh never stood a chance. He and Yahweh engage in a turf war for power, recognition and control. Yahweh plays with Pharaoh's head, for when Pharaoh is about to surrender, Yahweh hardens his heart again; or so indoctrinated, Pharaoh hardens his own heart. Sadly and outrageously, this divine manipulative action is premeditated.

In sum, it is dangerous to read the Exodus text merely for its liberative components. In exploring the text, it behooves us to see and live with the violence. Perhaps we can learn more about ourselves, and Yahweh, and how to live responsible lives, without needing to project our shortcomings on to others. We also learn that at the end of the day Yahweh remains, at least partially, clothed in mystery and ambiguity. Some of our questions were not the questions of the ancients, and thus the text cannot answer our queries. The good news is that this reality is an open invitation to experience more revelation.

Part II

SECOND REVISIT: MIRIAM

MIRIAM

Phyllis Silverman Kramer

Introduction

Despite the clear evolutionary trend in Bible interpretation, many of
the interpretive works of previous eras still dominate most Jewish
exegesis of the text, particularly those in synagogues and schools. The
compositions from talmudic and medieval times are particularly important in this respect; the Babylonian Talmud, *Genesis Rabbah* and
Rashi have been especially popular.

Subjective interpretation has played an important role in virtually
all Jewish understanding of the Hebrew Bible throughout the past 25
centuries, and remains a meaningful factor in contemporary efforts to
fathom the text. Until the late nineteenth century, virtually all Bible
scholarship reflected a male-oriented bias that re-affirmed and elucidated the patriarchal society of biblical times. Surfacing since then has
been an increasing concern among women regarding biblical interpretation and scholarship. Through their work, feminists have aimed
to do a number of things. They have tried to explore positive examples of women's positions in Scripture and find role models among
the biblical women. They have attempted to conduct critical studies of
the Bible texts that avoid sexist language and perspective, and even to
offer their own style of midrash that embellishes the Bible from a feminist point of view as earlier male writers did from a masculine one. In
truth, the work of modern feminist hermeneutics is a continuation of
biblical interpretation that has gone on through the millennia. This
paper will examine the two streams of Bible exegesis—the male and
the female—delineating the similarities and/or differences in the portrayal of Miriam. Her presentation in the Bible is that of an active and
controversial female—a family member, leader and prophetess. She
stands alongside of her brothers, yet she stands alone. She shows vivid
signs of independence despite being an appendage to her siblings.
She is outspoken yet subdued, quiet yet dominant. She is a multi-
faceted biblical figure, richly painted in midrashic literature. For these

personality traits as well as her unique actions during the evolution of a people, Miriam is a female to be studied in her own personal evolution and involvement in the history of this people.

Miriam in the Bible

Miriam, who appeared in isolated scenes scattered throughout Moses' life, was the most important female figure in the books of Exodus and Numbers, but the actual number of verses in which she appears was limited to 17 in the Pentateuch, and 1 each in Micah and 1 Chronicles. Scripture describes her as daughter, sister, leader, prophetess, and sister-in-law; her role in the history of the Exodus experience was appreciable, and she lived and acted with foresight at a pivotal time in her people's history.

The Bible contains no physical description of Miriam; her personality emerges only through her actions. As a girl (Exod. 2.4, 7-8), she appeared to be a dynamic individual who acted with alertness and swiftness when her brother Moses needed a nurse. Some 80 years later (according to the biblical chronology), she took a leadership role in the crossing of the Reed Sea (Exod. 15.20-21). Often she is linked to what her brothers were doing. She helped save Moses and later, after Moses had led the people across the Reed Sea, she led the women in song. This latter role was enriched by a further description of her joining the women in music and dance, a unique combination for a Pentateuchal female. Her integral connection with her brothers was seen again when she was punished with a skin affliction because of disparaging remarks she and Aaron levied against Moses (Num. 12.1-5, 9-15). The critical nature of her remarks showed her to be antagonistic toward Moses' Cushite wife and jealous of Moses to whom God spoke; because of this latter resentment she challenged God (Num. 12.2), expressing her bitterness verbally.

While Miriam was usually called by her name, she was also known as the sister of Moses and Aaron, as when she saved Moses at the bank of the Nile. Even though the text (Exod. 2.4) reads אחתו ('his sister'), the omission of her name from this passage may suggest she was denigrated and not the focus of the event, albeit she was the motivating force behind it.

Miriam had several crucial experiences at the water's edge. At the bank of the Nile, she proposed to bring her mother to Pharaoh's daughter so Moses could be nursed; years later, she led the women in song and dance at the edge of the Reed Sea. This symbol of water connected her with a natural force that gave life to Moses and the

Children of Israel. The verse following the death of Miriam (Num. 20.1) indicated a lack of water for the people (v. 2). While there was not necessarily a cause and effect relationship between the two events, the proximity of the two verses raises the possibility that, as Miriam was associated with water during her lifetime, after her death water was lacking. Just as her life and actions were connected with life-giving water, her death was associated with the lack of this vital essential. This link indicates the high regard and deep esteem the Pentateuch held for her.

Micah counted Miriam as one of the people's three leaders during the Exodus experience, along with Aaron and Moses (Mic. 6.4). Her being honored by such a description showed the key position she had earned, and her reputation was carried down through biblical tradition. Such esteem was accorded her despite her having sinned and her having been punished severely by God. And yet, because Micah's work might be construed, in a broad sense, to be an interpretation, questions arise as to how he has elected to list the three siblings. Since they are not listed in their order of birth (Moses, Aaron and Miriam), has he listed them in a hierarchical order of his own choosing? In 1 Chron. 5.29 Miriam's paternal parentage was noted, although the children were not listed in order of birth here either (Aaron, Moses and Miriam). Miriam, the first-born, was recorded last.

Miriam in Rabbinic Interpretation

Miriam's Name
The targumim translated the stories about Miriam literally and hence added little or nothing to the Bible story when describing her early life; midrashic texts regularly amplified the biblical verses. Some sources put forth an explanation for Miriam's name, saying it meant bitterness (associating the first element in her name with the Hebrew מר), and referred to how the lives of the people were embittered with hard work designed to break their spirits, if not their bodies (*Exod. R.* 26.1; *Cant. R.* 2.24; *Pes. R.* 15.11; *C.J.* 44.1;[1] and *Pes. K.* 5.9).

Miriam's Personality
Epithets for Miriam, such as Puah, Azubah, Jerioth, and Ephrath, gave an indication of her personality and physical appearance (*Soṭ.* 11b and 12a; *Exod. R.* 1.21; and *PRE* 45). A wide range of qualities emerged

---

1.   M. Gaster (trans.), *The Chronicles of Jerahmeel; or, The Hebrew Bible Historiale* (New York: Ktav, 1971), referenced as *C.J.* throughout this essay.

from the descriptions, resulting in a portrayal of her beauty, her gift of arousing passion in men, her paleness of color because she was an invalid, and her being forsaken by men because she was an invalid. This was certainly not the image the Bible presented. These characterizations might be a response to the Bible's failure to mention Miriam's husband or her children, if she had any.

Exodus Rabbah emphasized the word העלמה ('the young woman', Exod. 2.8) as a description of a personality quality, and a play on words of the root עלם resulted: when Miriam ran to get her mother to suckle the infant Moses, the word העלמה meant haste. Samuel opined she concealed (העלימה) her identity (*Soṭ.* 12b and *Exod. R.* 1.30). Midrashic amplification also suggested that Miriam was one of the midwives, namely Puah, assisting her mother Shifrah (*Exod. R.* 1.17). Miriam would have been five years old at that time, Aaron was two, and Moses would be born the following year (cf. Exod. 7.7). The sages said she used to escort her mother Yocheved, assisting her when delivering babies and attending to all her wants. Being so fervent in helping her mother was an early indication of her character (*Exod. R.* 1.13). Further personality traits were elucidated: she was called Puah because she cried out (פועה), and mothers gave birth. She also wept for Moses when he was put in the water. She disclosed (הופיעה) Moses' future leadership (*Eccl. R.* 7.3). *Soṭah* 11b identified Miriam as one of the midwives in Exodus 1—Puah, because she cried out through the Holy Spirit saying: 'My mother will bear a son who will be Israel's savior.'

Miriam the Sister

Miriam was commented about as a young girl who saved Moses, and as a mature woman who sinned by slandering him. After having prophesied that her brother would one day save Israel, Miriam watched him while he was in the river to learn his fate (*C.J.* 42.9; *Mek. Beshal.* 1; and *Mek. Shir.* 10).[2] Miriam stood at a remove so she would not be seen, thereby making it appear as if the baby had been forsaken.[3] When the baby was discovered by Pharaoh's daughter, Miriam's response to find a nurse to suckle him was interpreted by Malbim as God-inspired, that is, she had no dread of punishment. Her

2. *Jubilees* 47.4 offered a fascinating reason for Miriam's being at the river bank when it read 'during the day Miriam, your sister, guarded you from the birds' (see *OTP*, II, p. 138).

3. See Nahum M. Sarna, *Exodus* (JPS Torah Commentary: Philadelphia: Jewish Publication Society of America, 1991).

words to the princess indicated Miriam's astuteness. Cassuto said Miriam questioned the princess about calling a Hebrew to nurse the child, trying 'to give the impression that she is making the suggestion only for the sake of the princess'.[4]

Calling Miriam the sister of Aaron (Exod. 15.20) related to this time when she was, in fact, only Aaron's sister, prior to Moses' birth (*Soṭ.* 12b-13a, and *Meg.* 14a). It was understood that she and he were born before their parents separated in fear of Pharaoh's edict. Moses was born after their reunion entreated by Miriam.

Miriam the Leader and Prophetess

Miriam's role as prophetess was evident early in her life when she challenged her father for having divorced his wife (*Exod. R.* 1.17) to avoid having any children, and Amram capitulated and took Yocheved back. Miriam and Aaron accompanied their wedding procession, she 'carrying castanets and marching' (*Pes. R.* 43.4). Miriam challenged her father's actions and said he was wrong to abstain from a conjugal relationship with his wife. She reminded him that Pharaoh's edict intended to kill only male infants, and that by his abstaining from sexual relations with his wife he was not allowing for the possibility even of females to be born (*Soṭ.* 12a and *Pes. R.* 43.4). When Miriam predicted the birth of a son who would be a savior, her father praised her; when the infant was put into the Nile, the father chastened her and was skeptical about the prophesy (*Soṭ.* 13a and *Meg.* 14a). Actually, Miriam's prophesy was twofold: first, the birth of a son; and second, the son would redeem Israel (*Meg.* 14a; *C.J.* 42.8 and 44.2; and *Mek. Shirata* 10). As a result of this prophesy, she was listed as one of seven prophetesses, the others being Sarah, Deborah, Hannah, Abigail, Huldah, and Esther (*Meg.* 14a).

Similarly *The Chronicles of Jeraḥmeel*, in speaking of Miriam's prophesy, attributed her abilities to 'the Spirit of God' (*C.J.* 44.2). This was a singular theophanic description, connecting Miriam directly with the divine. This same section stated: 'Amram begat a son and daughter, Aaron and Miriam' (*C.J.* 42.8). Since Miriam was the elder child, one would have expected her name to be listed first (cf. 1 Chron. 5.29)!

Miriam, enjoying equality with her two brothers, was counted as one of Israel's three redeemers, and merited the respect of the people who waited for her when she suffered from leprosy, as the Shekinah lingered (*Lev. R.* 15.8). Their waiting was reciprocal for her having

---

4.   Umberto Cassuto, *A Commentary on the Book of Exodus* (trans. Israel Abrahams; Jerusalem: Magnes Press, 1967), p. 20.

waited at the Nile's banks to learn the fate of the infant Moses (*Soṭ.* 9b
and 11a; and *Mek. Beshal.* 1). Rabbi Joshua likened the vine in the chief
steward's dream (Gen. 40.10) to the Torah, and the three branches to
the three siblings: Miriam, Aaron and Moses (*Ḥul.* 92a and *Gen. R.*
88.5). Rabbi Berekiah stated that God said to Israel: 'I sent you three
messengers, Moses, Aaron and Miriam' (*Lev. R.* 27.6). Miriam was
referred to as a pedagogue, as were her brothers, and she was cred-
ited with having merited the well accompanying the people in their
wanderings. She was equated with her brothers concerning her leadership, the gift of the well bestowed upon Israel because of her merit,
and the well being taken away upon her death (*Pal. Targ.*). In each of
these instances, Miriam was treated identically with her brothers
(*Ta'an.* 9a).

Exegetes viewed Miriam as a woman, a righteous leader and a
prophetess. In Exod. 15.20 she was mentioned both as a prophetess
and the sister of Aaron. Rashi and Epstein explained why she was
called both prophetess and sister of Aaron, echoing earlier talmudic
statements (*Soṭ.* 12b-13a and *Meg.* 14a). She was specifically called
Aaron's sister because it was he who, despite the possibility of incur-
ring God's wrath and jeopardizing his life, pleaded for Miriam when
she was stricken with leprosy, showing feelings from his soul (Rashi
on 15.20). Sarna defined Miriam's two titles in a variant way. He
posited she was a prophetess like Deborah, Huldah and Noadiah, and
further explained the reference to being Aaron's sister as reflecting a
system of fratriarchy, where the eldest brother was in a position of
authority.

Miriam's Song

The targumim, when speaking of Miriam leading the women at the
crossing of the Reed Sea, echoed the biblical text and included a picture of Miriam with a chorus (*Targ. Onq.*) and the women dancing
while playing musical instruments (*Targ. Ps.-J.*); however, the implied
image is varied. Dancing, choral singing and the accompaniment of
musical instruments gave a variety of possibilities to the mental image
of the women's role at the Reed Sea.

Midrashim affirmed Miriam's righteousness, along with that of the
other women, as a result of their having prepared musical instruments in advance of the departure from Egypt. The timbrels used during the song were brought from Egypt. Implied was that the women
knew such an item would be necessary during the Exodus, and they
had planned for it almost intuitively, having faith a miracle might be
forthcoming (*PRE* 42 and *Mek. Shirata* 10).

In describing the presentation of Miriam's song, it was posited she began the song of praise to God and the women joined her (*PRE* 42). As Moses had led the men with a song, Miriam then led the women (*Mek. Shirata* 10). Later, Rashi said Moses sang his song to the men who then answered him; and Miriam sang the song to the women (Exod. 15.21). Considering the midrashim understood her role in the event at the sea to have been a major focal event in Miriam's life, and this was the first song in Scripture by a woman, it is shocking that some commentators did not comment on Miriam's singular role in these two verses (Exod. 15.20-21).

Ibn Ezra said Miriam was known as Aaron's sister in order to distinguish her from other women named Miriam. Therefore, when she sang her song, she would not be confused with anyone else. Ramban had no comment about Miriam and her song; rather he interpreted Aaron's relationship with Miriam as being one of honor, since he was the elder of her two brothers and a prophet. Rashbam's interpretation was that Miriam took the timbrel while still in the water, and sang her song. As Moses had been commanded by God to sing his song, Miriam was adjured to do likewise.

Sarna commented similarly about the Reed Sea episode, averring female musicians were recognized as being special in using the timbrels. Speaking specifically about the Song of Miriam, he wrote:

> This popular English title is somewhat misleading since the text states that Miriam recites only the first line of the **shirah**. However, a midrash has it that Miriam and the women actually recite the entire song. These verses affirm the custom, chronicled in Judges 11.34 and 1 Samuel 18.6, of women going forth with music and dance to hail the returning victorious hero, although in the present instance, it is God and not man who is the victor.[5]

Saadiah and Sforno did not comment about Miriam at the Reed Sea crossing.

The Issue of Slander

Commentaries about her grievous act of slander against Moses said: 'Miriam is consistently seen as the prototype of the slanderer.'[6] God's punishment of her was to be an example so others would learn not to engage in public or private slander, or of uttering malicious state-

---

5.   Sarna, *Exodus*, p. 82.

6.   Reuven Hammer (trans.), *Sifre: A Tannaitic Commentary on the Book of Deuteronomy* (New Haven: Yale University Press, 1986), p. 479. This quote was in a footnote for para. 275.

ments against anyone. Even though she was punished with a skin affliction, the people did not journey onward, but rather waited for seven days while she was quarantined outside the camp. (The connection between her having waited at the banks of the Nile to see what Moses' fate would be, and the people now waiting for her, was examined earlier.)

Who effected Miriam's punishment by deeming she had leprosy and sending her outside the camp? Reasoning that Moses and Aaron could not have done it, The Holy One must have bestowed great honor upon Miriam in that moment, declaring: 'I am a priest; I will shut her away, declare her a leper, and free her' (*Zeb.* 101b-102a). While Miriam had leprosy and was detained, the people waited for her.

Generally, midrashic sources were concerned with the adult Miriam, the woman who sinned and was punished severely, yet who merited the respect of her people and was rewarded with illustrious descendants; however the volume of material was not as replete as for her youth. Comments about her adult life focused indirectly on her when Moses prayed to God to heal her in Num. 12.13 (*PRE* 53). *Deuteronomy Rabbah* stressed the aspect of Miriam's slander, yet recognized her piousness. The congregation was warned not to slander as Miriam had done. She was smitten with leprosy for having told a lie and, despite her being considered faithful (*Deut. R.* 6.4), she was nevertheless punished as an example to future generations. Earlier, when Eve was created, God did not make her from Adam's mouth; nonetheless, Miriam exhibited slander (*Deut. R.* 6.5). Further, while Miriam sinned by using her mouth in slandering Moses, God punished her whole body (*Eccl. R.* 5.3). The midrash recognized that Aaron also had spoken against Moses (*PRE* 53), but nothing was raised about the unjust punishment Miriam received (*Deut. R.* 6.5 and *PRE* 53).

As a woman traveling through the wilderness with her people, Miriam exhibited controversial behavior and was punished by God. She voiced her disgruntlement, vehemently protesting that Moses was not the only person with prophetic puissance. Rashi said the sense of the root דבר 'speak' (Num. 12.1), was that they used stern language. Miriam's being mentioned first indicated she initiated the words, casting a disparaging remark against Zipporah, Moses' wife. Further, she questioned why God spoke only to Moses and not to them, given they were not divorced and Moses was.

When God's relationship with Moses was explained, and Miriam and Aaron did not capitulate, God became angered, departed and left Miriam stricken with leprosy, saying she deserved this humiliation

(*PRE* 53). A collection of sources, commenting on Miriam's transgression, showed that 'commentators differ regarding the exact content of Miriam's offensive utterance which is not recorded for us in the Torah'.[7]

Rashi posited Miriam was left leprous and white as snow, and quarantined outside the camp for seven days (also *PRE* 53). He further said the period of seven days was a concession on God's part. According to law, she could have been quarantined for 14 days (Rashi on Num. 12.14). Extrapolating from this adjustment on God's part, a reverence developed toward Miriam: that God would bestow special favor on her implied her singularity as a person and, despite her having sinned, remarkable care from a metaphoric surrogate parent!

Miriam's Well

References to Miriam's well permeated the talmudic comments about her. Mentioned twice in *Pes.* 54a, this well that traveled with the people in the wilderness was one of the ten items created on the sixth day of creation. In midrashim, Miriam's well was an important guiding sign in the travels of the people. Its placement showed the Israelites the position they were to take in the camp (*C.J.* 53.1). The well waters became rivers reaching all parts of the encampment. 'But do not think that they obtained nothing from the waters, because they produced all kinds of dainties similar to those of the world to come' (*C.J.* 53.17).

A connection was made between Miriam and the well because of the verse following the announcement of her death (Num. 20.2), stating there was no water for the assembled congregation (*Num. R.* 1.2). The well was rich in its gifts to the people, producing enjoyments, herbs, vegetables and trees. The well stopped providing water upon Miriam's death (*Cant. R.* 4.26).

Miriam's Death

Although there might be unfairness in Miriam being the one who was punished, and not Aaron, exegetes were in agreement in their praise of Miriam since the people waited for her when she was banished from the camp. Her importance was again emphasized when, upon her death, the people had no water. In addition, because of the proximity of the verses about the Red Heifer and her death (Num. 19; 20.1),

---

7.   Nechama Leibowitz, *Studies in Bamidbar (Numbers)*, (trans. and adapted from the Hebrew by Aryeh Newman; Jerusalem: WZO Department for Torah Education and Culture in the Diaspora, 1976), p. 129.

as the Red Heifer had died to expiate Israel's sins, so too did Miriam's death atone for Israel's sins (*PRE* 26).

Some comments were tinged with midrashic augmentations. Rabbi Eleazar said Miriam's death by divine kiss was the same as Moses' (*Cant. R.* 1.16). In *Targum Onqelos*, Aaron asked Moses to plead before God for Miriam since she had been with the people all through the difficulties in the wilderness, and Aaron wanted her to be able to complete the journey into the Promised Land.

Miriam and Gender Issues

Jewish commentators further affirmed Miriam's equality and elaborated on her specific role when interpreting Mic. 6.4. Rashi said she was to be a light for the women. Malbim averred she would be the person to teach the women about the good path of life. Abravanel said the three siblings were leaders, redeemers and teachers, Miriam's responsibility being to teach the women. He also referred to Miriam's well having been given to the people because of her merit. Ibn Ezra stated she would prophesy to the women about what God had spoken to Moses. Radak avowed she was one of the three prophets, while Altschuler called her one of three worthy, respectable leaders.

General Observations about Miriam in Rabbinic Literature

Rabbinic commentaries presented Miriam as a multi-dimensional personality. She was a strong-willed individual, unique in undertaking responsibilities as a young girl caring for her brother, and as a young woman in leading the women of Israel in song at a key moment in history. She was also a rebellious sister and sister-in-law when she cast aspersion on her brother Moses and her Cushite sister-in-law.

By not commenting on a number of verses, and by emphasizing others, the commentators left a somewhat incomplete and inaccurate picture of Miriam. They seemed concerned primarily with her youth and her actions related to Moses, rather than her rebelliousness and subsequent punishment. She was lauded for her alert and mature actions and thoughts at the river bank, extolled for her suggestion to Pharaoh's daughter, and praised for bringing her mother to nurse her infant brother Moses.

Miriam's qualities as a leader and prophetess commanded less attention in the rabbinic commentaries. A glaring omission was the reference to her song at the crossing of the Reed Sea. While explication was found about her defiance against Moses and his wife and, one could also say, against God in a broader context and her ensuing punishment, little was interpreted about how she led the women in the

Exodus. For example Ramban, Sforno and Leibowitz did not comment on any of the Exodus verses. The Babylonian Talmud contains no references to Miriam at the Reed Sea. Similarly, Ramban and Baruch Ha-Levi Epstein offered nothing on the verses in Numbers. Leibowitz, while not considered a feminist Bible interpreter, was the only female synthesizer/commentator. I was disappointed that she did not comment about Miriam at the Reed Sea crossing, recognizing the singular position Miriam played as a leader and a female.

Miriam was faulted and punished for her slanderous words. Most commentators admitted not knowing what Miriam's words of dissension and aspersion were (they expressed the feeling the comments were negative because of the semantic import of the word דבר with the preposition ב, meaning spoke against), and sources were not emphatic in ascribing specific words to her.

Conclusion

The biblical Miriam was presented as a responsible young girl at the Nile's bank, a dynamic leader of song at the Reed Sea crossing, and an instigating woman who slandered her brother Moses and challenged God. In no recorded episode did she function alone. Each of her actions related to an aspect of Moses' life: his infancy at the Nile's bank, his leadership at the crossing of the Reed Sea, his marriage and his singular relationship with God.

The portrait emerging from rabbinic literature was of a very strong-willed young girl, capable of foresight and prophecy and, according to midrashim, able to persuade her parents to effectuate a renewal of their conjugal relationship resulting in the birth of Moses. Commentators agreed about her qualities of patience, astuteness, and bravery. Thus, the emphasis on her alacrity as seen in the commentaries, rather than on Miriam's acting in a lame or faulting manner, may be interpreted as a positive characteristic.

The absence of rabbinic interpretation about Miriam at the Reed Sea seems blatantly unfair given that her maturity and spiritual development combined to allow her to have reached such a key position among the women of her people. Even Ramban, in giving an accolade to Aaron for being Miriam's brother, was concentrating on Aaron who, otherwise, was not conspicuous during the Reed Sea crossing; he was not speaking of Miriam alone at this moment of her glory.

The general sense of rabbinic literature was not strictly in accord with the grammatical significance of the phrase באהרן ותדבר מרים (Num. 12.1). The verb is third person feminine singular, indicating that Miriam was the one who spoke. However, I question the conjunction connected to Aaron's name and wonder if he, too, did utter a slanderous remark as well, or if she spoke *with* him. In any case, the grammar makes her the responsible person and Aaron, with no verb attached to his name, would be guiltless of having spoken. That he got off unscathed may reflect an understanding of the text as if it read ותדבר מרים באהרן, that is, she did the talking and he did the listening. This interpretation would make him an accomplice for having heeded her, but certainly not as guilty as she for her words. In addition, because God dispensed punishment for Miriam and not for Aaron, the commentators mirrored this difference, impugning and reproving only her. This was most inequitable and biased, if not sexist![8]

Miriam and Female Exegetes

Miriam's Name

Names in the Bible often provide clues to personality traits and actions. When examining the meaning of Miriam's name we find exegetical comments connecting the meaning of her name philologically to her life. As female exegetes examine Miriam's name, they relate the word מר, 'bitter', to the hardships and bitterness of her life. Her name 'embodied the condition of Israel at the time of her birth'.[9] Thus 'the meaning of her name is linked with the time of bondage in Egypt'.[10] Here we see a name linked to the fate or destiny of a nation, rather than restricted solely to the person.

The syllable meaning 'bitter' is combined with ים or water. Miriam, in a modern day midrash, defines her own name:

> My name is an amalgam of two Hebrew words—*mar*, meaning 'bitter', and *yam*, meaning 'sea'. My life was indeed bitter, like the waters we

8. The volumes of *Torah Shelemah* that included verses about Miriam were studied. The predominant number of interpretations depicted Miriam as the one who had committed slander and was punished. Understanding the literalness of the grammar of ותדבר, the implication here was that Aaron was totally guiltless. While there was room for thinking that Aaron was an accomplice in the act of slander, Miriam alone was held culpable. This schema reflected a pattern in the biblical interpretations seen in this portrait of Miriam, namely a dearth of explications about Miriam in her positive role at the Reed Sea, and an emphasis on her sinning through an act of slander. (In addition to the commentaries included in this paper, *Torah Shelemah* includes other midrashim and individual interpreters.)

9. Judith Antonelli, *In the Image of God: A Feminist Commentary on the Torah* (Northvale, NJ: Jason Aronson, 1995), p. 173.

10. Leila Leah Bronner, *From Eve to Esther: Rabbinic Reconstructions of Biblical Women* (Louisville, KY: Westminster/John Knox Press, 1994), p. 168.

encountered after crossing the Sea of Reeds, as it is written: 'THEY COULD NOT DRINK THE WATER OF MARAH BECAUSE IT WAS BITTER; THAT IS WHY IT WAS CALLED MARAH' (15.23).[11]

In fusing the water theme with Miriam's personality, the stories of Marah and Meribah are referred to:

> The ambiguity of this motif associated with Miriam seems to be reflected in two biblical wordplays on Miriam's name. Both appear in stories about the Israelites' lack of water, in the episodes of Marah and Meribah, each of which follows a reference to Miriam. The word *mar*, 'bitter', occurs four times in one verse soon after Miriam's song, echoing and reechoing a play on Miriam's name as MRYM, 'bitter sea' or 'water' (Exod. 15.24). Meribah means 'contentiousness' (Num. 20.13) and is linked in the episode which immediately follows Miriam's death with the word MRY, 'rebelliousness' (Num. 20.10, 24; 27.14). Both of these stories seem to be playing on Miriam's name; together, they offer the double connotation of bitterness and rebelliousness and suggest, perhaps, a complex view of Miriam consistent with the complexity of the water motif.[12]

Antonelli connects Miriam's strength of character with her name: 'Miriam did a lot of wonderful things for the Jewish people for which she should be remembered. Her name, meaning "bitter sea", indicates her capacity to swim against the tide of society when necessary.'[13] This insight pictures her as a determined individual capable of using inner strength.

If Miriam is an Egyptian name, the word *mar* can have a beautiful meaning. It might be 'derived from a term for "love" (*mer*), perhaps with the implication of "beloved"'.[14]

In a midrash, matriarch Sarah asks:

> Why does Miriam need so many names? Because during her life she follows the path of חסד, lovingkindness, comforting her people in distress, encouraging them when they lose faith, providing succor and song. Although her own lot is so often bitter, *mar*, she so sweetens the lot of others that she becomes beloved, *mer*.[15]

11. Ellen Frankel, *The Five Books of Miriam: A Woman's Commentary on the Torah* (New York: Putnam's Sons, 1996), p. 113.

12. Devora Steinmetz, 'A Portrait of Miriam in Rabbinic Midrash', *Prooftexts* 8.1 (January 1988), pp. 35-65 (55).

13. Antonelli, *Image of God*, p. 348.

14. Drorah O'Donnell Setel, 'Exodus', in Carol A. Newsom and Sharon H. Ringe (eds.), *The Women's Bible Commentary: Expanded Edition with Apocrypha* (Louisville, KY: Westminster/John Knox Press, 1998), pp. 30-39 (36).

15. Frankel, *Five Books of Miriam*, p. 113.

Miriam the Sister

Focal events in Miriam's life occur in her familial position as sister. 'Although the narrative concerning Moses' childhood tells of a sister (2.7), she is never explicitly named. The text states that she goes to call "the child's mother" (2.8), which seems strange if she is presumably her mother as well.' [16] Why is her name excluded?

> She responds: 'The three children in our family rarely appear together. So when my brother Moses first arrives on the scene, at the beginning of the Book of Exodus, only an unnamed sister is mentioned. Aaron is totally absent from the story. I first appear by name only after the crossing of the Sea of Reeds, and there I am identified only as *Aaron's* sister. Moses is absent from my genealogy.' [17]

Additionally disturbing is that Miriam, who was the key person or catalyst at the Nile's edge when Moses was set in the basket, is not named. In a midrash, Miriam says to Moses: 'Your cradle was to have been your grave. I made it into a life-barge instead. I led Pharaoh's daughter to your rescue... I brought your own mother's breasts to your lips.' [18]

When listed as a sibling her name does not appear first, although she is the eldest child born to Amram and Yocheved. In Num. 26.59 her name appears after those of Aaron and Moses, as it does in Micah and 1 Chronicles. Are we dealing with serious issues of gender bias and the manipulation of the text?

Miriam the Daughter

Miriam's role as daughter is integrally related midrashically to her gift of prophecy. She predicts to her parents the birth of a savior or leader for the people.

> When Moses was born circumcised and the house was then flooded with light, her father stood up and kissed her head, saying, 'My daughter, your prophecy has been fulfilled'. However, when Yokheved cast Moses into the Nile, Amram took his anger out on Miriam—he slapped her and said, 'Where is your prophecy now?' (*Sot.* 13a; *Meg.* 14a; *Exod. R.* 1.22 [which changes the story to have Yokheved slapping her]). [19]

In another midrash, a byplay occurred between parents and child. Amram and Yocheved visited their daughter when she was isolated

16. Setel, 'Exodus', p. 36.

17. Frankel, *Five Books of Miriam*, p. 103.

18. Norma Rosen, *Biblical Women Unbound: Counter-tales* (Philadelphia: Jewish Publication Society of America, 1996), pp. 100-101.

19. Antonelli, *Image of God*, p. 141.

from the people. He chastised her saying her current fate could have been predicted because of her personality traits. Afterward her mother tried to assuage the situation and Amram relented:

> Her father and mother sat with her on the ground. 'From the time you were small', her father said, 'I knew your fearless ways would bring you a bad end. I smacked you but did it do any good? No—you had to get your smack from God. So now you know!'
> Her mother brushed some dust from Miriam's robe. 'Miriam, child-saver, I don't like to see you look so broken. I recognized your inventiveness as a child. Seven days of punishment by God is an honor, if you look at it in a certain way...I'm sure if your father stops to think about it he'll agree.'
> Miriam's father stopped to think. After a bit he said, reluctantly, 'I mean, you weren't left behind, abandoned, which frankly I thought was going to happen. Imagine! All the people, stopped in their tracks and made to pitch their tents right there!...And then there's your well...it's sitting in one place just like the fire and the cloud. That's power, Miriam, there's no doubt about it. You're not being treated like some nobody with nothing to offer. I don't say I'm happy about this, but, now that I stop to think about it, maybe the family name isn't really smirched.'[20]

From this excerpt one must query where Amram's sympathy lay—with his daughter or his own egocentrism!

Miriam and Family Continuity
Miriam has been praised for her deep abiding concern for family relationships and continuity. Midrashim portray her as she

> functions wholly within the family, even though she functions for the benefit of the nation: she assists her mother in birthing the next generation, she compels her father to beget the nation's redeemer, she marries for the purpose of having children and gives rise to kingship, and she talks with her sister-in-law and with her brother about her concern with the continuity of leadership.[21]

Miriam essays to reconcile husbands to their marital unity. Adverse to her father's and to Moses' separation from their spouses, she risks her being to tell them so. To Miriam, family continuity must supersede public needs or direction and she is fervent in striving to effectuate this ideal. She is stricken with a skin affliction because of her

> concern for Moses' relationship with his family, for his separation from his wife and thus, we have suggested, his lack of involvement with his

---

20. Rosen, *Biblical Women Unbound*, pp. 99-100.
21. Steinmetz, 'Portrait of Miriam', pp. 57-58.

son. While Miriam's gossip is punished, it derives from the same concern which impelled her to stand watch over her infant brother and which, according to other midrashim, had driven her to chide her father into remarrying Jochebed and begetting a son. The merit of that early concern is held to Miriam's favor now, when once again she acts, albeit inappropriately, for the sake of continuity of family and of leadership.[22]

Continuity of leadership is intertwined with family continuity as Miriam lashes out at authority.

The young girl who turns up her nose at Pharaoh and who stands up to her father eventually criticizes Moses. And when she challenges the established authority, even though her criticism reflects a concern for the continuity of leadership and is couched in terms of family, appropriate to a woman's realm of responsibility, Miriam has stepped beyond her bounds.[23]

Although punished for slander, her motives have been recognized and affirmed. 'The synthetic portrait of Miriam concerned about the continuity of family and leadership highlights a concern which the rabbis read in the Exodus and Numbers narratives, a concern for the stability and survival of the nation born during Miriam's lifetime.'[24]

Miriam as Prophetess

Miriam, Deborah and Huldah are unique in that they 'are endowed with gifts of prophecy that transcend sex or gender'.[25] Of these three women, Miriam 'is the first person—not the first woman, but the first person—in the Hebrew Bible given this title in its general sense'.[26]

The *peshat* does not elaborate on what prophetess Miriam does; rather, her gift is described exegetically. In modern day thinking, one can imagine her saying:

When I was but a child of five, I chastised my father and all the Hebrew men for abandoning their marriage beds; when I was a leader of our free people, I upbraided my brother Moses for abandoning his marriage bed. Mine is the voice of joy, of victory, of power. I prophesy the redemption of all our people! My vision is clear and limitless. I see to the last generation![27]

22. Steinmetz, 'Portrait of Miriam', p. 50.

23. Steinmetz, 'Portrait of Miriam', p. 58.

24. Steinmetz, 'Portrait of Miriam', p. 59.

25. Roslyn Lacks, *Women and Judaism: Myth, History, and Struggle* (Garden City, NY: Doubleday, 1980), p. 90.

26. Alice Ogden Bellis, *Helpmates, Harlots, and Heroes: Women's Stories in the Hebrew Bible* (Louisville, KY: Westminster/John Knox Press, 1994), p. 102.

27. Frankel, *Five Books of Miriam*, p. xxii.

Miriam as prophetess does not fit the model found in post-Pentateuchal books. Her

> designation as a prophet and her unquestioned leadership of the victory
> celebration in Exodus 15 indicate that ancient Israelites were also famil-
> iar with forms of female authority that did not survive into later peri-
> ods... Although she is called a prophet, her actions do not follow the
> patterns of oracular speech generally associated with Israelite prophecy.
> They do, however, suggest ritual, perhaps ecstatic, dance and song.[28]

Miriam the Leader/at the Reed Sea/Her Song

In examining the role of Miriam as leader at the crossing of the Reed Sea, several themes become intertwined. A comparison is made between Moses and her as they both sing their song. The authorship of the songs is also questioned. Female exegetes look closely at the sociological/anthropological role of women as singers in the ancient Near East. As women sang in groups, they established leadership roles and contributed to the society at large in the public forum, especially at victorious occasions.

In an insightful article, Meyers writes about Miriam and the women of her time vis-à-vis the singing they did at the Reed Sea. She speaks of women meeting together in order to learn the songs and practice the playing of the musical instruments. These women form a sociological group that becomes most meaningful in their lives and binds them together into a unit. She then posits:

> The opportunity for the elevation of female status also occurs in women's
> groups in terms of the internal dynamics of such groups, which typi-
> cally have their own structures, values and hierarchies, thus affording
> prestige to the participants in relationship to their competence and
> accomplishments with the group itself as well as in public activity. If
> Miriam in fact was a dominant figure in such a group, her leadership
> abilities would easily have trancended the female context and exerted
> themselves in other community settings.[29]

In looking at the anthropological/sociological scene,

> Miriam's association with the Song at the Sea challenges several stereo-
> types about women in ancient Israel. It conveys an image of women as
> singers of war songs, which is supported by other biblical texts (Judg. 5,
> 1 Sam. 2.1-10). These militaristic hymns are among the oldest examples

---

28. Setel, 'Exodus', p. 36.

29. Carol Meyers, 'Miriam the Musician', in Athalya Brenner (ed.), *A Feminist Companion to Exodus to Deuteronomy* (Sheffield: Sheffield Academic Press, 1994), p. 227.

of Hebrew poetry. Although scholars have generally assumed that poetry, like other cultural creations, was exclusively the work of men, these examples raise the question of women's role in originating and developing poetic forms. Vocal and instrumental music, in addition to ritualized dance, may have recreated the sensations as well as the oral images of battle.[30]

In fact, she 'animates the musical life of Israel. If Jubal be its mythical father (Gen. 4.21), she is its historical mother. She inaugurates a procession of women who move throughout Scripture, singing and dancing in sorrow and joy'.[31] We can further add that 'Miriam emerges as the foundress of a women's song tradition. After all, she is the first woman in the Bible to break into a victory song'.[32]

The authorship of the song has been an issue for many centuries. Interpreters have opined that Miriam wrote the song sung by Moses. Today, women speak about Miriam's song as an appendage of Moses' praise.

> Scholars believe that Miriam was the author of the entire Song of the Sea, not just the first verse. Later, in the process of elevating Moses, the song was attributed to him. The Miriamic tradition was so strong, however, that it could not be squelched. As a result, the much-shortened version was appended. So Miriam was both preserved and diminished in importance, even as Moses was elevated.[33]

In many interpretations, Miriam's 'performance in Exodus 15 has been placed in the shadow of Moses' performance'.[34]

Brenner calls both Deborah and Miriam:

> great leaders...Miriam aspires to political leadership on the national scale...Miriam echoes Moses' words in her capacity as the women's leader. Both stories stress the opinion that women, even though they attain a high degree of political involvement and achievement, remain women—and Jewish Midrash elaborates this point further. As such, these female leaders are not depicted as independent figures; they are either led by men or have to share the leadership with them, in the literary area as well as in others. In other words, they are not presented as

---

30. Setel, 'Exodus', p. 35.

31. Phyllis Trible, 'Bringing Miriam Out of the Shadows' in Brenner (ed.), *Exodus to Deuteronomy*, pp. 166-89 (182).

32. F. van Dijk-Hemmes, 'Some Recent Views on the Presentation of the Song of Miriam' in Brenner (ed.), *Exodus to Deuteronomy*, pp. 200-206 (205).

33. Bellis, *Helpmates*, pp. 102-103.

34. van Dijk-Hemmes, 'Recent Views', p. 206.

possessing a talent for the independent poetic creativity which is almost
a standard feature of their male counterparts.[35]

Notwithstanding the foregoing comments, an aura of magnitude
lingers in regard to Miriam's role in the Reed Sea crossing. She
describes the impact she has made: 'Still, my song, though so much
briefer, today stirs the hearts of Jewish women, inspiring them to create new songs, poems, stories, meditations, interpretive commentaries, and prayers.'[36] Miriam's following thought is a mixture of
conflicting feelings she has as she thinks about her part in the history
of the Reed Sea experience: 'my only solo moment in the entire Torah
is at the Sea of Reeds, when I *echo* a single verse of my brother's song,
and even then I "chant for the women", not for myself'.[37] Finally, in a
poem entitled 'Miriam at the Reed Sea', there is a jubilant expression
that she felt toward God:

> The Lord lifted me, I felt His hands,
> and my song poured out
> and the timbrel shook in my fingers
> and my feet never touched the ground.[38]

The Issue of Slander

The most controversial, passion-arousing episode in Miriam's life involves her being punished by God for slandering Moses. Aaron,
whom she is with, escapes unscathed. While rabbinic interpreters fault
Miriam for her vindictive words, female exegetes defend Miriam for
her actions, adding a human and emotional dimension to their interpretation and looking at her as a real person with whom we may identify today.

Several themes surface from women's writings. The religious/God
issue, the rationale for Aaron's not being punished, the effects—
emotional and otherwise—upon Miriam of the punishment, and the
gender component are raised. The critical question asked by women
is why only Miriam was punished:

> That Miriam was the initiator of the offensive action against Moses we
> learn from the outcome: she is punished, then saved by Moses' plea on
> her behalf (vv. 9-15), while Aaron remains unscathed. The conflict, by

35. Athalya Brenner, *The Israelite Woman: Social Role and Literary Type in Biblical Narrative* (Sheffield: JSOT Press, 1985), pp. 55-6.

36. Frankel, *Five Books of Miriam*, p. 110.

37. Frankel, *Five Books of Miriam*, p. 212.

38. Barbara Holender, *Ladies of Genesis: Poems* (New York: Jewish Women's Resource Center, 1991), p. 35.

and large, is a power struggle between Miriam and Moses. God is on Moses' side, and therefore she loses. Nevertheless, she felt confident enough to bid for the supreme position of community leadership. In so doing she does not cite her alleged blood kinship with Moses himself, but regards prophetic gifts equal to Moses' as the basis for her challenge...The conclusion we might draw is that Miriam was an important enough figure in her own right—not only just a leader of women, not only just a woman identified as Moses' or Aaron's sister—to wish for greater authority.[39]

The issue can be addressed in the following way: 'Leprosy was sentence to the horror of a living death. Why is it given to Miriam and not to Aaron?'[40]

Another reason for his not being punished

is related to the role of Aaron as priest...that the Aaronic priesthood must be physically unblemished... Skin diseases such as that infecting Miriam are explicitly listed as a source of such uncleanness (Lev. 22.4)... Our modern question of "unfairness' to Miriam does not appear to have worried the ancient storytellers, at least they did not express any explicit concern for the difference in treatment of Aaron and Miriam.[41]

Sakenfeld refers to Aaron's being reproofed as a 'narrative impossibility'.[42]

The gender issue is clearly elucidated in this comment:

Miriam's claim to a position of authority comparable to Moses... threatens to blur the distinction between Moses' role and hers. Her claim challenges male hegemony. Punishment is swift and devastating. Miriam is put outside the boundary of patriarchal order, symbolized by the camp, where she becomes, literally, the outsider, the other—until she is allowed to come back *inside* the camp/symbolic order in her proper, submissive role.[43]

Exum lucidly combines the gender and punishment issues:

Gender politics are also at work, I suggest: as a man, Aaron poses no threat to the symbolic order. On the contrary, his proper place is inside it; he remains within the camp. While leaving Aaron unblemished and

---

39. Brenner, *Israelite Woman*, p. 53.

40. Beth K. Haber, *Drawing on the Bible: Biblical Women in Art* (New York: Biblio, 1995), p. 71.

41. Katherine Doob Sakenfeld, 'Numbers', in Newsom and Ringe (eds.), *Women's Bible Commentary*, pp. 49-56 (52).

42. Sakenfeld, 'Numbers', p. 52.

43. J. Cheryl Exum, ' "You Shall Let Every Daughter Live": A Study of Exodus 1.8–2.10', in Brenner (ed.), *Exodus to Deuteronomy*, pp. 75-87 (86).

unpunished, Numbers 12 effectively humiliates and eliminates the woman.[44]

Trible concludes: 'The male is spared, the female sacrificed.'[45]

Miriam, God, and the Punishment

Since it is God who inflicts punishment on Miriam, women have tried to figure out why it was so severe, so one-sided and so demeaning. Despite community outpouring, she nevertheless suffered.

> Miriam believes that God has spoken not only through Moses but also through herself and Aaron. Her words would seem to be in line with Moses' own wishes. According to the text, he does not want to be alone with all the authority. Yet God chastises Miriam severely for her audacious challenge to Moses.[46]

Lilith posits another reason why God chastised her: 'Perhaps God was punishing her for her bravado. So dependent had the people and her two brothers become upon her resuscitative powers that she grew too proud and had to be humbled.'[47]

The severity of Miriam's punishment is so great

> that Aaron pleads on her behalf... The mother figure of the nation becomes as a child, even a dead child, or aborted fetus, whose flesh is eaten away. In response to Moses' intercession, God justifies His punishment, reiterating the belittling of Miriam, for she is now compared to a shameful daughter.[48]

Frankel also focuses on the aborted fetus image and says:

> Miriam the healer loses her health, becoming—according to the Septuagint... 'like an abortion', or, as Aaron puts it, like a stillborn baby 'Who emerges from his mother's womb with half his flesh eaten away... (12.12). And so the woman whom Jewish legend identifies as one of the Hebrew midwives in Egypt becomes her own opposite'.[49]

Furthermore, 'leprosy turns out to be the punitive spitting of the Father'.[50]

44. Exum, ' "You Shall Let Every Daughter Live" ', p. 86.
45. Trible, 'Miriam', p. 177.
46. Bellis, *Helpmates*, p. 104.
47. Frankel, *Five Books of Miriam*, p. 214.
48. Ilana Pardes, *Countertraditions in the Bible: A Feminist Approach* (Cambridge, MA: Harvard University Press, 1992), p. 9.
49. Frankel, *Five Books of Miriam*, p. 213.
50. Pardes, *Countertraditions*, p. 10.

As God caused the infliction on Miriam so, too, did God have to be the healer. In Miriam's case, God's role was particularly unique:

> A person had to be examined by a priest to be declared a *metzora*, and again after seclusion to be declared *tahor*, yet Aharon could not perform this role with Miriam, since she was his relative. Nor could Moses, who was not a *kohen*. Therefore, it was God alone who examined her and decided whether she was *tamae* or *tahor* (*Zev.* 101b-2a).[51]

And so, after wreaking upon Miriam such an infliction, God had to effect the cure.

The Effects of the Punishment on Miriam
It could be expected that a woman of Miriam's stature could withstand life's vicissitudes and mature through life's tribulations. Not only would she be a role model, but she would be able to find inner strength and prevail when life seemed unkind to her. When she was in isolation, she took 'a journey inside herself to find there her parents, her husband, her kin, her neighbors, and whatever words she could locate for addressing God'.[52]

When Miriam came out of isolation, life for the people resumed a sense of normalcy. The pillar of cloud which had temporarily stopped now guided them once again. The well also functioned once again.

> And then—did Miriam lead them along the way? Or did the combined weight of sorrow, joy, rejection, and exaltation crack her heart at last, so that she died?

> Both, say the old legends, and ours must say the same. She both died and she persisted. She was ground down and she continued. She gave up and she endured.[53]

Even though Miriam did exemplary things throughout her life, 'for none of these positive behaviors are we commanded to remember Miriam. Rather, we are told to remember what happened to her on the way out of Egypt—the only negative thing ever recorded about her'.[54]

> In spite of the puzzle of her punishment, what remains clear is that Miriam maintains important status within the community... This is testament to the power and significance of her presence, and the devastation of her loss. Miriam's scant appearance and her departure leaves

51. Antonelli, *Image of God*, p. 351.
52. Rosen, *Biblical Women Unbound*, p. 110.
53. Rosen, *Biblical Women Unbound*, p. 110.
54. Antonelli, *Image of God*, p. 349.

us, with the congregation in the wilderness, parched, and thirsting to know more of her and her story.[55]

Miriam's Well

If there is a leitmotif in Miriam's story, it is that of water—the waters of the Nile and the Reed Sea. So, too, there is Miriam's well. Female exegetes have focused on this well and add to the richness of biblical interpretation in relating the theme of water to wisdom and nourishment. Frankel makes a connection between women and wells: 'Like water bubbling up mysteriously from the earth, nurturing fluids issue forth from women's bodies: menstrual blood to nourish life, the waters of birth, breast milk—and so many tears.'[56] In making the Bible relevant to our time, 'Miriam's well has become for us a symbol of Jewish women's creativity, spirituality, collective experience, healing, and wisdom'.[57]

During the people's wandering in the desert, following the Exodus, a pillar of cloud and a pillar of fire accompanied them. So, too, did Miriam's well 'which, according to biblical tradition, traveled with the children of Israel, guiding, guarding, and nourishing them throughout their wanderings'.[58]

The affiliation between Miriam and the well is further forged as she explains why the well was named for her:

> Because of my merits—my powers of prophecy, my protection of my baby brother Moses, my skillful midwifery among the Hebrew slaves, and my victory song at the Sea of Reeds—this well was restored to the Jewish people and was called by my name...'[59]

The ebb and flow of the water in her lifetime is poignantly described:

> In Jewish legend she is associated with a well, and like water she flows in and out of the books of Exodus and Numbers. At times Miriam is submerged, moving with the Exodus saga as a subterranean traveling companion to the people, then emerging at the water's edge, to play a central, if brief, role.[60]

The last major connection made between Miriam and the well is at her death: 'during the next thirty-nine years in the wilderness, the people got water through Miriam's merit from this rock, which was

---

55. Haber, *Drawing on the Bible*, p. 72.
56. Frankel, *Five Books of Miriam*, p. 227.
57. Frankel, *Five Books of Miriam*, p. 226.
58. Pardes, *Countertraditions*, p. 160 n. 7.
59. Frankel, *Five Books of Miriam*, p. 226.
60. Haber, *Drawing on the Bible*, p. 71.

known as Miriam's Well'.[61] Upon her death the well is reported to have functioned no longer. Antonelli concludes it is 'significant that the theme of water follows the death of Miriam as well as precedes it'.[62] In looking back over Miriam's life,

> the symbol of water also supports Miriam... Nature's response to Miriam's death is immediate and severe. It mourns, and the community suffers. Miriam, protector of her brother at the river's bank and leader in the victory at the sea, symbolized life. How appropriate, then, that waters of life should reverence her death. Like the people of Israel, nature honors Miriam.[63]

It is important to note how women express gratefulness to Miriam for the gift that was bestowed by God upon her and therefore on the wandering people:

> Miriam has been especially honored by our God. Wherever we wander in this wilderness, there is water. Wherever we camp, there is a well, or spring, of water to refresh us and our animals. Women say the well is God's gift to Miriam for her devotion to God and to the people of Israel ... Miriam gained much merit with God when she sang the people across the sea during our escape from Pharaoh's wrath... Miriam is strong and makes us feel brave.[64]

Miriam's Death

In the book of Genesis women's death is reported tersely, if at all, Rachel being the exception. Compared with her brothers, Miriam's death does not receive much coverage:

> Its very brevity, with absence of detail and no reference to a period of mourning, indicates her lesser status in the tradition in comparison with her two brothers. On the other hand, that her death is reported at all suggests her importance, and the location of her death geographically and narratively functions to raise her status closer to that of her brothers.[65]

A gender issue is related to her death as well:

> Although Miriam is brought back to the camp after being 'shut out' for seven days, she dies shortly after this harsh incident without uttering an additional word... For in Moses' day a woman with the gift of prophecy

61. Antonelli, *Image of God*, p. 365.
62. Antonelli, *Image of God*, p. 365.
63. Trible, 'Miriam', p. 180.
64. Alice Bach and J. Cheryl Exum, *Miriam's Well: Stories About Women in the Bible* (New York: Delacorte Press, 1991), pp. 43-44.
65. Sakenfeld, 'Numbers', pp. 52-53.

would have had to be silenced and then buried in the wilderness for daring to demand a central cultural position.[66]

Contextual hints often give clues about people. In Miriam's case, her death is juxtaposed with two major events: 'The death of Miriam is said to follow immediately upon the preparation and use of the waters of the Red Heifer because "as the Red Heifer effects atonement, so does the death of the righteous effect atonement" (*M. Qaṭ* 28a; *Lev. R.* 20.12; Rashi). This may be true, but it is equally significant that the theme of water follows the death of Miriam as well as precedes it'.[67]

Frankel addresses this part of Miriam's life in a midrash:

> OUR DAUGHTERS ASK: Why isn't there a period of national mourning when Miriam dies, as there is at Aaron's death? Hasn't she also been a national leader for forty years! And why does the Torah narrate Miriam's death in only a single unadorned sentence...(20.1), while her brother's death is divinely scripted in elaborate detail later in this same chapter?... We aren't even told how Miriam dies or when...
>
> THE RABBIS ANSWER: Miriam does get the death she deserves. She is one of only six people...who have merited death by the kiss of God... Miriam's death occurred on the tenth day of the month of Nisan... To memorialize her death, this day was long ago established as a fast day for all righteous women, a custom that has fallen into disuse.
>
> MIRIAM THE PROPHET ANSWERS: Perhaps it is time to revive this custom and properly honor my passing.[68]

Miriam and Gender Issues

Because of the feminist exegetical track with which this paper deals, a separate heading is included called gender. However, throughout this article, gender issues are intertwined. Under this particular theme, some of the problems emphasize Miriam's uniqueness within the patriarchal society and recognize how difficult it was for her to excel as she did. Other comments discern her remarkable personality and stress the extraordinary nature of the role she played in the birth of the Israelite nation.

The theme of power surfaces in many writings:

> In the early portion of the story the prophetess Miriam is one of a set of powerful transgressive females...who may be seen as colluding across ethnic and class boundaries and against patriarchal power to preserve the life of the hero, Moses.[69]

---

66. Pardes, *Countertraditions*, p. 10.

67. Antonelli, *Image of God*, p. 365.

68. Frankel, *Five Books of Miriam*, p. 225.

69. Alicia Suskin Ostriker, *Feminist Revision and the Bible* (Oxford: Basil Blackwell, 1993), p. 43.

Nunnally-Cox also speculates on the motif of power:

> Women are rarely named as tribal figures or national heroines, yet Miriam seems to carry a good deal of influence in her community. It is of great interest, then, that Miriam is the one to receive leprosy, in the minor mutiny against Moses, while Aaron remains untouched. Perhaps this suggests the kind of power Miriam held, and perhaps to the story-teller this seemed dangerous.[70]

In a modern day midrash which depicts different people visiting Miriam each day, the following episode is depicted:

> On the sixth day, the women of the community come, urging Miriam to give up assaults on power, or at least to seek power couched in femi-nine wiles and apparent submissiveness.
> 'Don't you know you catch more flies with honey than vinegar, Miri-am? And all men are flies!'
> 'Go away', Miriam answers. 'Things have gone too far for that now. I want the same right to speak out as my husband Caleb and my brother Moses, to say what I think, and act on it.'
> 'Poor Miriam', the women sigh. 'She hasn't a clue'.
> Then they leave her.[71]

The public–private motif is also placed in this gender category. Usu-ally women's position is in the home:

> The notable exception to this domestic focus, is, of course, Miriam. She serves as a reminder that even in cultures that emphasize domestic roles for women, some women do achieve public leadership. Miriam's story here typifies much of such leadership: it is exceptional, it is not re-garded as fully comparable to that of the men, and it is much more easily challenged, compromised, and undercut.[72]

Taken in the context of ancient Israel, the topic of patriarchy is raised. This has been seen earlier, but is necessary to focus on again here:

> Biblical clues suggest that Miriam was of equal stature with Moses and Aaron. Nevertheless her importance has been reduced, while Moses's story has been glorified. Even her song has been placed in Moses' mouth and she has been left with only the opening lines. At least with the clues that were left, we could surmise that the historical reality was more favorable to Miriam than the historical memory of her.[73]

---

70. Janice Nunnally-Cox, *Foremothers: Women of the Bible* (San Francisco: Harper & Row, 1981), p. 35.

71. Rosen, *Biblical Women Unbound*, pp. 107-108.

72. Sakenfeld, 'Numbers', p. 55.

73. Bellis, *Helpmates*, p. 231.

Burns posits:

> Women are rarely named in biblical genealogies. This, of course, is not
> so much a reflection of the female population of ancient Israel as it is a
> commentary on their position (or lack thereof) in patriarchal society,
> politics and religion. When they do appear in genealogical texts, their
> significance rests largely on their roles as wives or mothers of important
> figures. Miriam is an exception to this general pattern'.[74]

Women's position is illustrated by Frankel in a midrash related to
the slander incident:

> OUR DAUGHTERS ASK: Why doesn't Miriam speak for herself? In fact,
> why doesn't she speak a single word throughout this entire episode?
> Why does Aaron serve as her mouthpiece, as he did for Moses before
> Pharaoh?
>   MIRIAM THE PROPHET ANSWERS: Women rarely speak in the Torah,
> especially after the Book of Genesis. Clearly, this silence reflects our
> subordinate status in ancient Near Eastern society: to be seen—and even
> then, behind a veil—and not heard…we women who came out of Egypt
> were no longer a shaping force among our people. Not even I, matriarch
> of the ruling family, was granted a powerful voice. For here, in my bold
> bid for such a role, I was slapped down, whitened out, and silenced.[75]

Ostriker says that Miriam is one of a number of women who 'are
foregrounded as active agents at the beginning of a story, and disappear by the end of it'.[76] She 'begins triumphantly and fades into
disgrace and obscurity'.[77]

General Observations about Miriam by Female Exegetes
By way of summarizing the exegetical remarks of females, several
quotations have been chosen to illustrate the persona and the personality of Miriam. 'Both the Biblical and the midrash…are relatively
silent when it comes to assessing the figure of Miriam; mostly, they
characterize her through narrative, with little explicit comment abut
her nature.'[78] Female exegetes are filling in the lacuna today. Miriam
is becoming more of an all around person. She

> emerges from the bits and pieces as a multifaceted character: mediator,
> cultic figure, prophet, musician, beloved leader, strong even threatening
> personality. That she can be reconstructed at all from the fragments in

74.   Rita J. Burns, *Has The Lord Indeed Spoken Only Through Moses? A Study of the Biblical Portrait of Miriam* (Atlanta: Scholars Press, 1987), p. 97.

75.   Frankel, *Five Books of Miriam*, p. 212.

76.   Ostriker, *Feminist Revision*, p. 47.

77.   Nunnally-Cox, *Foremothers*, p. 35.

78.   Steinmetz, 'Miriam', p. 55.

scripture is cause for celebration. That she has been diminished by these same scriptures is cause for concern. Yet her story is not unusual, in the Bible or in history.[79]

Women are trying to extract enriching material about biblical females from the text. In the case of Miriam, and

In spite of diminution by the biblical text, she can be reconstructed as a multifaceted, strong, character. She begins her literary life as a mediator and part of the Pharaoh-defying women who save Moses. She emerges as an adult who has cultic, prophetic, and musical leadership in the life of the Hebrews in the wilderness period. She confronts Moses and loses, is punished by God, and is silenced. In the eyes of the people, however, and later in the voices of the prophets, she is celebrated.[80]

After finding a decrease in her importance in the Israelite nation's history, it was concluded that 'the actual narrative space accorded Miriam in the Torah is only a fraction of what Aaron receives. The Torah leaves us, then, with tantalizing hints concerning Miriam's importance and influence and the nature of her religious role, but she is by no means accorded the narrative attention the few texts concerning her suggest she deserves'.[81]

In looking at the overall presentation of the Exodus experience, Meyers determines:

Perhaps nothing epitomizes the range of ways that scholars have sought to understand the Exodus more than their attempts to grasp the role of Miriam in the seminal events of Israelite experience and in the biblical traditions that provide our imperfect and incomplete knowledge of Israelite beginnings. Issues of historicity, of literary presentation, of redactional bias, of editorial impositions—all of these concerns characterize attempts to reconstruct the flight from Egypt and to comprehend what place, if any, a woman held in the foundational drama of Israel's story.[82]

Frankel concludes her commentary of Deuteronomy with a declaration of hope spoken by Miriam:

And so I now chide you as God once chided the Children of Israel: How long will you continue to seek me in vain? I am not in the heavens or across the sea, but I am very close to you, in your mouth and in your

79. Bellis, *Helpmates*, p. 106.

80. Bellis, *Helpmates*, pp. 108-109.

81. Judith Plaskow, *Standing Again at Sinai: Judaism From A Feminist Perspective* (San Francisco: Harper & Row, 1990), p. 39.

82. Meyers, 'Miriam the Musician', p. 207.

> heart. Indeed, it is you who have lost me, but if you seek me, I will show
> myself to you. And together we will choose life![83]

Such a statement can be a catalyst for further study, increased identification with the text and meeting a challenge of educational hope.
This is a true goal of female exegesis—opening the door for increased
study of the Bible and finding, in the text, what is waiting to be discovered.

Conclusion

In examining the work of rabbinic tradition and that of female exegetes, similarities and contrasts surface. From the section headings in
both parts of this presentation, we find the females concentrated on
different parts of Miriam's life and on more aspects of the episodes
than did the rabbis. Looking at Miriam's life through the eyes of a
female has reaffirmed elements of rabbinic tradition and, more importantly, has greatly broadened and enhanced the scope and depth of
biblical interpretation. Women are asking more questions about Miriam herself, are comparing her with her brothers (as well as with other
biblical females), and are showing discontent with how she has been
perceived through the millennia. Women are finding a new place for
her at the crossing of the Reed Sea and explicating on Miriam's well
more expansively. While recognizing her foibles, they challenge the
reader of the Bible to accord her a more prominent place alongside
her brothers in the history of the Israelite nation. Where questions
were not asked by the rabbis, women are enjoining the reader to ask
these questions and they have begun answering them as well. Slowly
Miriam is becoming a more flourishing person in her people's past, a
most influential woman within the public sphere of their lives. The
stages of her life are now more replete with an understanding of her
indomitable role and invincible spirit.

One way to interpret Miriam's role at the Reed Sea is to read the
peshat, picture her only as a woman leading other women in song and
give no further exegetical elaboration. A second way to explicate these
verses is to recognize that Miriam's major leadership experience was
actually related to this one particular time when she led the women in
song. Rabbinic exegesis preferred the former route; female interpreters stressed the latter.

Two crucial questions, not addressed before but significant for our
understanding of the text, are: If Miriam was a righteous woman and

83. Frankel, *Five Books of Miriam*, p. 303.

needed to be punished in order to set an example for others, what might be assumed about Aaron's qualities if he went unpunished? What was God's relationship with Miriam so that the length of her punishment was lightened? Questions such as these need to be posed to further discussion about a major female Bible figure. If, when reading about Miriam's punishment, the reader does not raise speculations, the interpretation of her character may be said to be skewed and/or gender biased.

Female exegetes explore and try to imagine how Miriam achieved and effectuated her leadership, and what her rapport was with the women. While following behind the men, the women formed their own nucleus and had their own dreams. What was Miriam's position at their head? What role did she play with her brothers in the Exodus? While Aaron's position was missing from the text, Miriam's name appeared as she shared the spotlight, in song, with Moses. It was striking and unusual for a woman to be in this position.

If the richness of her personality is only seen as she watched her baby brother at the water's edge and responded by seeking his mother to nurse him, then we have been deprived of seeing Miriam as a multifaceted daughter/sister/leader/prophetess whose actions and reactions should provide modelling for qualities and values. The intensity of the Bible message and Miriam's position as a role model will have been weakened considerably, if not lost. Vital for the forthright presentation of Miriam, who was included equally with Moses and Aaron as one of the three leaders (Mic. 6.4), is a recognition of the variations in leadership between the three siblings, each demonstrating individual strengths. In assessing what they did, qualitative distinctions may arise indicating the varied facets leadership may take and the importance of each type. The unusual nature of a female in such a position must be acknowledged.

Rabbinic tradition seemed open to a more positive and autonomous role for Miriam as a child, preferring to have the woman Miriam closed off, hidden as it were, perhaps because she was an adult female. If we continue to reflect rabbinic tradition, and ignore the profundity of feminist biblical exegesis, Miriam's total portrait and contribution will have been lost, and a distorted picture of her will have been garnered. Incorporating modern interpretation by women into the compendium of Bible study will provide a richness that will enhance our understanding of the biblical narrative figures, so that they become more alive and relevant in our lives today.

MIRIAM RE-IMAGINED, AND IMAGINARY WOMEN OF EXODUS IN MUSICAL SETTINGS

Helen Leneman

Music based on texts about biblical women brings these women's stories to life with a fresh immediacy. Music is a universal art, a form of midrash (creative rewriting), and the most emotional medium for transmitting a story. Composers set biblical stories because they were inspired by the story and characters; their music brings new dimensions to both. This chapter will explore the texts of various musical settings written for Miriam and for imaginary women of Exodus. These texts will be translated, discussed and compared. Each will be treated as a 'musical midrash' that amplifies women's voices and gives their characters new dimensions.

Three genres of musical composition have dealt with the story of Exodus: songs, oratorios and operas. There are major differences in the length and possibilities in each of these. Since a song is the shortest medium in which to express a musical idea vocally, the Exodus text typically utilized musically is Miriam's song. An oratorio is a much more extensive musical setting, generally of a sacred text. Until modern times, the oratorio was the only permitted form for musical settings of biblical stories. It was considered unseemly or worse to present biblical characters acting out their stories on a stage until at least the late nineteenth century, and even later in some countries. Yet musical settings of biblical stories were very popular in the eighteenth and ninteenh centuries. A large percentage of Handel's oratorios are based on the Hebrew Bible,[1] and many later composers followed in his footsteps. An opera is a musical drama, usually based in its earlier centuries (sixteenth to eighteenth) on mythological stories. In the twentieth century, a form of opera known as *verismo*, or reality-based, became more popular. These operas dealt with real people in real-life situations, albeit often highly dramatic ones. Operas based on the

---

1. To name only a few examples, Handel wrote oratorios called *Deborah, Saul, Jephtha* and numerous others.

Exodus story fall somewhere between the earlier and later forms. This essay will discuss the following works:

1. Songs: *Miriam's Song* by Charles Avison
              Miriams Siegesgesang by Franz Schubert
              Miriams Siegesgesang by Carl Reinecke

2. Oratorios: *Israel in Egypt* by Georg Frederic Handel
              Il Mosé by Lorenzo Perosi
              Mosé by Adolph Marx

3. Operas: *Mosé in Egitto* and *Moïse et Pharaon* by Gioacchino Rossini
              Il Mosé by Giacomo Orefice

Songs

Two extensive concert arias and a short song are based on Miriam's Song at the Sea (Exod. 15.20-21). *Miriam's Song* by eighteenth-century English composer Charles Avison (1709–70) is set to the biblical text. According to the *Groves Dictionary*, Avison is considered the most important eighteenth-century English composer of concertos.[2] The text of this song is based quite literally on the Exodus verses in which Miriam sings God's praises. Avison composed this as a song in its own right; it is not part of an oratorio. The song is very bright, full of energy and bursting with the joy of victory. The very existence of this song would seem to indicate an interest in the biblical Miriam and a focus on her part in the story of the Exodus. Of course, this is conjecture. It is just as possible that Avison chose Miriam's and not Moses' song because he preferred to write for the soprano voice.

There are two concert arias called *Miriams Siegesgesang,* or *Miriam's Victory Song:* one is a setting for soprano, chorus, and piano by Franz Schubert (1797–1828); the other is a setting for soprano and orchestra by Carl Reinecke (1824–1910). It is more than likely that Reinecke was familiar with the Schubert work and was influenced by it.

The text for the Schubert song is a poem by renowned Austrian poet Franz Grillparzer (the complete poem in its original German is in the Appendix).[3] The poem conflates the Exodus narrative found in

2. *New Groves Dictionary of Music and Musicians,* I (London: Macmillan, 1980), pp. 748-51.

3. There is a score published by G. Schirmer & Co., with only an English text available. There are three different CDs on the market that include this work. (1) Hyperion Schubert Edition, *Complete Songs of Schubert,* vol. 31; Christine Brewer (soprano), Holst Singers; (2) Art of Classics, *Chöre der Romantik,* Intercord Klassische Diskothek ICOR 885-917; Krisztina Laki, (soprano); (3) *Works for Choir and Piano,* Thoroton CTH 2358; Markus Brutscher (tenor).

ch. 14 and the Song at the Sea of ch. 15. In other words, the original song contains mostly praise for God, which is also found in the Grill-parzer but with the additional dramatic description of the experience of the Israelites at the Sea. Schubert completed this work in the year of his death, 1828. He envisioned Miriam as a larger-than-life character, writing possibly the most demanding music for soprano he had ever written. In pianist and commentator Graham Johnson's words, 'It requires considerable stamina and an opulent voice able to ride triumphantly over a large chorus'.[4] In fact, when the work received its premiere in a private concert a few months after Schubert's death, no soprano could be found to sing it and a tenor was engaged instead.[5]

Johnson believes that Schubert wrote *Miriams Siegesgesang* as a result of his enthusiasm for the oratorio tradition of Handel.[6] The work opens with celebratory music in the brilliant key of C major, which is traditionally associated with jubilation. Miriam, the soprano soloist, opens, followed by the chorus. The text for this first section is (translation by Helen Leneman):

> Strike the timbrels, pluck the strings,
> let the sound be carried far.
> Great is the Lord at all times,
> and today greater than ever before.

The second section, which speaks of the shepherd and his flock, conveys a pastoral mode, with a totally different sound from the opening section. This musical shift in tonality and rhythm describes the calm that overtakes the Israelites at this point in the story:

> Out of Egypt you led the people,
> like the shepherd, with his protecting staff.
> Your staff was the clouds, your arm the fire's heat.
> Go forth, a shepherd leading your people,
> with your strong arm and fiery eyes!

The references to clouds, fire and strong arm are all biblical, deriving in part from Exod. 14.24: 'The Lord looked down upon the Egyptian army from a pillar of fire and cloud.'[7] Later, as the sea is parted, the music becomes more turbulent, suspenseful and dramatic; on the phrase 'A new land', Miriam soars to a high C over the chorus and

---

4. Graham Johnson, in liner notes and commentaries to CD volume 31 of the Hyperion Schubert Edition, *Complete Songs of Schubert*, p. 58.

5. Johnson, *Commentary*, p. 58.

6. Johnson, *Commentary*, p. 58.

7. All biblical translations are from the Jewish Publication Society *Tanakh* (Philadelphia: Jewish Publication Society of America, 1962).

piano. The reference to a 'crystal wall of waves' is loosely based on Exod. 15.8: 'The floods stood straight like a wall; the deeps froze in the heart of the sea.' After the Israelites have crossed over, the music returns to the calm 'shepherd' theme that opened this section:

> The sea hears your voice
> and becomes land when the people approach:
> the sea becomes land.
> Shrink from the monstrous sea,
> look at it through the crystal wall of waves.
> We trust in your voice
> and tread joyously on the new land.

Then, when Pharaoh gives chase, the music again becomes exciting, conveying panic and rapid movement. The dramatic musical imagery expands the biblical text. Only the opening words are sung by Miriam alone; the chorus soon takes over and, as the tempo and urgency quicken, Miriam and the chorus call out to one another as in an echo:

> But now the horizon darkens
> as horse and rider free themselves.
> Trumpets sound, armor glistens—
> it is Pharaoh and his followers.
> Lord, it grows dark with danger,
> helpless are we,
> while they have men and chariots.
> And the enemy, flushed with a murderous glow,
> Pushes forward, toward the safe passage,
> ever forward.
> But listen! what sighs, what moans and cries,
> wails and cursings.
> An assault!

As the word 'assault!' is repeated a second time, the tempo increases and the key shifts to C minor, which reflects a sort of reverse, or dark side, of the original C major of the song's opening. It expresses victory tinged with the defeat and death of the foe:

> An assault! It is the Lord in his wrath.
> The tower of water collapses
> all around them.
>
> Man and horse, chariot and rider,
> all twisted and tangled
> in the dangerous net.
> The spokes of their chariots are broken,
> dead are horse and rider.

The next section once again takes on a new key and tempo, suggestive almost of a funeral march. Tone-painting is effective in Miriam's image of Pharaoh being dragged to the bottom of the sea, as the lowest range of the voice is utilized in that passage. The passage borrows from Exod. 15.5, 10: 'The deeps covered them; they went down into the depths like a stone... They sank like lead in the majestic waters.' The music is calm but also plaintive when the sea has completed its task. Miriam sings this passage as a solo, which is then echoed in full by the chorus:

> Are you coming up for air, Pharaoh?
> Up, then down, down to the bottom,
> black as your heart.
>
> And the sea has fulfilled its task;
> silently its waves roll on,
> never revealing what it conceals:
> at once desert, grave and coffin.
> The Lord has fulfilled his terrible task,
> the sea's waves flow silently;
> who could guess what they hide—
> grave and coffin of the impious.

The work ends with the chorus's repetition of the opening passage ('Strike the timbrels, pluck the strings', etc.), sung here as an elaborate fugue, a musical form Schubert was just beginning to explore at the time of his early death. This triumphal conclusion conveys tremendous excitement and exultation.

Another concert aria called *Miriams Siegesgesang* appeared some years later, though it apparently was never recorded or even published commercially. The composer was Carl Reinecke. The text for the Reinecke song is not attributed, and is assumed to be by the composer himself (the German original can be found in the Appendix).[8] Reinecke was a German composer, teacher, administrator, pianist, and conductor. He received his music education from his father, a music theoretician and author. He was a teacher and later director at the famed Leipzig Conservatory from 1860 until his death in 1910. During his tenure, it became one of the most renowned conservatories in Europe. Reinecke was always conscious of his position as representative and guardian of tradition. He is most well known for his piano and flute works.[9]

The poem Reinecke used is closer in spirit to the original Exodus 15,

---

8.   The score at the Library of Congress is a lithograph of an autograph edition; the publisher is Breitkopf & Härtel, Leipzig.

9.   *Groves Dictionary*, XV, pp. 718-19.

with its focus on singing God's praises, than the Grillparzer poem. Musically it bears some similarity to the Schubert setting. For example, Reinecke also opens his song in the bright key of C major. The opening bars are actually a recitative for the soprano, a few brief unaccompanied measures in which Miriam proclaims:

> Behold, the Lord has done great things for us, thus let us rejoice.

Then Miriam continues, in a melody not very unlike Schubert's, with:

> Walk along the reed sea with drums.
> The Lord has triumphed, the Lord has triumphed!
> Our chain has been broken.
> Sing, roar! The pride of the mighty is broken,
> the pride of the mighty is broken.

There is no chorus, but Reinecke apparently supplied drama with his rich orchestration, which includes numerous wind instruments and a prominent harp. It is very possible that he chose these instruments to re-create an 'ancient' sound, or to highlight instruments similar to those of the time of Exodus.

The victorious sounds are briefly softened as the tempo slows and most of the instruments stop playing as Miriam sings:

> The Lord has spoken, and down into the reed sea vanished rider and horse.

(This line is loosely based on Exod. 15.5, 10.) Then, with a few musical and verbal variations, the hymn of praise resumes:

> Walk along the reed sea with drums!
> The Lord has spoken, our chain has been broken.
> Glory to the Lord, to the conqueror glory,
> His breath our sword, and his word our spear.

This last line, the most original in the poem, is repeated many times, each time with a slight change in rhythm, until a completely new melody appears. This melody is then used for the next few lines:

> Behold, who told the waiting people, who told them that thousands have fallen?
> Not one got away! Not one got away!
> The Lord looked out from the fiery cloud and tossed the enemy into the sea.
> The Lord has triumphed, our chain has been broken.

The 'fiery cloud' is another reference to Exod. 14.24. After another brief recitative, the song returns to the opening theme but, unlike Schubert, Reinecke introduces it in a new key. The concluding section becomes increasingly dramatic and exciting, and Miriam is once again called on to sing a high C, this time soaring above the orchestra and executing a trill before the final chord, when the entire orchestra joins in after her final notes:

> Glory to the Lord, the Lord has triumphed
> and the pride of the powerful is gone.
> Glory to the Lord, Glory to the Lord.

Some of the similarities to the Schubert setting indicate that it inspired Reinecke to write his own setting of Miriam's victory song. Musical differences exist, of course, since they wrote in different periods. Of greatest interest to the biblical scholar is the elaboration in these two works of Miriam's original two-line song found in the Bible. Did these poets believe Miriam's song had been truncated, as many modern scholars do? Or did they think Moses' song should have been attributed to Miriam, since women were usually the singers of victory songs in ancient Israel? Or did they just want to write a dramatic victory song for Miriam based on more than two lines of biblical poetry? The answers to these questions might only be found in a stray reference in the composers' correspondence, but since *Miriams Siegesgesang* was a very minor work in the full corpus of both composers' outputs, it is doubtful that any reference was ever made. In any case, such a study is beyond the scope of this essay.

Oratorios

An oratorio is an extended musical setting of a sacred text. Because it is not meant to be 'acted', the music does not 'describe' characters in the story. The most well-known oratorio based on Exodus is *Israel in Egypt* (1738) by Handel. There are no 'named' characters; the text is from Exodus and Psalms. Verses from the song at the sea are divided among chorus and soloists, with several taken by a soprano or by two sopranos in a duet. Miriam is introduced before singing a line from her own song, which concludes the oratorio. Though an oratorio is far longer than a song, in the case of Miriam the two settings described above paint far more descriptive a portrait of her character than does this entire oratorio, which is only meant to narrate the biblical story.

Several nineteenth-century oratorios based on Exodus are listed in the *Groves Dictionary*: the most well-known composers represented are Anton Rubinstein (1891) and Camille Saint-Saëns (1851); but these scores have not been located. Another score not located is that of *Mosé* (1900) by Lorenzo Perosi (1872–1956). Perosi was an ordained priest

who served as choirmaster of St Marks, and later as music director of
the Sistine Chapel. He entered a mental hospital in 1922. At the turn
of the century his numerous oratorios were very successful. His music
was considered 'naive and eclectic'.[10] He rejected the 'vulgar oratorio'
of the eighteenth and ninteenth centuries, for what he perceived as
their dependence on opera. In his 12 oratorios he returned to the
seventeenth-century format, but on a larger scale and with the addition of post-Wagnerian material. Most of his oratorios are in two parts
and in Latin, distributed among different voices. His stated goal was
to attain a more serious religious expression than could be found in
the previous two hundred years of Italian oratorios. He utilized Gre-
gorian chant and a quasi-liturgical mode, especially in his choruses. It
would be interesting to discover how large a part Miriam was given
in *Il Mosé*, but this score can only be found in a handful of libraries
around the world.

In an obscure oratorio, *Mosé* (1841 by Adolph Bernhard Marx (1795–
1866), Miriam sings two extensive arias. Additional female characters
who are created are a queen (consort to Pharaoh) and Pharaoh's
mother, who also sings an aria. Marx was a German-Jewish music
theorist, author and composer. He had a career as a lawyer and then
an editor. Marx's contemporaries were not very encouraging: Men-
delssohn refused to perform *Mosé* in 1841 in Leipzig; Schumann, who
praised Marx's earlier works, criticized *Mosé*. However, it was apparently performed often, even by Liszt in Weimar in 1853.

There are three extensive arias for women in this oratorio, which
does attempt to attribute emotions to Miriam not found in Exodus.
The text is presumably by the composer, since it is not attributed to
anyone (the German originals are in the Appendix).

Marx's music is fairly conventional, yet he injects tenderness and
pathos into Miriam's arias that render her appealing. This would seem
unusual for the oratorio form, but less so for the eighteenth century in
general, when Romanticism was flowering. In her first aria, *'Hebt
Euch'* ('Get Away'), Miriam's music is gentle and sad, as the lyrics
demand:

> Get away from me,
> let me cry bitterly.
> Don't try to comfort me
> about the destruction of my people.

The text of the aria sung by Pharaoh's mother sounds like excerpts

---

10. *Groves Dictionary*, XIII, p. 675.

from Proverbs in many places. This character, who of course does not
exist in the biblical text, gives Pharaoh home-spun advice about caring for the poor and needy, and tries to frighten him about the all-
powerful Hebrew God. It is intriguing to think that though Pharaoh
'knew not Joseph', his mother might have been old enough to remember him. Was Marx writing a modern midrash on the story? He certainly took a lot of interest in the female characters, to the point of
adding one of his own. His music, but even more his texts, add a fresh
dimension to the story:

> Listen, women,
> teach your daughters to cry!
> and let them teach one another to lament.
> Death has overtaken us,
> choking the children in the streets.
> Dear child, hear me, your mother,
> as I open my mouth
> to recount the old stories
> our fathers told us.
> Dear child, don't despise the poor,
> and don't look down on or afflict the needy
> in their sorrow,
> Don't turn away
> so they should not complain about you.
> For the one who made the poor man
> hears his prayer
> when he laments with a sad heart
> about you.
> Don't let yourself seem wiser
> than your elders.
> Don't follow your bad inclination
> else you bequeath it.
> Don't think, who will stand against me?
> But see, they serve one Lord,
> powerful over all gods.
> He is one, the almighty,
> all-powerful, a terrifying king.
> In the days that are now gone,
> I heard it from the elders.

The setting for Miriam's second aria is the Sea of Reeds. It is both a
soliloquy and a paean to God:

> Why are you sad, my soul,
> and so restless, so restless within me?
> Wait for God, I will thank him
> for helping me with his countenance.
> Your torrents are roaring,

and the deep waters are rushing all around us.
All your waves and billowing water
rush over me.
I say to God, my rock,
can you forget me?
That day God let his goodness be known,
and at night
I sing to him and pray to God
for my life.

This aria has a flowing, lyrical melody that paints a Miriam of deep feeling and warmth. Even though he was limited by the oratorio form, Marx succeeded in creating through his music and text a believable and very human Miriam.

Operas

The most striking element in opera librettos dealing with Exodus is the addition of female characters not found in the original story. The biblical story often seems merely a familiar and attractive peg on which to hang a standard romantic opera plot. The librettist for Rossini's *Mosé in Egitto (Moses in Egypt)*, A. Tottola, based his text on Francesco Ringhieri's 1747 tragedy *L'Osiride*, or *Osiris* (the name of an Egyptian god). Rossini set the story of Moses twice, once in Italian and later in French. The Italian version was first performed in 1818. The three-act opera was then revised as a Grand Opera in four acts as *Moïse et Pharaon, ou Le passage de la mer rouge (Moses and Pharaoh, or the Passing Through the Red Sea)* in 1827. The story only vaguely resembles the biblical original. Pharaoh has decided to free the captive Hebrews, and Moses hears a voice predicting that the Hebrews will at last reach the Promised Land. Pharaoh's son Osiride (Aménophis in the French version) wants to keep the Hebrews in Egypt because he is in love with Moses' niece, Miriam's daughter Elcia (Anaï in the French). This added female character is necessary for the romantic plot to unfold. (Miriam is known as Amenosi, Aaron's sister, in the Italian, and Marie, Moses' sister, in the French). Moses obscures the sun to demonstrate his powers. Osiride's mother Amaltea (Sinaïde in the French), another additional female character necessary to the plot, advises him to comply with his father's wishes and marry the daughter of the king of Assyria. Moses and the Israelites refuse to worship the god Isis, and Moses extinguishes the flame on the temple altar, which leads Pharaoh to banish the Hebrews.

Elcia is captured by Osiride but returns to her people and joins them as they escape across the Red Sea, as Moses miraculously parts the waves. The drama is supposedly heightened (as if that were necessary) by the unexpected last-minute return of Elcia.

The plot of *Moïse* is similar to the Italian version, but the names of the characters have been changed and additional episodes have been added. Any resemblance to the original biblical story at this point has been largely obscured. In this version, Moses and the Israelites await the return of his brother Eliezer, who has gone to Pharaoh to plead the Israelite cause. (In the Bible, Eliezer is actually the son of Moses and Zipporah. Moses' brother Aaron did occasionally plead the Israelite cause.) Act 2 is substantially the same as the first act of *Mosé in Egitto*. The third act includes an extended ballet in the Temple of Isis; inclusion of a ballet was conventional in French operas of that era. Rossini was ultimately far more loyal to the conventions of his day than to creating a believable musical drama. The final act adds a scene between Aménophis and Anaï where he tells her he will give up the throne if she will marry him; Anaï chooses to follow her people. Aménophis warns them that Pharaoh will attack them, and he rejoins his father. But once again, of course, Moses splits the sea and the people are saved.

There is one interesting plot difference: there is a scene between Elcia and Osiride in *Mosé in Egitto* where she pleads with Osiride to marry the Armenian princess (yet another created female character serving as a plot device) and let her go with her people. When Osiride threatens to kill Moses a bolt of lightning kills him, and Elcia expresses her despair in an extended aria. In *Moïse* Sinaïde, the Pharaoh's wife, sings the same aria as Elcia sings in the Italian version, but to express *joy* rather than *grief*. The same aria functions well in both contexts, proving Rossini's theory that music is not imitative of particular emotions. The *Groves Dictionary* refers to this as Rossini's 'conscious artificiality'.[11] It is for this reason that his music does not succeed in differentiating between characters and certainly cannot be employed as musical midrash. Much like Handel, Rossini tended to use the human voice as an instrument, not an expression of individual character.

The 1904 *verismo* opera *Il Mosé* by Giacomo Orefice (1865–1922),[12] based on the dramatic poem by Angiolo Orvieto, certainly succeeds where Rossini did not. Orefice graduated in law in 1886 and was first

---

11. *Groves Dictionary*, XIII, p. 562.
12. Edited and published by Edoardo Sonzogno (Milan, 1905).

active as a pianist. Most of his compositions were for the stage. *Il Mosé*
was first performed in Genoa in 1905. This telling of the Exodus story
bears more resemblance to the original than do the Rossini operas.
Orefice paints a Miriam of many more dimensions than the biblical
Miriam: passionate, strong, warm, and loyal to her brother and her
fellow Israelites. The role is for a mezzo-soprano, a lower and richer
voice than soprano. Opera composers have the advantage of instantly
creating a certain character type by using voice type. In operatic con-
vention young, virginal females are always sopranos (maybe it was
believed a woman's voice also changes!), while older or more seduc-
tive women are inevitably mezzos. For this reason, it is particularly
noteworthy that Orefice chose to cast Miriam as a mezzo.

In the story Khiti, an Egyptian princess (another added female
character), is in love with Moses. She tries to seduce him, to persuade
him to run away with her. Miriam rushes in; Moses at first does not
recognize her, saying he thought she was 'far away in her land'. He
explains to Khiti that his nursemaid was Miriam's mother. He swears
to protect Miriam, in memory of 'his sweet childhood'. In her aria *'Era
inondato di pace'* ('It overflowed with peace'), Miriam reminisces about
their joyful childhood. The musical setting, according to a note by the
composer, is 'based on a Hebrew chant'. It has a tranquil, incantatory
quality (translated by Helen Leneman):

> That sweet refuge was overflowing with peace
> On the fleeting current of the green Nile.
> Blessings that came from you
> rained upon my people.
> We were no longer Hebrews for Pharaoh!
> Loaded with golden baskets, a faithful messenger
> would come often to this rustic place.

Miriam now tells Moses who he really is. Khiti begs him not to listen. Smendes, an Egyptian in love with Khiti, overhears and sends
Egyptian soldiers to take Miriam and Moses away. Moses kills one of
the soldiers. In the following scene, the Israelites all bow down to
Moses. It is interesting that Orefice obviously had enough contact
with Jews to learn a 'Hebrew chant' for use in his opera, yet knew so
little of authentic Jewish practice of his day that he would have the
Israelites bowing to Moses.

In the next act, Smendes has married Khiti and they have a son.
Darkness has covered everything (one of only three plagues described
in the opera; the others would have probably been too difficult to
stage). Pharaoh makes a grand entrance. All bow 'as to a god'. This is
probably more realistic than the Israelites doing the same to Moses.

Pharaoh boasts of having chained and imprisoned Moses. In the next scene Moses, Miriam and Aaron sing 'no chains can hold me'. They praise their God, while inside their own temple the Egyptians praise theirs, probably a very effective scene on stage. Moses calls on God for vengeance—'Blood!'—and suddenly all water turns to blood, including fountains and the Nile itself (another plague which could be demonstrated dramatically on stage).

Pharaoh defies Moses. But when Khiti's son is struck down, she pleads with Moses to save him. He tells her only Pharaoh can do that. The child dies, then all Egyptian first-born children die. This, of course, is the final plague, and probably the easiest one to dramatize. Pharaoh sends the Israelites away.

Act III takes place in the desert. Moses has been gone 40 days. The Israelite men are grumbling, but the women keep their faith. Miriam is shocked that the people would doubt Moses and in a rousing, dramatic aria, *'Chi distese le palme?'* ('Who stretched out his hands?'), she reminds them of all Moses has done for them:

> You doubt him who redeemed Israel?
> And who was it that stretched out his hands over the raging waves,
> Who raised the abyss of the sea, letting Israel pass through?
> Who hurled the troops of our enemies
> into the sea's path, and then made the wave crash down upon them,
> annihilating Egypt?
> Who granted life to the dying
> by showing the bronze serpent?
> And who brought forth a spring
> from the dry rock of the mountain?
> It was Moses! Moses! Moses!
>
> (The others retort: But he won't return!
> The cloud of fire has swallowed Moses
> in the night of the misty mountain.)

Continuing in her role as leader and protector of her people, Miriam responds to the crowd in her final aria, *'La nuvola lo protegge'* ('The cloud protects him'). Only Miriam apparently understands both the cloud, and the light on Moses' face, to represent God. This aria starts as a gentle song and shifts in the middle to the bright key of C major to musically depict the light Miriam sees shining on Moses' face:

> The cloud protects him, it doesn't swallow him.
> I see him descending now;
> The trace of mysterious brightness
> sparkles again.
> Moses' entire face shines
> with the glory radiated by God.

The Midianite women in the camp are the Israelite men's lovers; they cured them of the plague with their special potions (the alleged involvement of the Midianite women is loosely based on Num. 25.1-3). Midianite women and Hebrew men are seen embracing in the moonlight. There is an orchestral interlude representing an orgy with the Midianite women. This orgy becomes worship of Baal-Peor and the golden calf. Moses appears and shatters the tablets on, and together with, the golden calf. This story merges parts of a later story, in Exod. 32.19-20 where, however, the women are absent.

Miriam and the other Hebrew women come out of their tents singing hymns to God. Miriam pleads for mercy for the Israelites. Moses relents; he approaches Mount Sinai, and is enveloped by a cloud. Miriam knows this is God. After an orchestral interlude depicting a storm, trumpets are heard proclaiming 'the glory of Adonai' (Orefice's words). A voice from the mountain proclaims 'You shall have no other gods'. The Israelites bow and say 'amen'. (Perhaps Orefice witnessed parts of a synagogue service when worshipers were partly bowing, and adopted this as a dramatic device.)

In the fourth act, Joshua helps Moses climb Mount Sinai to see the Promised Land (the librettist confused Mount Nebo with Mount Sinai). Moses sings an aria with its musical theme based on a Hebrew chant, as in Miriam's first aria. Moses blesses the tribes and dies.

Of interest in all these operatic settings is the increased number of female roles and the central part they play. In Rossini's case, this is mostly due to operatic conventions and the need for romantic interest. It is not known how often the Orefice opera was performed, or when it dropped out of the repertoire. It apparently has never been recorded, probably because the general interest in the Bible and biblical characters diminished greatly after the early years of the twentieth century. Perhaps in the new millennium we will see new inspiration to the opera composers of today, or to today's conductors and opera producers, and Miriam will be seen and heard in the flesh on an opera stage once again.

Miriam as re-imagined by eighteenth, nineteenth and twentieth century poets and composers emerges as a multi-dimensional woman leader with a powerful voice. For any reader of the Bible who longs for a Miriam of flesh and blood, songs, oratorios and operas will partially fulfill that longing. As for other female characters, such as the midwives, or Jochebed, they did not find a place in romantic or exotic plots, but librettists and composers did imagine other women populating the story of Exodus. Even if all these women are imaginary, artistic imagination can propel Miriam and other women beyond the pages of the Bible, to a place where their voices can be heard in many harmonies and languages.

APPENDIX

Miriams Siegesgesang (Carl Reinecke)

(A special note of appreciation to Henry Silberman and Herta Pollak for deciphering the German manuscript)

> Siehe, der Herr hat Grosses an uns gethan dass sind wir fröhlich:
> Wandelt mit Pauken das Schilfmeer entlang!
> Der Herr hat gesiegt, der Herr hat gesiegt, unsere Kette zersprang.
> Singet, donnert denn des Mächtigen Stolz ist gebrochen.
>
> Der Herr hat gesprochen, und unter im Schilfmeer ging Reiter und Ross.
> Wandelt mit Pauken das Schilfmeer entlang.
> Der Herr hat gesprochen—unsere Kette zersprang.
> Ehre dem Herrn, Ehre dem Herrn dem Eroberer Ehre Herrn!
> Sein Hauch unser Schwert und sein Wort unser Speer!
>
> Siehe, wer meldete dem harrenden Volk den Fall seiner Tausende?
> Keiner entrann! Keiner entrann!
> Der Herr sah hervor aus der feurigen Wolke.
> Wandelt mit Pauken das Schilfmeer entlang,
> Der Herr hat gesiegt, unsere Kette zersprang.
> Ehre dem Herrn, der Herr hat gesiegt und der Stolz des Mächtigen ist gebrochen. Ehre, Ehre dem Herren.

Miriams Siegesgesang (Franz Grillparzer)

> Rührt die Cymbel, schlagt die Saiten,
> lasst den Hall es tragen weit.
> Schlagt die Saiten, lasst den Hall es tragen weit,
> gross der Herr zu allen Zeiten,
> heute gross vor aller Zeit.
>
> Aus Egypten vor dem Volke
> wie der Hirt, den Stab zur Huth,
> zogst du her, dein Stab die Wolke,
> dein Stab die Wolke,
> und dein Aug' des Feuers Gluth.
> Zieh' ein Hirt vor deinem Volke,
> stark dein Arm, dein Auge Gluth.
> Und das Meer hört deine Stimme
> thut sich auf dem Zug, wird Land.;
> und das Meer wird Land.

Scheu des Meeres Ungethüme,
Schau'n durch die krystall'ne Wand.
Wir vertrauten deiner Stimme,
traten froh das neue Land.

Doch der Horizont erdunkelt,
Ross und Reiter lösst sich los.
Hörner lärmen, Eisen funkelt,
es ist Pharao und sein Tross.
Herr, von der Gefahr umdunkelt,
hilflos wir, dort Mann und Ross.
Und die Feinde mordentglommen,
drängen nach, den sichern Pfad,
jetzt und jetzt.

Da horch! welch Säuseln! Wehen, Murmeln,
Dröhnen, Sturm!
'S ist der Herr in seinem Grimme,
einstürzt rings der Wasser Thurm,
Mann und Pferd, Ross und Reiter
eingewickelt, umsponnen,
eingewickelt im Netze der Gefahr,
zerbrochen die Speichen ihrer Wagen,
todt der Lenker,
todt das Gespann.

Tauchst du auf, Pharao?
hinab, hinunter, hinab, hinunter
in den Abgrund,
schwarz wie deine Brust.
Und das Meer hat nun vollzogen,
lautlos rollen seine Wogen,
nimmer gibt es, was es barg,
eine Wüste, Grab zugleich und Sarg.

Arias from Moses, *by Adolph Marx*

Miriam's aria:
Hebt euch von mir,
lasst mich bitterlich weinen.
Müht euch nicht, mich zu trösten
über di Verstörung meines Volks.

Pharaoh's mother's aria:
So höret nun, ihr Weiber,
lehret eure Töchter weinen!
Und eine lehre die andere klagen,
der Tod ist auf uns gefallen,
die Kinder zu würgen
auf der Gasse und die Jünglinge der Strasse.

Liebes Kind gehorche mir,
deiner Mutter ich will meinen Mund aufthuen
und alte Geschichte aussprechen,
die unsere Väter uns erzählet haben.
Liebes Kind, verachte den Elenden nicht,
und betrübe den Dürftigen nicht
in seiner Armuth.
Und wende dein Angesicht
auf dass er nicht über dich klage.
Denn der ihn gemacht hat,
hört sein Gebet
wenn er mit traurigen Herzen
über dich klaget.
Lass dich nicht klüger
dünken denn die Alten.
Folge deinem Muthwillen nicht,
ob du es gleich vermagst.
Denke nicht, wer will mir's wehren
Denn siehe, sie dienen einem Herrn,
mächtig über alle Götter.
Einer ist es, der Allerhöchste,
allmächtig, ein gewaltiger König
und sehr erschrecklich.
In dem Tagen, die nicht mehr sind,
habe ich es von den Vätern gehört.

Miriam's aria:
Was betrübst du dich meine Seele,
und bist so unruhig, so unruhig in mir?
Harre auf Gott, ich werde ihm noch danken,
dass Er mir hilft mit seinem Angesicht.
Deine Fluten rauschen daher!
dass hier eine Tiefe und da eine Tiefe brausen
Alle deine Wasserwogen und Wellen
gehen über mich.
Ich sage zu Gott, meinem Fels,
Kannst du meiner vergessen?
Der Herr hat des Tages verheissen
seine Güte, und des Nachts
singe ich ihm und bete zu Gott
meines Lebens.

DREAMING OF MIRIAM'S WELL

Alice Bach

Midrashic storytelling, revisioning the biblical narrative from one's own perspective, points toward a contrapuntal, nomadic style of reading. Such a reading eludes the borders of accepted reading conventions and makes no claims for historical truth. As a student of modern midrash, I am challenged by the power of narrative expansion—and as a student of ancient haggadic midrash I feel constrained by scholarly reliance upon the dating and provenance of each text in determining its authenticity—and value. Several years ago, for a volume of the *Feminist Companion*, Athalya Brenner asked me to write a response to several articles on Miriam.[1] As part of that work, I wrote a narrative midrash in dialogue to illustrate what I had interpreted as Miriam's pacifist cry at the sea,

> Sing to the Lord, for he has triumphed gloriously.
> Horse and Rider he has thrown into the sea.

In the text of Exodus 15 the elements of warfare—the horses, the riders, their armor and their shields, the chariots—point toward a male culture. If, as Carol Meyers argues in that same volume,[2] there were communities of female performers, might they not have been rejoicing in the destruction of the dominant male culture, exemplified by and encoded within the language of warfare?

> Sing to the Lord, for he has triumphed gloriously.
> Horse and Rider he has thrown into the sea.

A classical echo of a lyric that appeals to the elements of women's culture over militaristic ideals is attributed to Sappho:

---

1. Athalya Brenner (ed.), *A Feminist Companion to Exodus to Deuteronomy* (Sheffield, UK: Sheffield Academic Press, 1994).
2. Carol Meyers, 'Miriam the Musician', in Brenner (ed.), *Exodus to Deuteronomy*, pp. 207-30.

> Some say the cavalry corps
> Some infantry, some again
> Will maintain that the swift oars
> Of our fleet are the finest
> Sight on dark earth; but I say
> That whatever one loves, is.[3]

While I found support for my pacifist reading in this lyric of Sappho, I could find no classical Jewish commentary or midrash that read Miriam's song in the way that I had. Perhaps pacifism is a modern category. My search has persisted among the modern midrashim, for I believe that pacifism is an important element to feminist theory. However, if the classical midrashist holds the power to narrate, he also has the power to block other narratives from forming or emerging. Perhaps that explains the absence of expansions beyond those haggadic midrashim that award the famous well to Miriam, water to sustain Israel, because she had first watched out for her baby brother Moses when he was rescued from the treacherous water of the Nile.

As I watch contemporary films and read novels based on the biblical book of Exodus and listen to feminist Seder prayers about Miriam, I listen for Miriam's Song at the Sea, and I hear no echo of my construction of Miriam as a peacemaker, singing for the end of warfare at the edge of the sea. Of course I know I am walking disputed territory. Like many of my generation, I was trained to halt at the border of classical haggadic midrash, the province of the *darshanim*. But doesn't that give a reading pride of place to the ancients? If texts can yield meaning only when situated in context, one's reading positions are limited. For context itself is a contrived and preferential construction. But echoes persist, and I still find myself needing to justify reading any texts against any others.

The central question for this paper revolves around the Scylla of defining midrash as a formalist closed genre and the Charybdis of viewing midrash as a dynamic juggling of cultural memory that reinvents itself at each border crossing. What is the significance for the narrative critic if the midrash was collected by groups of *darshanim* during the so-called classic midrashic period ending in the ninth century CE, after an unknown period of oral circulation and transmission, or written ten years ago as a biblical expansion by Israeli writer Amos Oz, or American Cynthia Ozick? Modern haggadic midrash differs not only in its being created within the past two hundred years but,

3.   Mary Bernard, *Sappho: A New Translation* (Berkeley: University of California Press, 1958), frag. 41.

even more importantly, it is written by a named author. Thus, modern midrash is considered to be a creative work of a known author, as opposed to a collection, cloaked in the mystery and authority of 'the rabbis'. For a feminist reading, it seems imperative to use the tools of cultural criticism to dig beneath the masculine codes in which the ancient texts and their ancient expansions were written.

Certainly, I am not the first scholar to wonder about the authenticity of midrash composed after the classical period. The august Shalom Spiegel, while not concerned with feminist issues, has argued against the tradition which considers the creation of authentic midrash to have been cut off before the last millennium.

> With the sacred writings of the Jews there traveled to the nations of East and West who had adopted them…traditions and tales current among the Jews. Along with the Bible they spread far and wide, having their imprint many a celebrated center of art and literature, gaining at times a surprising hold upon the popular imagination.[4]

Two of Spiegel's insights are important to my own thinking: his understanding that narrative grows and remains fluid, and that it develops with a society's *current* traditions and tales. Thus, midrash reflects the time in which it is written more than some reified adherence to biblical or classical accuracy. The Exodus midrash created by Jeffrey Katzenberg and the kids at DreamWorks reflects their desire to keep current movie audiences not only entertained but also reassured that it's a small world after all. The *Prince of Egypt* was conceived, according to the DreamWorks founding trio, during the initial burst of excitement of inventing the company in 1994.[5] In a meeting at Spielberg's house, the talk turned to animation. Spielberg said he wanted to do a project with the grandeur of *The Ten Commandments*. 'What a great idea,' Geffen said. 'Let's do it.'

At first, Katzenberg didn't recognize the risks of treading on such literally sacred ground. Then it hit him. 'The Moses story is central to three of the world's major religions,' Katzenberg told an interviewer from *Time* magazine. 'It is so much more complicated, so much more challenging than simply making a movie.' His eye fixed firmly on audience demographics, Katzenberg illustrates perfectly Shalom Spiegel's

---

4.   Quoted in Judah Goldin, *Studies in Midrash and Related Literature* (Philadelphia: Jewish Publication Society of America, 1988), p. 395.

5.   *Time* magazine 152.24, 14 December 1998. For many further articles and reviews concerning the *Prince of Egypt*, see

http://www.time.com/time/magazine/1998/dom/981214/cover1.html
and follow links.

second point about the surprising hold midrashic creations have upon the popular imagination. Here is where Spiegel speaks directly to the DreamWorks boys, masters of marketing Moses to a multicultural audience. Katzenberg continues, 'Just putting together the script raised enough delicate questions to fill the Red Sea. How to portray the Egyptians as cruel slave masters without antagonizing the Arab world?' 'We were very careful with skin tones to show that the slave population was multicultural, multiethnic', says Tzivia Schwartz-Getzug, an expert in interfaith relations who was hired as liaison to the religious community: 'And in the Exodus scene, you actually see some Egyptians going with the Hebrews.' Spiegel expected midrash to reflect the community that has created it. Nevertheless, I consider it a blessing that he did not live to see the *Prince of Egypt*.[6]

However, there were plenty of religious experts involved in the project. A focus group of the faithful, rabbis, evangelical Christians and Muslim specialists convened in Hollywood to vet the film script, in the twentieth century's version of the meeting in Javneh. And these canon-makers of caution took their job very seriously. The result is not surprising: the film sometimes looks starched as a vicar's surplice, sounds stodgy as a UN fundraising pitch. What is lacking is any trace of irreverence or wit within the dialogue or narrative. The most imaginative sequence for me is the hieroglyphs that come to life. The most charitable comment I can make about the parting of the Red Sea is that it is an homage to Mr DeMille.

And what of my major concern: the wily Miriam? One would think that DreamWorks would capitalize upon the young girl who brokers a deal with the pharaoh's daughter to reunite her brother with his biological mother. But alas, Disneyesque casting has sent spunky Miriam to the bottom of the sea, more little mermaid than biblical prophet. Sandra Bullock makes no attempt to camouflage her well-known voice. Even when she is telling Moses of his Hebrew heritage, her sugar-coated accent sounds too much as though she's recently returned from the mall. She is too fizzy to be completely believable as a beleaguered slave laborer in danger of getting lashed across the back if she takes too much time churning out the bricks. A couple of times I

6.   *Prince of Egypt* (1997). Directed by Brenda Chapman, Steve Hickner, and Simon Wells. Written by Philip La Zebnik and Nicholas Meyer. Produced by DreamWorks Inc. Running time: 97 minutes. Cast: Val Kilmer: Moses/God; Ralph Fiennes: Rameses; Michelle Pfeiffer: Tzipporah; Sandra Bullock: Miriam; Jeff Goldblum: Aaron; Danny Glover: Jethro; Patrick Stewart: Pharaoh Seti; Helen Mirren: The Queen; Steve Martin: Hotep; Martin Short: Huy.

thought Bullock was about to ask Moses if he wanted to super-size his fries. Thus, Miriam the prophet is relegated to perky sister status, a narrative strategy meant to please a cartoon audience that expects only Moses to be super-sized. Perhaps Spiegel's prodigious imagination had not counted on the wonder that is DreamWorks. Who holds the power to narrate is in my view what is truly at issue. Surely the genre of midrash benefits from cultural readings which avoid the privileging of high art over popular culture. For midrash, like any narrative text, reflects the cultural milieu of its creators. Gap-filling activity also reflects the interests of the midrashist. There is no whole picture that waits to be filled in by midrash, since the perception and filling of a gap lead to other gaps.

While Sandra Bullock's real swell Miriam was still cluttering up my mind, I came across an ancient midrash called the *Book of Miriam*. Well trained, I looked for its provenance. Translated into English by Canadian philosopher Leonard Angel, the book had apparently never before appeared in English.[7] Indeed, it had not been widely available in published form either in the original Hebrew, or in the Teutsch Miriam (a Yiddish form which appeared in Bohemia in the late fourteenth century). So it was no surprise that I had never come across this text. According to Angel a decision had been taken over half a millennium ago, in 1472 CE, to restrict access to the work to the few women who then possessed the physical manuscripts, to those women's daughter, to those women's daughters and so on. I thought this odd since medieval women's access to literacy, much less to sacred texts, would have been doubtful. As a result of physical attacks on the few European manuscripts by the husbands of the women studying the book, only a single German copy is extant, and is to be found in the city of Bonn. Outside of Europe there was a copy in a small town near Marrakesh, and it was this Moroccan copy that was now in the hands of Miriam HaCohen, a student of the renowned Sarah al-Fasudi, the maturate of the Miriamic study circle in the early twentieth century. Finally the text manuscript was shown to Professor Angel, who was authorized by the aged Miriam HaCohen to make an English translation. I had a transitory doubt that a man would be allowed the responsibility to translate this book preserved by women, but Miriam HaCohen was old and frail, and time was running out. She had no daughter to entrust the manuscript to. Might this work be an antidote to the simplistic Miriam of the Boys' Life of Moses?

---

7.   Leonard Angel, *The Book of Miriam* (Mosaic Press, 1997).

From the few passages Angel had reprinted from the Hebrew, I saw that the Hebrew was difficult and, according to Angel, much of it had been written in an elegant Rashi script. Related in poetic form (translated by Angel), the narrative tells of several named Israelite women going to the Egyptian pharaoh Picol to plead for the Israelites' freedom. The first is Adah, who plays a familiar role:

> Adah was wearing flowing garments, white, gold, and blue
> Sea green border, a nose ring, earrings, anklets
> A silver comb in her hair, jewelry adorning her crown,
> Her left shoulder bare. Bells that tinkled as she moved
> Among scarves of finest gauze,
> Trailing fragrance of anointing balm, myrrh, and frank
> Moving softly like a cat.
> Picol was captured.[8]

Now that she has Picol's attention, Adah warns him that his sons and daughters will be killed because the ruler 'has extended his dominion at the cost of Heaven'. And then she reveals the prophecy from God: 'Come live with us, be free in God's land, you, your children, your children's children.' Picol remembers words from the Hebrew prophet:

> God gives this land to all of us
> You too will not be counted, if you're among us
> Beat your swords into ploughshares.

But Picol's heart was hardened. After consulting with the male elders, Miriam dances with timbrel and drum for Picol, first to gain his confidence, then to show him signs and wonders. On the first day,

> She seemed to him a fog
> Picol, amazed, shouted
> His fear was gone.

Next day, Miriam danced, her veils flowed.

> Picol listened. It seemed to him Miriam was lost within a cloud of gnats.
> The gnats were buzzing him.
> Picol shouted: the gnats were gone. Picol was still afraid.[9]

The pattern is set for the days of the dance. Next day Miriam danced, led Picol to his harem, and lo! The women fell, screamed, rocked in agonizing pain. Next day, Miriam danced upon the portico,

---

8.   Angel, *Book of Miriam*, p. 234.
9.   Angel, *Book of Miriam*, p. 235.

the heavens opened. Hail. Next day and next day and next day Miriam danced, and in her song she said:

> The fields will be bared by locusts
> The crops will be spared by none.
>
> Next day, Miriam sang and danced and closed her eyes and Picol closed his eyes.
> When she ceased to sing, he was lost in darkness, could not open them.
> Picol shouted but his mind was lost in darkness.
> Picol was still afraid.
>
> Next day Miriam danced and sang, Now look at me, whom—do—you—see
> She bowed and darkened her face until Picol saw his son. Bloodied, staggered, limping, dripping red.[10]

OK, you all get the drill. But don't dismiss the power of the text that quickly. The next part of the narrative contains the midrash I had been searching for.

> When Adah and Miriam returned, Picol escorting them
> Fringe garmented and rainbow sleeved,
> a guest of the Hebrews
> The Hebrew elders, Picol, and all his retinue saw the folly of war.
> They said, 'War is madness'.
> Picol emptied his harem, destroyed his palace immersed in a cold and bitter spring
> Became astonished, even he himself, a Hebrew
> Taking the name Lamadyah, saying because I learned of Yah
> And from Yah and from his people
> And his people, one tenth the Philistines
> Immersed that day, in the cold, bitter spring
> Taking Hebrew names, women, men, children, all of them.
> The Hebrew elders gave them gifts, cattle, flocks, and to each, a newborn heifer not to be fatted, not to be killed, but for milking,
> All the days in which it would be milked.[11]

This is the teaching of Miriam, who came from the desert, from Sinai: *God is the womb of the world.*

Katzenbach and the DreamWorks crowd seemed to teeter on the brink of transforming Miriam into a New Age persona, and used her to justify their one world theme. If only they had found the *Book of Miriam*. The scene in which Miriam becomes the plagues for the pharaoh would have made a dynamic musical mime number, with anima-

---

10. Angel, *Book of Miriam*, p. 236.
11. Angel, *Book of Miriam*, pp. 242-43.

tion crossing the boundaries of human possibility. Some of the Egyptians left Egypt with the Israelites in both these cultural productions. Lest you think that I have eclipsed the great scholars for a glitzy world of animation, I shall evoke the memory of Father Freud, who speculated that Moses was actually an Egyptian who passed single-deity worship derived from Akhenaton to the Jews.[12] More recently German scholar Jan Assmann, author of *Moses the Egyptian*, argues that Moses and Hebrew monotheism are a memory of Akhenaton, whose name was purged from all lists of rulers when the priests of Amon retook power.[13] Perhaps Katzenbach was merely tapping into a *Zeitgeist* that renders Israel not chosen by God, but derivative of a much older culture. A collective unconscious longing for the fleshpots of Egypt. And what of Leonard Angel, and his discovery of the *Book of Miriam*? I must admit that this is not a clockwise midrash. Rather it falls backward through time, going counterclockwise. The *Book of Miriam* is an invention of Angel, the Canadian philosopher, who cast his fictive Miriam in the genre of targum and midrashic commentary.

Angel's creation argues for accepting midrash as a hybrid strategy, heterogeneous and unmonolithic, one that intermingles midrashic versions regardless of their place in the chain of chronology. Midrash has historical roots certainly, but midrash is not an object to be described; neither is it a unified corpus of symbols and meanings that can be definitively interpreted. Midrash rides the back of culture, contested, temporal, emergent. Read together, the film and the novel reveal an interesting contrast: the film follows the subjectivity of the ancient male-centered midrashists. Indeed, even the feminist reading of Trible in creating her mosaic of Miriam does not separate the woman from the patriarchal culture of triumphal warfare. The *Book of Miriam* is a true midrash of the Other. As such, it debates the historical and political construction of identities and Self/Other relations. It allows the voice of the Other to come through the level of the doxa text. This Miriam has been de-doxified and, as such, she has sung a revolutionary Song of the Sea.

---

12. Sigmund Freud, *Moses and Monotheism* (repr.; New York: Random House, 1987 [1939]).

13. Jan Assmann, *Moses the Egyptian: The Memory of Egypt in Western Monotheism* (Cambridge, MA: Harvard University Press, 1997).

THE AUTHORITY OF MIRIAM: A FEMINIST REREADING OF NUMBERS 12 PROMPTED BY JEWISH INTERPRETATION*

Irmtraud Fischer

Miriam is the only woman who is called a prophetess in the Torah, the first five books of Moses. Even though today she is one of the best-known female figures of the First Testament, it is extremely difficult to apprehend who she was. She is present at the Exodus, where she provides a theological interpretation of the rescue at the Reed Sea (Exod. 15.20-21; Mic. 6.4). In Exod. 15.20 she is identified as Aaron's sister, and in other texts as the sister of Moses (Num. 26.59; 1 Chron. 5.29; cf. also Exod. 2). After a conflict with Moses, Miriam is struck with leprosy (cf. Num. 12; Deut. 24.9) but is taken back into the community. She dies in the wilderness of Kadesh and is buried there (Num. 20.1). This is roughly all we know of Miriam—paltry in comparison to her male siblings, Moses and Aaron! Among the Miriam narratives that introduce to us a great woman of Israel's early history, Numbers 12 is a thorny text for women. In it we learn of a conflict between Moses and Miriam—and Aaron. God settles it, but Miriam is the only one to be punished. It is for this reason that feminist theologians in particular read Numbers 12 as a classic text of marginalization, where women are written out of their leadership positions and their life achievements devalued in relation to those of men.

1. Was the Story Told Originally in That Way?
Tensions in Numbers 12: Solution, Part One

On account of alleged internal discontinuities, scholars have judged the text as it exists today not to be a literary unit. The following points are cited as the most noticeable tensions and dualities:

*   Translated by Barbara Rumscheidt and Martin Rumscheidt. This essay is dedicated to Mag. Evi Krobath on the occasion of her seventieth birthday. It was first published in: Maria Halmer et al. (eds.), Anspruch und Widerspruch: Festschrift für Evi Krobath (Klagenfurt: Mohorjeva Hermagoras, 2000), pp. 23-38, and is printed by permission.

- The dual causes for the conflict: at one time the conflict is said to have arisen because of the woman whom Moses had married (לקח), while in vv. 2, 6-8, it is about whether God spoke to Moses alone or also with Miriam and Aaron.
- In v. 1 the predicate is in the third person singular feminine, which refers to Miriam alone, but the subjects named are Miriam *and* Aaron.
- The cloud is the sign of God's presence, but it is *after* the cloud has already disappeared that Moses speaks with God and God with Moses.
- Miriam *and* Aaron question whether Moses alone received God's word; but Miriam is the only one who is punished.

Such grave inconsistencies call for explanation. There are two fundamentally different possibilities for resolving these tensions.

a. *A Source-Critical Solution, Dissolving the Tensions in Terms of Different Authorship*
In the tradition of historical-critical study, an explanation for the tension is sought by means of the literary development of the text itself. Accordingly, the phenomenon of dual causes for the conflict has primarily been explained in terms of different authorship: two sources, yielding two approximately equal stories about Miriam's leprosy. In my judgment, at least as far as the traditional demarcation and dating is concerned, presupposing the two Pentateuch sources, Yahwist and Elohist, is no longer tenable. Rejecting this approach also frees one from the need to extract two roughly equivalent narratives that in some sense have to result from two such presupposed sources. But in choosing not to seek a solution in source-related material in Numbers 12, one still needs to pursue a literary-critical accounting. A possible literary-critical endeavour to provide an explanation[1] would be to regard the causes of the conflict, given in v. 1 aβ-b, as a late expansion and, consequently, to classify the argumentation about the Cushite woman as a later addition to the narrative, which originally was a literary unity.

b. *A Solution, Explaining the Tensions from the Intention of the Narrative*
The solution I support and I substantiate later takes the narrative as an original unity. The tensions are not relevant for literary criticism

---

1.   A survey of the research on this pericope and a synopsis of the source-critical proposals in scholarly studies is presented in Ursula Rapp's dissertation, presented to the University of Graz in the year 2001. I recommend this study.

but for the narrative's intention, because the dualities involved here are by no means criteria signalling a literary development of the text itself. The Hebrew text reveals some textual problems that in current translations of the Bible are so reduced that they become unnoticeable. Accordingly, in what follows I address briefly some problems relevant to the interpretation.

1.1. *Who Is Acting in v. 1?*

The text begins with a third person singular feminine form of the verb 'to speak'; its subject is Miriam. But Miriam *and* Aaron are named as the speaking subjects. The best-known German Bibles, the Ecumenical Bible, the Zürich Bible and the Luther Bible, all make the verb form plural. This accommodation not only renders the problem invisible but also produces the side effect that it becomes even more incomprehensible—as well as more hostile to women—that Miriam is the only one who is punished. The punishment of Miriam is predicated on the depiction of Miriam in v. 1 as the driving force of the conflict: in order to specify that punishment falls alone on Miriam, the feminine singular has to be kept. Jacob Milgrom[2] calls attention to other actions done by men and women together under the leadership of women, all of which are spoken of in terms of the third person singular feminine form of the verb (cf. Judg. 5.1; Est. 9.29). Hence Num. 12.1, where female dominance is specified grammatically, is no peculiar case. The accommodation introduced in German translations of the Bible, namely to include Aaron, writes Miriam out of the position of dominance.

1.2. *How Is the Conflict Carried Out?*

In my judgment, the key to finding a solution to the narrative lies in the translation of v. 1. The term דבר במשה is translated as 'spoke *about* Moses' (Ecumenical Bible), '*against* Moses' (Zürich and Luther Bibles). This suggests that Miriam and Aaron speak '*about*' Moses in his absence. But this translation presents the difficulty that in what follows immediately (v. 2) in the same text, speaking '*to*' (דבר ב) is constructed with the very same ־ב; how can one translate this as 'has the Lord spoken only *about* Moses?' I can find no argument that would support translating one and the same linguistic phrase differently in two successive verses, other than the exegete's helplessness in face of the narrative content. Thus, I argue in favour of a uniform translation: 'And Miriam—and Aaron—spoke *to* Moses because of the Cushite

---

2. Jacob Milgrom, *Numbers* (JPS Torah Commentary; Philadelphia: Jewish Publication Society of America, 1989), p. 93.

woman.' Clearly, this is a situation of open rather than concealed conflict.

1.3. *What Conflict Is Spoken of Here?*

If דבר ב is translated as 'to speak to', another difficulty does arise. Verse 2 begins the direct speech that follows with ויאמרו, 'and they said'. This clearly includes Aaron in the action while in v. 1 it was Miriam alone who spoke, with Aaron simply being mentioned alongside. Furthermore, it must be noted that two different verbs are used for the two exchanges, verbs that themselves introduce different arguments of the conflict.

Verse 2 is a quotation that obviously presents the words in which Miriam and Aaron reveal the reason for their question to Moses. Direct speech clearly requires an introduction; therefore the two synonymous verbs are not to be queried on grounds of source criticism.

But now, v. 2 uses דבר, 'to speak', to denote God's speaking with human beings, in the sense of communicating a word of God, whereas conversation among human beings is expressed in terms of the root אמר, 'to say'. In v. 2 דבר, 'to speak', is understood as prophecy, as it is in the prophetic law of Deut. 18.9-22 which establishes the basic understanding of prophecy within the Torah. Prophecy is denoted both times with the root דבר, 'to speak'. Thus, in both contexts we are dealing with the reception of a word from Yhwh that designates the true prophet.

As the text continues, it becomes apparent that Numbers 12 clearly distinguishes between אמר, 'to say', and דבר, 'to speak', inasmuch as the latter is used to denote only *prophetic* speech (vv. 2, 6, and 8), whereas the former introduces an exchange of words or conversation. But for Miriam's speaking, and for her and Aaron's speaking with Moses, v. 1 uses דבר, 'to speak', as does v. 8 that refers back to v. 1. This choice of this word clearly qualifies her speaking as communicating a word from God. For that reason, I interpret the conflict-laden verbal process that Miriam initiates and Aaron participates in as a conflict for reasons of prophetic speech rather than a normal quarrel among people. When Miriam—and also Aaron—*speak to Moses* they do so, within the confines of Numbers 12, *in the form of prophetic speech!*

1.4. *What Is the Reason for the Conflict in verse 1?*

How are we to understand the reason for the quarrel that, according to v. 1, is obviously related to the Cushite woman? From the subsequent text we learn no more about this woman. According to Exodus

2, 4 and 18, Moses is married to Zipporah. She is the daughter of the priest of Midian whose name according to one tradition is Reuel but according to another Jethro. Is this Cushite woman the same as Zipporah, or is it a reference to another woman?

The reason for the conflict is often assumed to be that Miriam and Aaron are showing their opposition to a woman from a foreign tribe. If Cush is understood as one of the peoples of Africa—as is often the case in the First Testament—then in exegesis the conflict is often interpreted as being for reasons of racism: Miriam and Aaron are opposed to her because she is a woman of colour![3] But Cush may also be located in the region of the Gulf of Aqaba, which allows one to identify this woman with Zipporah, Moses' wife according to Exodus 2. Biblically, one can substantiate this by referring to Hab. 3.7, where Cush appears in parallelism with Midian. Habakkuk's prayer locates Yhwh's 'origin' in the region where the Midianites had settled.

Certainly, Jewish tradition does not interpret this Numbers passage in terms hostile to foreigners. It sees the point of conflict in terms of Moses neglecting his marital duties to his Cushite wife, precisely *because* of his prophetic activity (cf. *Exod. R.* 1.13). The Exodus midrash also identifies the Cushite woman with Zipporah. According to *Exodus Rabbah*, she complains to Miriam that Moses no longer sleeps with her. However, despite their prophetic office, Miriam and Aaron did not abstain from sexual relations with their partners. Moses teaches wonderfully but does not deliver wonderfully: this is how Jewish tradition expresses the issue of failing to fulfil the commandment given at creation (*Yeb.* 63b). The ancient tradition of Judaism that always interprets the final canonical text establishes here a connection between the woman and the prophetic task of Moses. However, the Jewish interpretation once again is the cause of questions about whether the direction taken by interpretations is the correct one.

In accordance with Jewish tradition, Marie-Theres Wacker[4] also identifies the Cushite woman with Zipporah, since Wacker follows the direction indicated in the final text, namely that the wife had to have something to do with the subsequent prophetic conflict. For Wacker Zipporah, called the Cushite woman in this chapter, represents Moses' legitimating figure; Zipporah is from priestly descent and in her family Moses received the revelation of the god Yhwh.

3. Marie-Theres Wacker, 'Mirjam', in Karin Walter (ed.), *Zwischen Ohnmacht und Befreiung: Biblische Frauengestalten* (Fraventorum; Freiburg: Herder, 1988), pp. 44-52. On p. 48 she refers to an interpretation of this text by Hugo Gressmann.

4. Wacker, 'Mirjam', p. 49.

Such a thesis does allow for the possibility of combining the two causes of the conflict. But the text itself provides no background material that would point explicitly to a tradition of Zipporah, in the sense of a *priestly* legitimation of prophecy.

If one studies the tradition of Zipporah in detail, it becomes apparent that she is the wife of Moses who, according to Exod. 4.19-26, goes with him to Egypt and, on the way there, administers apotropaic circumcision to their son in order to save her husband from Yhwh's attack. The next time we hear of Zipporah in the course of the biblical narrative is in Exod. 18.1-12. All three of the German translations to which I have referred have v. 2 say that Moses 'sent back' Zipporah. The Masoretic Text has שלוחיה, 'her sending away'. שלח אשה (in the pi.) is a common technical term for 'get a divorce' (cf. e.g. Deut 21.14; 22.19, 29). Thus, the rarely used שלוחיה can indeed be understood to mean 'divorce'—as Jewish tradition testifies—and not the temporary dismissal insinuated by these German translations of the Bible. And in connection with Num. 12.1 this would mean that the cause of the conflict was not Moses' marriage to a Cushite woman but his divorcing Zipporah.

1.5. *The Cause of the Conflict According to Verses 2-16*
In v. 2 Miriam and Aaron express their doubt that Yhwh spoke only with Moses. As already demonstrated above, the way the text is formulated does not mean that this is a conversation within an encounter with God; it is an authorization with a prophetic word. In this action, Miriam and Aaron act as equals. (The masculine plural formulation used here is typical of androcentric language systems for describing actions performed by men and women together.) Yet here, Miriam and Aaron do not question that Moses is a prophet. There is no doubt about this. What they question is that Yhwh spoke with Moses *only*, which would be equivalent to saying that Yhwh had *not* spoken with them. Moses' prophetic office is not in dispute. But Miriam and Aaron claim that they too have the ministry of prophecy besides Moses, whose ministry they fully acknowledge.

The Torah associates both Miriam and Aaron with prophecy, each on one occasion: Miriam in Exod. 15.20 and Aaron in Exod. 7.1. In the Pentateuch, their prophetic function is neither their original nor their primary function. But the same is to be said about Moses as well. It is only Deuteronomy that makes Moses what he is from the postexilic period until this day in Jewish, although not in Christian, tradition: the prophet par excellence (cf. Deut. 18.15; 34.10).

2. Who Is behind the Three 'Siblings' at the Time of the Text's Composition? The Sociohistorical Location of the Conflict

On the narrative level, the issue is a conflict among the three leading figures in the Exodus. Now, Numbers 12 is not an early text that transmits an old tradition; it is demonstrably of postexilic origin. In whose interest is it to tell such a story in the days of Persian rule? To answer that question, we have to separate this conflict from the story of the rivalry among the three 'Levi's offspring'—as they are quite obviously *not* depicted in this text—and enquire about the sociological groups behind it. And that obviously leads to a discussion about different forms of prophecy and their sociological background. Behind the conflict there are groups that claim to have the ministry of prophecy themselves and, in fact, oppose those who see themselves to be successors to Moses. This suggests that the priesthood is not at all prepared to let itself be severed from the Torah that is to be actualized in concrete existence, and to be restricted to the Torah for sacrifice. But according to v. 1, the driving force in the conflict is a group that relates itself back to Miriam. What group if not one dominated primarily by women would do that? In this context, Renate Jost and Rainer Kessler[5] have shown that the search for such groups leads one to women prophets in the days of Persian rule (cf. Ezra 13; Neh. 6.14). According to the narrative of Numbers 12, the two groups—of prophets and priests—apparently face the threat of losing their authority in favour of the omnipresent Moses-office, which regards prophecy to be the interpretation of the Torah.[6] If the conflict is to be located in the days of the Persian rule, then Aaron clearly represents the priesthood and Miriam one of those prophetic groups that continue the work on the prophetic books. (For an indication of women's presence in such work, consider the abundance of female metaphors in the second and third parts of the book of Isaiah.) The dominant group continuing that tradition of Moses would then be found in the group around Ezra

5.   On this see Renate Jost, 'Die Töchter deines Volkes prophezeien', in Dorothee Sölle (ed.), *Für Gerechtigkeit streiten: Festschrift Luise Schottroff* (Gütersloh: Gütersloher Verlagshaus, 1994), pp. 59-65, and her *Frauen, Männer und die Himmelskönigin* (Gütersloh: Gütersloher Verlagshaus, 1995), pp. 180-90; Rainer Kessler, 'Mirjam und die Prophetie der Perserzeit', in Ulrike Bail and Renate Jost (eds.), *Gott an den Rändern: Festschrift Willy Schottroff* (Gütersloh: Gütersloher Verlagshaus, 1996), pp. 64-72.
6.   I substantiate this thesis in my monograph *Tora für Israel: Tora für die Völker* (SBS, 164; Stuttgart: Katholisches Bibelwerk, 1995), pp. 117-24.

who, like Moses, traces his lineage back to priestly forefathers; and the one around Nehemiah who, according to the narratives, works together with Ezra and the Levites (Neh. 8.9-12) and, in full accord with the Deuteronomic tradition of Moses, binds the people to the Torah. Interestingly enough, Ezra the priest is not depicted there in terms of cultic function but in the tradition of Moses! If it is precisely in scenes involving the whole people (cf. Neh. 5.1-2; 8.2 onwards) that women are referred to explicitly, this may serve as another indication that women markedly influenced the discussion at that time about the Torah and its interpretation.

The group whose arguments were finally communicated in the books of Ezra and Nehemiah happen to be the same group that in postexilic Judah exercised its muscle, opposing any marriage with foreign women and even supporting the divorce of existing mixed marriages. (Ezra 10; Neh. 13). Now, in these texts favouring the dissolution of mixed marriages by divorce, we do not find the same choice of words as in the Zipporah text of Exod. 18.2, but this is not required. For Exod. 18.1-7 is clearly an older tradition, and as such attests to the more common choice of words for divorce. That Exod. 18.2 was understood in this way is shown by later Jewish tradition for Numbers 12.

3. *Prophecy as Interpretation of the Torah: Solution, Part Two*

Based on such a postulation of groups that in the days of Persia stood behind Miriam, Aaron and Moses, we need to look again at the connection between the causes of the conflicts with the wife of Moses on the one hand, and the prophetic office on the other.

3.1. *Not Two But One Cause of the Conflict!*
If Numbers 12 connects the question of authentic prophecy with that of the Cushite woman, and if it is correct to posit that *groups* stand behind the three leading *personalities*, the quasi-different motives for the disputes with Moses can be explained on the basis of one sole cause: Num. 12.1 understands Exod. 18.2 to be about Moses' divorce from Zipporah. He sent her and her children back to her father's house. Based on Exod. 18.2, Moses is co-opted as an example in the issue of mixed-marriage divorces by the group that opposes exogamous marriages. The very group that calls for the dissolution of those marriages portrays itself in this matter as the sole authority in the interpretation of Torah (cf. Neh. 13.1, and its recourse to Deuteronomic community law). If the passage is understood this way,

Miriam's as well as Aaron's question suddenly fits in quite naturally. According to v. 1, the group behind Miriam calls to account what Moses stands for, namely that the Cushite woman had been sent away because she was a foreigner. The Moses group can appeal to a corresponding action of Moses in the Torah. The group tracing itself back to Aaron is in sympathy with Miriam and sides with her. In v. 2 the Moses group is questioned concerning its exclusive claim to represent prophecy, a claim that is clearly based on its assertion that its interpretation of the Torah is correct, that is, in succession with the prophecy of Moses.

Thus, the verse is to be understood precisely the other way around. It is not Miriam and Aaron who are against the Cushite woman whom Moses took to be his wife; it is not they who are opposed to mixed marriages or hostile to foreigners. It is the converse, as we may also learn well from Jewish tradition: Miriam and Aaron side with the Cushite woman and accuse Moses of having separated from his wife!

Given this interpretation, the argument that the group is laying claim to authentic prophecy has to be brought into conformity with that of the group of prophets opposed to Ezra–Nehemiah. That there was, at the same time, massive resistance against the dissolution of mixed marriages and against the prohibition to enter into such marriages is shown beyond doubt by the book of Ruth. 'Miriam' represents precisely the group that, in Ruth, calls for the acceptance of the foreign, Moabite woman. If not an all-female group, it is probably a group with an overwhelming presence of women. We learn from Neh. 13.28 that even the high-priestly family of 'Aaron' is affected by the separation of mixed marriages! But those groups do not simply let themselves be silenced. They agitate against a harsh course in matters of mixed marriages and, in their argumentation, they appeal to God's word: Yhwh has also spoken to us! In so doing the group that is the opposition in the mixed marriage issue claims for itself the prophetically legitimated interpretation of the Torah. That it is a matter of interpreting the Torah and not merely of contemporary marriage policy is apparent from the fact that the three leading figures of the Torah have to bear this conflict.

Now, if we proceed with the exegesis of the text wearing these glasses, we will discover who emerges from this conflict victoriously.

3.2. *The Unique Status of Moses*

Yhwh personally places Moses above all human beings on the face of the earth in meekness (v. 3) and declares him to be sacrosanct. The fact that Moses speaks with God and God with Moses *after* the cloud has lifted manifests Moses' unique status. Yhwh's conversation with him proves the fact, declared by Yhwh, that Moses alone is the one with whom he speaks directly, from 'mouth to mouth' (v. 8); but, with Miriam and Aaron, he speaks as with 'ordinary' prophets. With them Yhwh speaks by the mediation of the institutionally ordered possibility of an encounter with God. That possibility is furnished by the Tent of Meeting during the journey in the wilderness; it is symbolized here by the cloud that depicts the sign of God's presence. The disappearance of the cloud before the conversation with Moses confirms the difference that God had declared between Moses and the other two leading persons (vv. 6-8). Thus, it is not to be queried on grounds of source criticism, since the disappearance of the cloud serves a narrative function.

The text concedes that the groups around 'Miriam' and 'Aaron' have prophetic capacity like 'Moses', because God himself speaks to all three (אמר, v. 4); and by the manner in which God speaks to them in v. 6. Miriam's question (v. 1) and the reference back to it (v. 8) are expressed in the root דבר, 'to speak', reserved in Numbers 12 for prophetic speech; accordingly, her question to Moses is understood as prophecy in the sense of an actualization of the Torah. And thus the interpretation of the law, as manifested by the two groups 'Miriam' and 'Aaron', is acknowledged to be legitimate. Like Moses, Miriam and Aaron participate in an epiphany of God in the tent of revelation (vv. 4b, 5), but not in the direct talk of God with Moses (vv. 7-8).

The different kinds of prophecy are clearly hierarchically ordered in vv. 6-8; there are ordinary prophets who are also gifted with the word of God and to whom Yhwh gives himself to know in vision and dream. And then there is Moses above them all, for God speaks to him from mouth to mouth and he can see Yhwh without dying. Divine legitimation therefore raises him above questioning. According to the Deuteronomic law on prophecy, the office of Moses has priority over all other prophets who nonetheless are accepted as prophets.

3.3 How Is the Conflict Settled?

The conflict is settled hierarchically by Yhwh himself, but substantively in favour of Miriam. She is and remains a prophetess but not one of equal status with Moses. If one understands v. 3 and its reference to Moses' meekness—scholarship occasionally calls the verse 'baroque'—the way it is delineated above, it could lead towards the solution of the mixed marriages question. As the meekest of all humans on the face of the earth, Moses has more than richly fulfilled the divine instruction by letting go of his foreign wife. Therefore he cannot be held up as the norm in the matter of mixed marriages or, at best, as an example that cannot be attained anyway. And so Miriam would have been right in relation to mixed marriages: what Moses did cannot be forced upon the entire people. His privileged position before God and his outstanding humanity are not everyone's norms. Therefore his demeanour cannot be universalized. God declared Miriam to be right in the matter, but God also chastises her because she did not acknowledge Moses' extraordinary position as such. For seven days she has to bear shame. For seven days she has to put up with the father's patriarchal, humiliating spitting in her face and is excluded from the community. But the social sanctions of the patriarchally organized community comes to an end after the seven days and Miriam can be assured of the sympathy of the waiting people for whom, against the rigorists, she won the more humane solution.

3.4 Who Is Punished?

Miriam is punished but not Aaron. Indeed, a leprous high priest may be an absurdity; but the impossibility of telling a story about a leprous high priest in no way diminishes the palpable misogyny of the text. The fact that, with shaking knees, Aaron sides with Miriam permits one to assume that the 'Aaron' group and the 'Miriam' group had entered into an alliance. But Aaron escapes any kind of punishment and, hence, emerges from the conflict less weakened than Miriam. Aaron acknowledges Moses to be his lord (v. 11), and reverts to the status into which he had been placed as a prophet according to Exod. 7.1: Aaron is not the prophet of God but of Moses!

Miriam's punishment is hard indeed but, from the outset, it is limited to seven days and has no further consequences. The people are behind Miriam. They side with her and refuse to move on without her. The journey in the wilderness is resumed only after seven days, when her leprosy has disappeared and she has been brought back into the camp.

The authority of the prophetic group of women around 'Miriam' would seem at first glance to have come to an end. However, when one looks more carefully it is indeed apparent that Miriam and Aaron are distinguished, but also that Numbers 12 shows Aaron in a fairly unfavourable light and lower in the hierarchy than Moses. Yet God does not punish Aaron. Nor, however, is Miriam met by the customary fate of death that visits all who rise up against Yhwh,[7] a fate to

---

7.   Cf. Ursula Rapp, 'Das Buch Numeri', in Luise Schottroff and Marie-Theres

which the story of the wilderness journey makes repeated reference (cf. Num. 16–17). Even sons of the high priests are taken away; Miriam, however, remains alive! Thus, Numbers 12 cannot be one of the narratives about such rebellions; within the scope of the narratives of the journey in the wilderness, this chapter must have a different intention.

4. If You Desire to Understand a Text, Do Not Tear It from Its Context! Numbers 12 and Its Context

Is it really the intention of this narrative to document God's displeasure with women in positions of leadership? If one reads the narrative in its context, the answer is, unambiguously, NO!

4.1. Numbers 11: How Narrowly Is One to Define the Scope of Prophecy?

Using the image of God as a mother who is pregnant, gives birth and has to care for her child, Numbers 11 outlines the duties and responsibilities of the person in leadership who, according to Num. 11.10-15, is Moses alone. The text knows nothing of cooperative leadership. Moses alone bears responsibility and he is overburdened. He wants to quit and refuses before God to go on alone, bearing all responsibility by himself.

The solution to the dilemma of an overburdened Moses is the division of leadership responsibilities among the 70 elders (Num. 11.16-23). It is not a new solution in the Torah: Zipporah's father had already proposed it in Exodus 18! The group that speaks in that text through Zipporah's father pleads for a division of responsibilities given to those in leadership positions. Indeed, it does not deny Moses' predominance but it clearly argues that others, too, ought to shoulder responsibility. In Exodus 18 a judicial decision is at issue. In Numbers 11 the issue is prophetic leadership that is to be seen in relation to having received the spirit (Num. 11.24-30). As soon as the spirit, רוח, passes from Moses on to the chosen they become prophets. Even those chosen ones, who do not yet heed the call to gather at the Tent of Meeting, begin to prophesy (v. 26).

Young Joshua considers this to be inappropriate (v. 28), but Moses has no problem with it. He accepts the fact that the spirit also acts outside the company of those who are called. Indeed, Moses desires that the prophetic spirit be democratized and he admonishes the

Wacker (eds.), *Kompendium Feministische Bibelauslegung* (Gütersloh: Gütersloher Verlagshaus, 2nd edn, 1999), pp. 54-66 (57).

young Joshua (v. 29). Zealousness, for Moses, is set over against the democratization of the spirit and Moses rejects the former. He wishes that Yhwh will let the spirit come upon all, not only upon the 70 oldest men. He pleads for this like Joel (ch. 3), who speaks of the gift of the spirit on the old and the young, the free and the unfree, men and women. Numbers 11 recounts no divine response to Moses' wish for the democratization of the spirit. It is the spirit's coming upon people not present at the gathering that, alone, shows that Yhwh is on their side.

How do the stories told in Numbers 11 interpret the Miriam narrative following immediately in Numbers 12, and vice versa? In ch. 12 Moses does not defend himself, which corresponds to his reaction to Joshua. When one has read ch. 11, it is apparent that Moses is not the only one who has the spirit. In this respect, Miriam's question is significantly softened by the context, because 'prophecy for all' was what Moses had wished for. It is said immediately before that he did not understand that as an attack on his own authority. It is with the person of Joshua that the party of rigorists is identified in ch. 11. But Joshua is not just any man; he is the successor of Moses who, according to Num. 14.30, shall see the land.

If we read this story as reflecting conflicts of interests, it becomes rather clear that Moses' successors are considerably more confined in their view of the world than he is. For Moses' wish for the democratization of the prophetic spirit legitimates in the canonical sequence of texts even Miriam's question. Numbers 12 could therefore be a text originating from the rigorist party.

4.2. *Numbers 12 in the Context of Exodus–Deuteronomy: Why Is Only Miriam Punished?*

When one goes on reading the canonical text beyond Numbers 12 one comes upon the spy narratives that dominate the subsequent wilderness journey narratives, and are focused on the three leading figures. After the spies who had been sent out had in their report poured contempt on the land, Yhwh vowed that everyone over 20 years of age would have to die in the wilderness (Num. 14.26-35). It is clear from God's view that Miriam, Aaron and Moses would have to die before they have reached the boundaries of the Promised Land. The reason for the decision that Moses and Aaron must die is given in the story of the waters of Meribah (Num. 20.2-13; see esp. v. 12 and the reference in v. 24), where their guilt is defined. That story follows immediately upon the short notice of Miriam's death and burial (20.1), together with a similar notice concerning Aaron (20.22-29). Moses dies in the same year (cf. the dating in Num. 33.38-39 and Deut. 1.3), according to Num. 14.34, in the fortieth year of the wandering in the wilderness, immediately before the entry into the Promised Land (Deut. 34).

If one reads Numbers 12 in the context of these events of the journey in the wilderness period, it becomes obvious that a narrative needs to be found also for Miriam's death, naming her guilt, since she is no longer present at Meribah. In my opinion, that narrative is provided in Numbers 12. Precisely for these contextual reasons, Miriam is depicted as a ringleader. She exclusively is punished, so that her rebellion against Yhwh is quite manifest and her death can be said to be the result of her trespass against God. Thus, in its function, Miriam's leprosy story (Num. 12) corresponds to the Meribah story of Moses and Aaron (Num. 20.2-13).

In the context of these Pentateuchal narratives, one can now speak only in a rather limited way about punishment being meted out exclusively to Miriam. The explicit hostility to women is present when one tears Numbers 12 out of its context, but it is in no way the message of the narrative. The tension around the action and subsequent punishment in relation to Miriam and Aaron forms the framework of the story and, for that reason, cannot be dismantled in classic source-critical fashion, for there would be no story left.

5. *What Does Numbers 12 Say to Women Today?*

In concluding, I would like to venture a daring actualization for the situation of women today. From its context, Numbers 12 ought not to be read as a pure text of terror for self-aware women. It is true, the fact that only the woman is punished and not the man who participates in the conflict cannot be discussed away; but it is clear that a guilt narrative also exists for Moses and Aaron.

Despite all the injustice that leaps out at us at first reading, the story of Numbers 12 could be read even as a text of political realism, of empowerment for us women in patriarchally constituted religious communities. When we rise up in a discussion to make an intervention and assert that God speaks also to *us*, we may well be right, but still be punished, treated with contempt for a while and excluded from the community. I do not want to trivialize the injustice of such events. Obviously, it is the case that patriarchal, hierarchical religious communities reach for the weapon of humiliating their members, even when it is acknowledged that such members were right in what they were presenting. After all, the divinely legitimated authority of hierarchy is under no circumstances to be questioned in principle!

As women, we must sometimes ask ourselves what is of greater value to us: our own reputation or the issue we have come to judge right before God. Just like secular communities, religious communities are marked by power relations. I do not argue that existing power relations be upheld when, as a Catholic woman at the end of the second millennium, I maintain that sometimes the way that is practicable in the perspective of political realism is better, particularly when we do not lose sight of the overall picture. Numbers 12 offers us at least this one consolation: the people will refuse to move on, the seven days will pass and the issue settled as we had proposed. But, during this Exodus from oppressive and inadequate structures, we ought not to let the nostalgic longing for the fleshpots of Egypt overtake us with the maxim: Better unfree but without worry about survival.

Part III

THIRD REVISIT: DAUGHTERS

THE DAUGHTERS OF ZELOPHEHAD AND WOMEN'S INHERITANCE: THE BIBLICAL INJUNCTION AND ITS OUTCOME

Tal Ilan

In the Torah the example of the right of a daughter to inherit is unique. The initial biblical law, handed down to Moses at Sinai, ignored the issue altogether (see, e.g., Deut. 21.15-17, particularly v. 17).[1] Inheritance was a matter for men, since it entailed the transition of property from one person to another. The basic assumption of the law is that women, rather than owning property, are in themselves a form of property.[2] The episode that challenges this situation is that of the daughters of Zelophehad in Num. 27.1-10. Modern scholars usually assign this text to the priestly source, namely probably the latest editor of the Torah, dating to the late sixth century BCE or even later.[3] This means that much of biblical law was by then in existence, and if the episode presents itself as an addition to an existing legal corpus, it may very well be correct.

The episode proceeds as follows. The daughters of Zelophehad had been orphaned in the desert without male siblings and, realizing that the patrimony of their clan was at risk, they presented themselves before Moses, demanding that their special case be incorporated into

---

1. All commentaries on Numbers seem to agree on this. See George B. Gray, *A Critical and Exegetical Commentary on Numbers* (ICC; Edinburgh: T. & T. Clark, 1903), pp. 397-98; Martin Noth, *Numbers* (OTL; London: SCM Press, 1968), p. 211; J. Sturdy, *Numbers* (Cambridge Bible Commentary; Cambridge: Cambridge University Press, 1976), pp. 193-94; Philip J. Budd, *Numbers* (WBC, 5; Waco, TX: Word Books, 1984), pp. 299-300; Jacob Milgrom, 'Excursus 63: The Inheritance Rights of Daughters', in *Numbers* (JPS Torah Commentary; Philadelphia: Jewish Publication Society of America, 1990), pp. 482-84; Eryl W. Davis, *Numbers* (NCBC; Grand Rapids: Eerdmans, 1995), pp. 268-70. And see particularly N.H. Snaith, 'The Daughters of Zelophehad', *VT* 16 (1966), pp. 124-27.

2. This issue has been debated at great length in the literature, often with apologetic overtones. Since I have already dealt with it elsewhere I will not repeat the arguments here, and see my *Jewish Women in Greco-Roman Palestine* (Tübingen: J.C.B. Mohr, 1995), p. 88 and particularly n. 97.

3. See initially Gray, *Numbers*, p. 397.

the law and that they be allowed to take over their father's inheritance. After due deliberation and reference to God, Moses concluded that the women were making a valid point. Thus, the biblical law was transformed so that henceforth daughters who had no brothers became the rightful heirs of their fathers. The last chapter of Numbers (36.1-12) presents a further amendment on this law. The men of the tribe of Manasseh present themselves to Moses and complain that, by allowing the daughters to inherit, females marrying into other tribes will pass the tribe's patrimony to others. The complaint of the Manassites is duly noted, and the law of the daughters' inheritance is further amended, so that an heiress is forbidden to marry outside the tribe. The position of this chapter, at the end of the book of Numbers, makes it appear as an afterthought. Gray, therefore, suggested that it is an even later addition, appended to the Priestly source by one of the Torah's final redactors.[4]

In 1988 Katherine Doob Sakenfeld published an important feminist-critical article on the episode of the daughters of Zelophehad in Numbers 27 and 36.[5] She used this story as a point of departure for a theoretical discussion of feminist modes of interpretation and outlined three feminist-critical approaches, all of her own creation—(1) literary; (2) literary-cultural; and (3) historical—with which to analyze it. She displayed how these approaches could produce conflicting interpretations and contradictory messages for feminists of a community of faith seeking some guidance or solace in the biblical text. The purely literary approach can produce an interpretation that uses the episode of the daughters of Zelophehad to celebrate women's independence and personhood, and the interest the biblical text shows in their well-being. The literary-cultural approach seeks to limit this over-joyous stance by suggesting a patriarchal background and a set of concerns that, probably, produced the story. These concerns have to do with what patriarchal societies view as a tragedy—the death of a man with no male heirs. The historical approach seeks to place the story within a historical framework; and in this way, perhaps, to glean insights into the historical position of women at the time the text was produced. Sakenfeld's observations are of major importance.[6] I shall refer

4. Gray, *Numbers*, p. 477.

5. K.D. Sakenfeld, 'In the Wilderness Awaiting the Land: The Daughters of Zelophad and Feminist Interpretation', *Princeton Seminary Bulletin* 9 (1988), pp. 179-96.

6. In a footnote I find it necessary to remark that for people like myself, who belong to no community of faith, the biblical text remains a historical and literary text with no voice of authority. Yet its historical and literary importance is not

occasionally to her contradictory exegetical observations in support of my analysis which, in fact, adopts her third approach. Ultimately, though, I seek to venture beyond the biblical text, and to encompass its historical consequences and aftermath in the development of Jewish law and in its canonization.

The special features of the daughters of Zelophehad episode are manifestly clear. The brotherless daughters' right to inherit was not handed down at Sinai, and yet it became law. It is one of very few examples in the Pentateuch of a precedent dictating the decisions of the Jewish lawmakers.[7] These examples had very important consequences for the development of Jewish law. They suggested, already within the Torah itself, that the divine corpus of law was not complete, and supplied only the groundwork on which the complete structure should be built. Incidents like that of the daughters of Zelophehad form the basis of the ideology of the 'Oral Torah', namely the Jews' right, also handed down at Sinai, to interpret and expand on the existing legal code.[8] In the episode of the daughters of Zelophehad Moses had to fill in the gaps that the Torah left. He was, of course, fortunate that in his case the problems could be directly presented to God himself (Num. 27.5).[9] Like Moses, Jewish lawmakers over the centuries would now have to issue innumerable ad hoc decisions based on the guidelines dictated by the Torah. Unlike Moses, however, not having a direct line of communication with God, the Jewish lawmakers' decisions would have to be based on their own sense of justice, the prevailing circumstances and their ingenuity. It is for this reason that the rabbis, themselves lawmakers but designating themselves 'expounders' (דרשנים), claim that the daughters of Zelophehad were also 'expounders' (דרשניות, *b. B. Bat.* 119b).

Of no less significance is the feminist aspect of this episode. The first persons that challenge divine law and succeed in bending it in

diminished thereby, and Sakenfeld's observations still remain valid. However, for me, since the text does not need to be 'saved', the historical approach is the most useful.

7. Together with Lev. 24.10-22—the man who curses God; Num. 9.6-14—the enactment of the second Passover for those unclean for the first; and Num. 15.32-36—the Sabbath violator.

8. And see already J. Weingreen, 'The Case of the Daughters of Zelophchad', *VT* 16 (1966), pp. 518-22.

9. Note Sakenfeld's first (literary) approach, which suggests a distinction between the divinely sanctioned law on the daughters' right to inherit, and the humanly grafted law of their need to marry in the family ('In the Wilderness', p. 182).

their favor include women.[10] This may suggest to the reader several interpretive points of view—some of them lamenting women's position in Judaism, some lauding it. On the lamentable side, one may claim that the fact that one of the first Israelite laws that had to be emended by precedent had to do with women's position 'suggests that God's own decrees given through Moses may have overlooked an important point'.[11] Laws that were supposedly given to the Sons of Israel turned out to be just that—laws for sons, not for daughters. On the other hand, on the laudable side, one may point out the sensitivity Scripture shows to injustice toward women, hastening to correct it.[12] This example, one may surmise, should probably serve as a guideline for future Jewish lawmakers who, based on the example of Moses, will listen to women's complaints and correct wrongs inflicted upon them.

This essay is interested principally in the immediate ramifications this episode had for the position of women in Judaism. First we may note that this law is presented in the Bible as a benevolent innovation on the part of the biblical lawmaker (probably over and against contemporary Semitic law codes). However, as Zafrira Ben-Barak has shown, the daughters' right to inherit where there are no sons is the rule, rather than the exception, in the ancient Near East.[13] Why the biblical lawmaker did not incorporate this commonplace piece of legislation into his original program requires an explanation. One suggestion that immediately springs to mind is that while some Semitic peoples, probably those more urban, had considered the situation of a daughter with no male siblings—in Israelite law, which reflects primarily a tribal society, this was a new concept. Previous to this adaptation, the property of a man who had died leaving no sons would have reverted to his closest male relatives, most likely his brothers.

Surprisingly, this rather draconian system where women's rights are concerned, has now been partly corroborated from 'Jewish' documentary papyri of the Judean desert dating to the second century CE. These documents represent the legal transactions of Jews living in the Nabatean township of Maoza, at a point in time when the Nabatean

10. Sakenfeld's third mode of interpretation (historical; 'In the Wilderness', pp. 184-85).

11. Sakenfeld, 'In the Wilderness', p. 181.

12. Sakenfeld, 'In the Wilderness', pp. 184-85; and see also Davis, *Numbers*, p. 298: 'The present law marked a new departure in Israel in the rights and privileges of women.'

13. Zafrira Ben-Barak, 'Inheritance of Daughters in the Ancient Near East', *JSS* 25 (1980), pp. 22-33.

Kingdom became the Roman province of Arabia. Hannah Cotton assumes that the law reflected in these documents, although clearly written for Jews, was neither biblical nor rabbinic, since the documents were written by and for the local courts of law. Cotton devoted a series of articles to the issue of women's inheritance. Her work shows that a close reading of some of the documents from the Babatha archive reveals that, if a father made no provision for his daughter prior to his death, then, even when he had no other offspring, she was *not* likely to inherit his property. Rather, the male heirs of his (in this case dead) brother were the more likely candidates to his inheritance.[14] Cotton asserts that this legal practice is not only not Jewish, but neither is it Roman nor Greek. We may therefore assume that it best reflects the Nabatean legal system. One may speculate that these Semitic peoples, who had adopted sedentary ways relatively late, probably still adhered to a legal system similar to the one followed by the ancient tribal Israelites. This, of course, is extremely conjectural, but in some ways supports the assessment suggested here: that the incorporation of the daughters of Zelophehad incident as a legal precedent indeed points to an initial situation whereby daughters were not considered possible heirs, and a later (probably rather recent) development where they were considered as such in some cases.

The biblical daughters-of-Zelophehad amendment was a halfway reform of the law. As a general principle, to be applied legally in other cases, it served a useful purpose. It pointed the way to the future Jewish lawgivers as innovators. However, on the question of a woman's right to inherit according to Jewish law, its outcome was detrimental. This claim has to be explained. Scripture does not always spell out its approach to women's rights. The laws are, of course, formulated in male language, but since 'masculine/male' is also the generic form in Hebrew, a broad application of the law could include women. Thus a reference of Scripture to 'sons' could, according to some schools of interpretation, refer to sons *and* daughters. For such an interpretation to take hold, a favorable disposition on the part of the lawgiver toward the issue was required, to be sure. Theoretically, at any rate,

14. Hannah M. Cotton and Jonas C. Greenfield, 'Babatha's Property and the Law of Succession in the Babatha Archive', *ZPE* 104 (1994), pp. 211-21; Hannah M. Cotton, 'Deeds of Gift and the Law of Succession in the Archives from the Judaean Desert', *Eretz Israel* 25 (1996), pp. 410-16 (Hebrew), and somewhat more modified in *idem*, 'The Law of Succession in the Documents from the Judaean Desert Again', *SCI* 17 (1998), pp. 115-23.

such a disposition could be (and is indeed sometimes) found among Jewish lawmakers.[15]

However, although one group of rabbis could occasionally revoke a legal decision made by another, the situation is somewhat more complex when Scripture itself already spells out the gender discrimination. We may greatly compliment the biblical legislator who incorporated the daughters-of-Zelophehad episode in Numbers for improving women's position with relation to inheritance, compared to what it had been before. However, the discriminatory character of the definite new ruling is still apparent. It does not assume that daughters, as a rule, share in the father's estate. Furthermore, the ruling is clear-cut. If a legislator will, in the future, wish to incorporate women as full heirs, he will be going against the specific words of Scripture, which qualify their legal rights in the area of inheritance.[16] This is not to say that exegetical attempts to tackle the daughters-of-Zelophehad case as indicating the daughter's right to inherit, at all times and under any circumstances, were not made; but these attempts are usually displayed in Jewish sources as bordering on the heretical. These examples will now be discussed.

In a literary composition that presents the Sadducees arguing with the Pharisees over the issue of the daughter's right to inherit, we find the Pharisees strongly defending Scripture's position on the limited applicability of this law, while the Sadducees uphold the daughter's right to inherit:

> The Sadducees argue as follows: The daughter of the son and the daughter should be equivalent to one another. For they interpret the passage (about the daughters of Zelophehad) as follows: Now if the daughter of my son, who inherits by virtue of my son, can inherit indirectly from me, my daughter, who inherits by virtue of direct relationship to me—is it not a matter of logic that she should inherit from me? They said to them: No. If you claim that the daughter of the son inherits, who does so only through a stronger claim than the brothers of [her]

15. I have recently dealt with this issue with regard to the interpretive school of Rabbi Ishmael; see Tal Ilan, ' "Daughters of Israel Weep for Rabbi Ishmael" (*mNedarim* 9:11): The Schools of Rabbi Aqiva and Rabbi Ishmael on Women', *Nashim: Journal of Jewish Women's Studies and Gender Issues* (in press). And see further below.

16. See P. Neeman, 'The Daughter's Inheritance in Torah and Halakhah', *Beth Mikra* 47 (1971), pp. 476-89 (Hebrew), particularly p. 483: 'Even though the makers of the Halakhah could not contradict the words of the Torah...and could not completely alter the principle of the daughters inheritance... they looked for ways to sweeten the law and weaken its influence on the daughters of Israel' (my translation).

father, will you say so in the case of the daughter, who inherits solely
through her direct relationship to the deceased (i.e. her father) (*y. B. Bat.*
8.1, 16a).[17]

We know very little about the historical Sadducees, except that they
were a Jewish group who opposed the Pharisees and died out some-
time after the destruction of the Second Temple. Since the Pharisees
became the forefathers of present-day Judaism, we are usually taught
to view them in a more favorable light than their opponents. In the
rabbinic text at hand, however, the Sadducees are the ones who try to
improve women's position by circumventing the biblical injunction.
Because this is a rabbinic text, the Sadducees are portrayed as using a
logical principle—a fortiori (קל וחומר)—to derive this principle. Logical principles of this sort are typical rabbinic instruments for interpreting Scripture. There is no independent historical data that could induce
us to suppose that it was also acceptable to the Sadducees. In their
own legal language, the rabbis have the Sadducees argue that if a man
had a son who died and left an only daughter, this daughter, based on
the daughters-of-Zelophehad precedent, would inherit along with her
uncles. The man's own daughters, however, would not. The Sadducees argue by a fortiori that this cannot be the intention of the biblical law, since a man's own daughter has a greater claim on him than
his granddaughter does. If the Pharisees agree that this [grand]daugh-
ter has a right to inherit, they must then assume also that the daughter
has one too.

If the Sadducees never employed such exegetical techniques in their
interpretation of Scripture, they probably did hold the view that
daughters, like sons, were heirs of their fathers. The Pharisees, however, turn out to be strict legalists, following the word of the biblical
law closely: The biblical law says that daughters do not normally inherit and the biblical law, so they maintain, should be followed.[18]

On the same page of the Palestinian Talmud the rabbis have, next to
the Sadducees, also the sages of the Gentiles (חכמי גויים) expound the
daughters of Zelophehad biblical text, in order to infer the principle
that sons and daughters share equally in the inheritance:

> The sages of the gentiles say: The son and the daughter are equal, since
> they expound (דרש) 'If a man die and have no son, then you shall pass

17. The text is found also in the *t. Yad.* 2.20, where the Pharisees' opponents are
the Boethusians. And cf. also *b. B. Bat.* 115b.
18. Neeman, 'Daughter's Inheritance', pp. 488-89, claims that this position was
adopted as a result of sectarian (party-political) line and not out of any true concern for the plight of the daughters of Israel.

his inheritance to his daughter' (Num. 27.8). This means that if he has sons, they are equal. They answered them: It is further written: 'and if he have no daughter' (Num. 27.8, 9)…here too he has no son (*y. B. Bat.* 8.1, 16a).

The exegetical technique that the rabbis assign to the Gentiles is another principle which they themselves occasionally employ. They have the Gentiles read the biblical verse stressing the daughter's inheritance as devoid of context. By itself, it could imply that daughters inherit by default; but when there are no sons, they inherit the sons' share as well. The rabbis' answer is the usual one given in such cases, that is, to return the verse to its biblical setting and thus deprive it of a privileged unattached status. Obviously, placing the sages of the Gentiles in the position of Torah exegetes arguing with the rabbis is not an indication that the former had, all of a sudden, begun to learn the Hebrew Bible in order to deduce legal decisions from it. Rather, it is an indication that the rabbis knew that, in other legal systems of their immediate surroundings, sons and daughters shared equally in their father's estate.

These two examples come from the Palestinian Talmud. The Babylonian Talmud also assigns the view that sons and daughters inherit equally to a heretical group. It assigns this view to Christians.

> Imma Shalom, the wife of Rabbi Eliezer, was Rabban Gamaliel's sister. There was once a philosopher in their neighborhood, who gained a name for himself for refusing to accept bribes. They came to mock him. She brought him a golden lamp and presented herself before him. She said: I inherited property in the House of the Nasi. (The philosopher) said to them: divide it. (Rabban Gamaliel) said to him: it is written to us: Where there is a son the daughter shall not inherit. (The philosopher) said to him: Since the day you were exiled from your land the Law of Moses has been withdrawn and another book has been introduced in which it is written: A son and a daughter shall inherit equally. Next day (Rabban Gamaliel) brought him a Lybian ass. (The philosopher) said to them: I have cast my eyes to the end of the book and it is written there: 'I have not come to add to the law of Moses' [cf. Mt. 5.17]. And it is written there: Where there is a son a daughter shall not inherit'. (Imma Shalom) said to him: Your wisdom shines like a lamp. Rabban Gamaliel said to him: An ass came and kicked the lamp (*b. Šab.* 116a-b).

The philosopher in this story is evidently Christian, as his reference to a new law (=New Testament) and his almost exact quotation of a passage from the New Testament indicate. The role of Rabban Gamaliel and his sister in this story is twofold: discrediting the integrity of the judge, and discrediting Christianity. The first goal is achieved by the siblings pretending to be rivals. Their action is coordinated so as to prove that the judge accepts bribes. The second goal is attempted (though not completely attained) by demonstrating the disparity between Jewish and Christian law on the daughter's inheritance.[19] Since this issue is nowhere discussed in the Gospels, we may surmise that early Christians adopted the Hellenistic and Roman law on this issue, and that this fact was known to the Jews.

The fact that Gentiles, Christians and even Sadducees held the position that daughters should be allowed to inherit with the sons put the rabbis in an ever-diminishing minority. Yet, even within rabbinic circles we find an exegetical attempt to derive from the daughters-of-Zelophehad episode an equal right to inherit for daughters. This idea is voiced in a midrash found in the early halakhic compilation of the *Sifre* on Numbers:

> Whence do we learn that a daughter inherits? Since it is written: 'And every daughter that inherits (יורשת) territory in the tribes of Israel' [Num. 36.8]. Does this refer only to the daughter? [How do we know if] it refers also to the son? It is an a fortiori case. If daughters, who are inferior (הורע כוחן) to sons, inherit, how much more so sons, who are superior (כוחם.ייפה) to daughters (*Sifre Num.*, Pinehas 134).

This text displays a bold departure from the plain meaning of Scripture, somewhat similar to the approach the rabbis assign to the sages of the Gentiles. It ignores the entire narrative thrust of Numbers 27, instead latching on to the linguistic phenomenon that describes the daughters as heirs. Since the word 'inherits' in the feminine (יורשת) is applied in this chapter specifically to women (and not to men), using the feminine declination, should we perhaps suspect that daughters alone inherit from their fathers? This is indeed an inverted position taken by the exegete. It is immediately put to right by applying to the verse the logical principle of a fortiori, which employs the near axiom that this cannot be the intention of the text since it is well known that sons are privileged with relation to daughters. Thus since the text explicitly makes daughters inherit, this implies that sons do too.

Although this text is not placed in a polemical context, it is so isolated that it is seldom quoted and never taken as normative. It is found in a compilation assigned to the school of Rabbi Ishmael. In light of this, it is not surprising that in the *sugya* (pericope) in the Palestinian Talmud which assigns the heretical view that, in inheri-

---

19. Further on this issue see Tal Ilan, *Mine and Yours are Hers: Retrieving Women's History from Rabbinic Literature* (Leiden: E.J. Brill, 1997), pp. 110-18, and particularly pp. 115-18.

tance, a daughter is equal to the son to Sadducees and Gentiles, Rabbi Ishmael is lumped together with these two:

> Rabbi Ishmael says: Scripture has distinguished this estate from all other estates in the Torah, since in all other cases it is written: 'and you shall give' and here is written 'you shall pass' (Numbers 27.8). With 'pass' the law is that a daughter inherits (*y. B. Bat.* 8.1, 16a).

In this literary composition Rabbi Ishmael is again using a linguistic anomaly associated with the daughters-of-Zelophehad story (albeit a different one) to promote the same view, namely that daughters should inherit equally with sons. This text indicates that the rabbis who compiled the Palestinian Talmud were aware that this idea was also reviewed (sometimes favorably) among the sages of Israel and not just among heretics. However, Rabbi Ishmael never became part of the consensus. His great opponent, Rabbi Aqiva, became the founding father of the Mishnah, the legal text that eventually attained canonical status. Furthermore, the competing school of Rabbi Aqiva (albeit based on a verse from the book of Deuteronomy) produced a contradicting ruling, stating specifically that daughters are not included in the law of inheritance (*Sifre Deut.* 215).

Those texts clearly indicate that the mainstream rabbinic school of thought was not prepared to challenge the law laid down by Scripture, according to which daughters inherit only where there are no sons. To be sure, daughters' inheritance rights were psychologically close to most rabbis' hearts, many of them having daughters themselves and worrying about their future and welfare. It is, therefore, not surprising that the legal situation was never completely left at that. The rabbis of future generations invented all kinds of legal instruments with which to circumvent their own draconian endorsement of the biblical injunction.[20] The most common one was the deed of gift. This instrument—a deed written by the father, in which he presents his daughter in his lifetime with part of his property—was useful because it apparently circumvented not just the Jewish legal system, but also all other legal systems under which Jews lived and which also limited the daughters' inheritance rights.[21]

Since the biblical law of inheritance is clearly spelt out, and since the deed of gift as a Jewish legal tool is an innovation, in their legal

---

20. For a thorough review of the material on this subject see particularly Judith Hauptman, *Rereading the Rabbis: A Woman's Voice* (Boulder, CO: Westview Press, 1998), pp. 177-95.

21. Still relevant for this issue is Reuven Yaron, *Gifts in Contemplation of Death in Jewish and Roman Law* (Oxford: Clarendon Press, 1960).

discussions the rabbis had to make sure that their formulation of the latter did not appear to be a violation of the former. Thus, the discussion of the deed of gift in rabbinic literature is constructed in such a way that no one would suspect its real character. After all, deeds of gift could be written on behalf of friends, distant relatives and other possible beneficiaries. In effect deeds of gift, particularly those formulated so as to be executed after the death of their author, were the forerunners of the Jewish will. Yet all Jewish deeds of gift from the Judean desert and all those found in the much earlier Jewish archive of Elephantine, dating from the Persian period, were written on behalf of women—wives and daughters.[22] Clearly, the ramifications of the daughters-of-Zelophehad episode were at work here.

Deeds of gift and other forms of maintenance for daughters and women are often discussed by the rabbis.[23] Thus, the rabbis invented a fixed sum of money that a father was obliged to deposit in his daughter's marriage contract (*ketubbah*) on her marriage (*m. Ket.* 6.5). They further decreed that, although a daughter does not inherit the father's estate, if she is not married she should be maintained from it (*m. Ket.* 13.3). Although these rulings do much to insure the daughter's welfare, they invariably make her a dependant of her father (when a minor), her husband (who receives for safekeeping the assets of a woman's marriage contract, *m. Ket.* 6.1; 8.5), or her brothers (who, as the father's heirs, should supervise her maintenance). Any property a woman may come to own in her own right depends entirely on the goodwill of her father who can, if he wishes, write her a deed of gift and make her economically independent. If no such goodwill exists, however, the woman remains dependent on others throughout her life and is placed in a disadvantaged position if forced to independence through widowhood or divorce. Ironically, much of this reduced status is to be attributed to the initial goodwill toward women displayed by the biblical author, who composed the episode of the daughters of Zelophehad for the sole purpose of elevating women's legal status within Jewish law.

---

22. See my discussion of this issue in *Mine and Yours are Hers*, pp. 143-47.

23. On these see, e.g., Z. Falk, 'The Daughter and Widow's Inheritance in Bible and Talmud', *Tarbiz* 23 (1952), pp. 9-15; Neeman, 'Daughter's Inheritance'; Hauptman, *Rereading the Rabbis*, pp. 177-95; and as a corrective see further T. Ilan, *Integrating Women into Second Temple History* (Tübingen: J.C.B. Mohr, 1999), pp. 204-205.

SERAH AND THE EXODUS: A MIDRASHIC MIRACLE

Leila Leah Bronner

As the reward for the righteous women who lived in that generation
[Exodus] were the Israelites delivered from Egypt

(*b. Soṭ.* 11b).

The period of the Exodus was a time of crisis in Israelite history and
also a time of impressive women. In the Scriptures, many women
play crucial roles in saving the Israelites from extinction under the
cruel edicts of Pharaoh, and the midrash (the rabbinic retellings and
lore on the Hebrew Scriptures) embellishes the deeds of the women of
the time of the bondage in Egypt and the departure. If we read only
the Scriptures, we would not count Serah bat ('daughter of') Asher
among these women, but the midrash invents a number of stories that
credit Serah with a role in facilitating the Exodus. Indeed, by her
assistance to Moses the Exodus is made possible.

Serah appears three times in the Scriptures, each time as a name on
a genealogical list:

(1)   Asher's sons: Imnah, Ishvah, Ishvi and Beriah, and their sis-
      ter *Serah* (Gen. 46.17).
(2)   The name of Asher's daughter was *Serah*. These are the clans
      of Asher's descendants (Num. 26.46).
(3)   These are the sons of Asher, Imnah, Ishvah, Ishvi and Beriah,
      and their sister *Serah* (1 Chron. 7.30).

To the modern reader genealogical lists of names appear unimportant
and tedious, but genealogical lists are of great importance in Jewish
tradition. They affirm that the history of Israel was no human acci-
dent, but was instead the result of divine purpose and plan in history.
They provide an unbroken link with the remote past, hence a firm
basis on which to build the future. In the Bible lineage is usually
traced through the male, and females are mentioned only in rare instances. The fact that Serah is mentioned no less than three times by
name in genealogical lists is remarkable in itself. Her triple appear-

ance may be what made her seem to the sages extraordinary enough for them to want to embroider marvelous, even myth-like stories about her. The company Serah keeps may also have something to do with it: not only does Serah live during a time of exemplary women, but her closest male relations are among the giants of Israelite history: Jacob (her grandfather), Joseph (her uncle) and Asher (her father).

The Bible is a laconic, elliptical and at times ambiguous text, and the filling in of the biblical account is a basic procedure in the midrashic mode of interpretation. Midrashic narratives often involve magnificent flights of imagination and spectacular feats of conjuring stories from the slightest of clues. In the midrash there are several imaginative stories describing Serah's life.

The shortest of the midrashic references to Serah is a gloss on Gen. 46.17, found in the highly discursive seventh- or eighth-century CE Aramaic translation of the Pentateuch known as *Targum Pseudo-Jonathan*:

> And Serah their sister, who spoke and was therefore worthy of entering Gan Eden [Paradise], because she brought good tidings to Jacob, saying: 'Joseph lives'.[1]

The *Sefer Ha-Yashar*, which is from thirteenth-century CE Europe, has a lengthier story:

> And...[the sons of Jacob] went along until they came nigh unto their houses, and they found Serah, the daughter of Asher, going forth to meet them, and the damsel was very good and subtle, and knew how to play upon the harp... And they took her and gave unto her a harp, saying, go now before our father [Jacob] and sit before him, and strike upon the harp, and speak these words... She took the harp, and...she came and sat near Jacob. And she played well and said, and uttered in the sweetness of her words, 'Joseph my uncle is living, and he ruleth throughout the land of Egypt, and is not dead'. And she continued to repeat and utter these words, and Jacob heard her words and they were very agreeable to him. And Jacob blessed Serah...and he said unto her, 'My daughter, may death never prevail over thee, for thou has revived my spirit'.[2]

---

1. *Targum Pseudo-Jonathan* on Gen. 46.17; my translation. The Hebrew text can be found in *Mikra'ot Gedolot Genesis* (5 vols.; Jerusalem: B.B. Berman, 1985).

2. M.M. Noah (ed.), *The Book of Yashar* (repr.; New York: Hermon Press, 1972 [1840]), pp. 166-67. See also *Targum Pseudo-Jonathan* on Gen. 46.17; A. Ben Jehiel, *Sefer Hadar Zekainim* (B'nai Brak: Institute for Dissemination of the Commentaries of the Ba'alei Tosafot, n.d.) (Hebrew), p. 116. A.Z. Chefez (ed.), *Midrash Avot* (Warsaw: n.pub., 1904) (Hebrew) p. 45.41.

For reasons that are unclear, *Sefer Ha-Yashar* finds it necessary to have Serah, Jacob's granddaughter, rather than Jacob's sons, tell him the news that Joseph lives and to have him respond to the news by blessing her. We see here the beginning of the construction of Serah's spiritual powers, her power to guide people in distress.

The midrashic literature also invests Serah with the secret knowledge of how to identify the redeemer of Israel from captivity in Egypt. This knowledge had been transmitted through the males of the family, but in the eleventh- or twelfth-century CE commentary known as *Exodus Rabbah* Serah is suddenly given this knowledge.

> The sign of [God's] visitation which He communicated to them, for they had this as a tradition from Jacob, Jacob having handed down the secret to Joseph, and Joseph to his brothers, while Asher, the son of Jacob, had handed down the secret to his daughter Serah, who was still alive. This is what he told her: 'Any redeemer that will come and say to my children: "I will surely visit you" shall be regarded as a true deliverer'. When, therefore, Moses came and said these words, the people believed him at once.[3]

The midrash narrates that the people accepted Moses as their redeemer once he said the words that Serah received from her father. Thus, Moses' recognition as the redeemer is dependent on Serah and, even more crucially, on the people's willingness to trust her assertion that his words identify him as the redeemer.

In midrashic lore Serah's most significant act is locating the elusive bones of Joseph.[4] The Bible records that Joseph asked his brothers to promise him that, on departing from Egypt, they would take his bones back to the land of Canaan:

> So Joseph made the sons of Israel swear, saying, 'When God has taken notice of you, you shall carry up my bones from here'. Joseph died at the age of one hundred and ten years; and he was embalmed and placed in a coffin in Egypt (Gen. 50.24-26).

3. *Exod. R.* 5.13-14. All quotations of the *Midrash Rabbah* are cited by biblical book name, followed by *R.*, and are from *Midrash Rabbah* (trans. H. Freedman and M. Simon; 7 vols.; New York: Soncino, 3rd edn, 1983).

4. For more on the subject see J.L. Kugel, *In Potiphar's House* (San Francisco: HarperSanFrancisco, 1990), ch. 5. Kugel, who is primarily concerned with studying the image of Joseph in ancient haggadic sources, devotes attention to Serah's part in so far as it clarifies the Joseph problem. Until recently only a few brief references to her were to be found in biblical and Judaic encyclopedias. See further J. Heinemann, *Agadot ve-Toldotehen* (Jerusalem: Keter Publishing House, 1974) (Hebrew), pp. 49-63. He describes Serah as playing an important role in the midrashic episodes about Joseph's bones.

Further it is written: 'And Moses took the bones of Joseph with him; for Joseph had solemnly sworn the people of Israel, saying, "God will visit you; then you must carry my bones with you from here"' (Exod. 13.19). Why did the rabbis feel the need to create the story of Joseph's inaccessible bones? It grows out of the Jewish concern for burial of the dead. Genesis mentions only the embalming of Joseph and the place-ment of his body in a casket, but not the location of burial. This left a gap that rabbinic midrash moved in to fill.[5]

Various rabbinic sources inform us that Moses could not redeem the people and leave Egypt because he could not find the place of Joseph's grave. Three versions tell the tale of Moses' recovery of Joseph's bones. They are found in the *Mekilta deRabbi Ishmael*, an exegetical Midrash compiled and redacted in Palestine before the end of the fourth century CE; the *Tosefta*, a collection of additions to the Mishnah from after the end of the fourth century CE; and *Soṭa*, a trac-tate in the Talmud dating from the fourth to the sixth century CE. The version of the *Mekilta*, which may be the most elaborate, describes the Israelites' preparations to leave Egypt, depicting them taking booty from the Egyptians while Moses was occupied with finding the bones of Joseph. How did Moses eventually discover where Joseph was buried? In all three sources the sages tell us that Serah, daughter of Asher, survived from the time when Joseph died and was buried, and that she showed Moses where Joseph's casket was to be found. She told him that the Egyptians had fashioned a metal casket and dropped it into the middle of the Nile. The version in the *Mekilta* reads:

> *And Moses took the bones of Joseph with him.* This proclaims the wisdom and the piety of Moses. For all Israel were busy with the booty while Moses busied himself with the duty of looking after the bones of Joseph. Of him Scripture says: 'The wise in heart takes on duties' (Prov. 10:8). But how did Moses know where Joseph was buried? It is told that Serah, the daughter of Asher, survived from that generation and she showed Moses the grave of Joseph. She said to him: 'The Egyptians put him into a metal coffin which they sunk in the Nile'. So Moses went and stood by the Nile. He took a table[t] of gold[6] on which he engraved the Tetragrammaton, and throwing it into the Nile, he cried out and said: 'Joseph son of Jacob! The oath to redeem his children, which God swore to our father Abraham has reached it fulfillment. If you come up, well

5.   The *Testament of Simeon*, a pseudepigraphic source, says that Joseph's cas-ket was hidden by the Egyptians because they had been told that should Joseph's body leave Egypt, they would be visited by darkness and plague. H.C. Kee (trans. and introduction), 'The Testaments of the Twelve Patriarchs', in *OTP*, I, pp. 787-88.

6.   A variant reading says 'bundle' rather than 'tablet'.

and good. But if not, we shall be guiltless of your oath'. Immediately Joseph's coffin came to the surface.[7]

The *Tosefta* provides another version of these events:

> How did Moses know where Joseph had been buried? They tell: Serah daughter of Asher was [a survivor] of the generation [of Joseph], and she went and said to Moses, 'In the River Nile Joseph is buried. And the Egyptians made for him metal spits and affixed them with pitch (to keep him down)'. Moses went and stood at the Nile River and said, 'Joseph, the time has come for the Holy One, blessed be He, to redeem Israel. Lo, the Presence is held up for you, and the Israelites are held up for you, and the clouds of glory are held up for you. If you show yourself, well and good, and if not, we are free of the oath which you have imposed upon our father'. Then the coffin of Joseph floated to the surface and Moses took it and went his way.[8]

The talmudic version reads:

> It is related that Serah, daughter of Asher, was a survivor of that generation. Moses went to her and asked, 'Dost thou know where Joseph is buried?' She answered him, 'The Egyptians made a metal coffin for him which they fixed in the river Nile so that its waters should be blessed'. Moses went and stood on the bank of the Nile and exclaimed, 'Joseph, Joseph! the time has arrived which the Holy One, blessed be He swore, "I will deliver you". and the oath which thou didst impose upon the Israelite has reached [the time of fulfillment]'… Immediately Joseph's coffin floated [on the surface of the water].[9]

Only in the talmudic version is Moses said to go to Serah for help with his problem. In both of the earlier sources she is mentioned without any introduction at all. She simply appears suddenly and instructs Moses where to look. In all versions he follows her directions with no hesitation, and immediately locates Joseph's river-bottom tomb. Although Moses still faces the problem of raising the casket, Serah plays no role in this part of the recovery operation, perhaps because the raising of the casket has magical and miraculous elements

7.   J.Z. Lauterbach (ed.), *Mekhilta de-Rabbi Ishmael* (3 vols.; Schiff Library of Jewish Classics; Philadelphia: Jewish Publication Society of America, 1933–35), I, pp. 176-77.

8.   *t. Sot.* 4.7; quoted from J. Neusner and R.S. Sarason (ed.), *The Tosefta: Translated from the Hebrew*. III. *Nashim* (trans. J. Neusner; New York: Ktav, 1979), pp. 162-63. The Hebrew may be found in M.S. Zuckermandel (ed.), *Tosephta: Based on the Erfurt and Vienna Codices* (Jerusalem: Wahrmann Books, 1970), pp. 299-300.

9.   *Sot.* 13a. Quoted from I. Epstein (ed.), *Babylonian Talmud* (London: Soncino, 1952). All subsequent references to books of the Babylonian Talmud will be indicated by *b.* followed by the book name.

which are usually associated with prophets rather than prophetesses, or perhaps because midrashic tradition places succeeding prophets like Elijah and Elisha in the line of Moses and they perform similar miracles, such as causing an iron ax head to float upon the water (2 Kgs 6.5).

Another narrative account of Serah's involvement in the Joseph incident is external to rabbinic sources, appearing in the *Tibat Markeh*, a collection of Samaritan writings dating from the fourth century CE. This account describes the Israelites in Egypt, sacrificing at Raamses and moving on to Sukkot. When they want to leave Sukkot, however, a pillar of fire blocks their way. Frightened, Moses and the elders wonder what wrong they might have done. The elders go out to speak to all the tribes in an attempt to ascertain that no sin has been committed. When they come to the tribe of Asher, Asher's daughter Serah comes to meet them. Gifted with special insight, she is able to inform them that no evil has been committed, the problem is simply that Joseph's bones had been forgotten:

> Serah the daughter of Asher went hurrying out to them. 'There is nothing evil in your midst. Behold, I will reveal to you what this secret is'. At once they surrounded her and brought her to the great prophet Moses and she stood before him…[saying] 'Hear from me this thing that you seek: Praise to those who remembered my beloved [Joseph], though you have forgotten him. For had not the pillar of cloud and pillar of fire stood still, you would have departed and he would have been left in Egypt. I remember the day that he died and he caused the whole people to swear that they would bring his bones up from here with them'. The great prophet Moses said to her, 'Worthy are you Serah, wisest of women. From this day on will your greatness be told'… Serah went with all the tribe of Ephraim around her, and Moses and Aaron went after them, until she came to the place where he was hidden.[10]

The final association of Serah with the events of the Exodus is a story told in an important later rabbinic source. Serah is described as looking down from heaven and listening to the discussions of important religious matters by the rabbis in the house of study. Then:

> from the teacher's seat R. Johanan sought to explain just how the waters of the Red Sea became a wall for Israel. Even as R. Johanan was explaining that the wall of the water looked like a lattice, Serah, daughter of Asher, looked down and said: 'I was there. The waters rising up like a wall for Israel were shining because the radiance [of such personages as

10. Z. Ben-Hayyim (ed.), *Tibat Markeh: A Collection of Samaritan Midrashim* (Jerusalem: Academy of Science, 1988) (Hebrew), p. 98; my translation.

Moses and Aaron who had drunk deep of Torah's waters] made the waters shine'.[11]

In all of rabbinic literature, Serah is the only woman who interrupts a discussion in a house of study and corrects a sage.[12] Beruriah, the female scholar of the Talmud par excellence, is often depicted as discussing and differing on legal matters with male scholars, but she always seems to be outside the house of study.

Serah does, however, show up once more in the rabbinic literature. A midrashic gloss on the biblical verse, 'Wisdom is better' (Eccl. 9.18), says that this refers to the wisdom of Serah the daughter of Asher.[13] This midrash identifies Serah with a wise woman from the Bible who lived hundreds of years after the Exodus: the wise woman of Abel who saved that city from slaughter at the hand of Joab, King David's commander-in-chief (2 Sam. 20). How does the midrash justify Serah's reappearance at a much later time? This story stems from the midrashic interpretation of the genealogical information about Serah given in the Scriptures. That she entered Egypt is evident from the list in Genesis, and that she was still alive during the census taken prior to the Israelites' entry into the land of Canaan is evident from the list in Numbers. This led the rabbis to declare that she lived for hundreds of years.

The extraordinary longevity of Serah implied in the Scriptures was eventually turned by the rabbis into the statement that Serah 'did not taste death' and was 'one who entered paradise'. We recall that *Targum Pseudo-Jonathan* describes her as 'one who entered paradise',[14] and the *Sefer Ha-Yashar* elaborates how Serah came to merit entry into paradise. She is movingly described as singing good tidings to Jacob about the fate of his son Joseph. Jacob is so comforted that he blesses her, saying, 'My daughter, may death never prevail over thee, for thou hast revived my spirit'.[15] By suggesting that she never tasted

11. Quoted from *Pesikta de-Rav Kahana* (trans. W.G. Braude and I.J. Kapstein; Philadelphia: Jewish Publication Society of America, 1975), p. 212. The Hebrew may be found in S. Buber (ed.), *Pesikta de Rab-Kahana, Beshalah* (Vilna: Romm, 2nd edn, 1925; repr. Lyck: Selbstverlag des Vereins Mekize Nirdamim, 1968), p. 86, para. 117.

12. The institutional context for this incident, whether synagogue, house of study (*beth hamidrash*), or somewhere less formal, is not specified in the account; since a beth hamidrash was the usual setting for rabbinic teaching, it seems justifiable to set this event in one.

13. *Gen. R.* 94.9; *Eccl. R.* 9.18 (2).

14. *Targum Pseudo-Jonathan* on Gen. 46.17.

15. Noah (ed.), *The Book of Yashar*, pp. 54, 92-99; cf. Chefez (ed.), *Midrash Avot.*

death and that she entered *Gan Eden* (the Garden of Eden, a term often equated with paradise), giving her quasi-immortal status, the rabbis place her in an exalted category nearly on par with Elijah, the eternal prophet.[16] As a result, Seraḥ sometimes appears in midrashic and talmudic discussions of the seven biblical figures whose successive lifetimes span the whole history of humankind: Adam, Methuselah, Shem, Jacob, Seraḥ (or sometimes Amram, the father of Moses), Ahijah and Elijah.[17]

Seraḥ emerges in these texts as an usual woman. Women of her historical era were not often depicted either as leaders or as advisers to men, but Seraḥ in the midrash is an adviser to Moses, the great teacher, leader and prophet. She is also unique in her longevity, bestowed on her in midrashic tradition by an interpretation of the blessing bestowed on her by her grandfather Jacob. Even more curious, however, is that the midrash describes Seraḥ as a helper of her people and as a daughter or sister or granddaughter, but not as mother or wife. In both scriptural and rabbinic literature the marital status of women is usually given; and if the Scriptures do not describe a woman as married, the midrash often invents a marriage for her in some narrative expansion. The most prominent female leaders in the Bible, such as Deborah and Huldah, are identified in the Scriptures as being married and the names of their husbands are given. Miriam, for example, is described as unmarried in the Bible but is given a husband in the Talmud.[18] Yet Seraḥ's marital status is not even discussed by the rabbis. It may be that, in the evolution of the Seraḥ legend, the sages accepted the extraordinary figure they had fashioned on her own

For further information on those who entered paradise, see L. Ginzberg, *Legends of the Jews* (trans. H. Szold; 7 vols.; Philadelphia: Jewish Publication Society of America, 1959–68), V, p. 356, nn. 294-95.

16. Haggadic sources in the Talmud and midrash enumerate a large number of men and women who were worthy of entering paradise, but it is not always stated that they did not taste death, as is said of Seraḥ. The following are mentioned in various sources: Abraham's servant Eliezer, Seraḥ, Pharaoh's daughter Bithiah (1 Chron. 4.18), Othniel, Abigail and the matriarchs, Hiram, Elijah, Jonah, Baruch, Ezra (only in the Pseudepigrapha), Enoch, Jabez, Ebedmelech the Ethiopian, Jonadab ben Rechab.

17. *ARN* 38.103; cf. *b. B. Bat.* 121b, which also speak of seven saints, where Seraḥ is replaced by Amram, the father of Moses. See Ginzberg, *Legends of the Jews*, II, p. 116; V, p. 356 n. 294; V, p. 359 n. 321.

18. L.L. Bronner, 'Biblical Prophetesses through Rabbinic Lenses', *Judaism* 40 (1991), pp. 171-83, 175-77; *b. Soṭ.* 12a; *Exod. R.* 1.17. Josephus and the Talmud operated out of the same tradition. He too ascribes a husband to Miriam; see Flavius Josephus, *Ant.* 3.2.4.

merit, and then were so awed by the wisdom of their own creation that they did not feel the need to marry her off. Of course, Seraḥ's legend was probably influenced by the fact that her lineage is righteous. Two of the three genealogical references to Seraḥ in the Bible describe her as 'sister' while the third reference speaks of her as 'daughter' (Num. 26.46), but in rabbinic literature she is always referred to as Seraḥ daughter of Asher, thus emphasizing her good lineage.

In the ancient world family bloodlines and traditions were believed to determine to a great extent a person's character. For women, subject as they were to male authority, this was even more true, as a brief detour to look at the midrashic lore on Naamah illustrates. Just like Seraḥ, Naamah is only a name on a list in the Bible, although Naamah appears only once, in Gen. 4.22, as the daughter of Lamech and Zillah, sister of Tubal-Cain; yet, the rabbis create a number of stories about her. They explain that the name of Naamah means 'pleasantness' but that her charms were used to serve idolatrous ends: she is described by the rabbis as the mistress of dirges and songs, playing to the temple idols made by her brother.[19] Later rabbinic literature about her is even more negative: she is said to have led the angels astray with her beauty and to have been the mother of the devil Asmodeus and, like Lilith, she slays little children and appears to men at night. Just as Seraḥ's good lineage results in stories of exemplary actions, Naamah's wicked forebears prompt stories of wickedness. Consciously or not, the sages may have created a binary opposition between Seraḥ, the saint, and Naamah, the sinner. Because they had fashioned from the merest mention of a name in Scripture an exceptional woman, perhaps they felt compelled to create, from similarly scant materials, an odious one.[20]

But it also seems to me that the rabbis would have been hard put to

19.	*Gen. R.* 23.3.

20.	While rabbinic exegesis very rarely fashions women almost out of whole cloth into figures of significance, good or bad, the midrash abounds with creativity regarding obscure biblical men. A case in point is Ḥur (Exod. 17.10-12; 24.14). Although ostensibly groomed as Moses' successor, he mysteriously disappears from the biblical scene. Like Seraḥ, Ḥur becomes a significant figure in the haggadic traditions of the midrash and Talmud. His sudden disappearance is explained by claiming that he was murdered by the Israelites because he refused to join them in making the Golden Calf (*Exod. R.* 48.3; *b. Sanh.* 7a). He was the ancestor of both Bezalel, the architect of the sanctuary (Exod. 31.2) and of Solomon, builder of the temple (1 Kgs 6–7; Buber [ed.], *Midrash Tanḥuma* on Exod. 12.1; *b. Soṭ.* 11b). In *Exod. R.* 16–17 he is said to be the son of Miriam, Moses' sister.

create stories of a wicked woman given the bravery and redemptive actions attributed to the women of the Exodus in the Bible. If, for instance, we look only at the women directly associated with Moses, we find that, as Eileen Schuller notes, 'Moses is surrounded by six women and, in fact, owes his very life to them'.[21] The midwives, Shifrah and Puah (Exod. 1.15), not only defy Pharaoh's command to kill every male child born to the Israelites but also supply newborns with food and water. Jochebed, the mother of Moses, hides the newborn child from Pharaoh (Exod. 2.3). Miriam, Jochebed's daughter, watches from afar until the daughter of Pharaoh rescues Moses from the river (Exod. 2.4). The daughter of Pharaoh rescues Moses from the bulrushes and brings him up as her own son (Exod. 2.5). Zipporah, the wife of Moses, circumcises their son so that her husband's death is prevented (Exod. 4.24-27).

If the midrash says anything about these women, the tales are primarily pleasant and wondrous. For Shifrah and Puah, the midrashic sources decide to identify Shifrah with Jochebed and Puah with Miriam and then spend a great deal of time discussing the meaning of the names 'Shifrah' and 'Puah'. They explain that 'Shifrah' refers to the fact that the Hebrews were fruitful and multiplied in her days or, alternately, that it indicates that she straightened Moses' limbs. 'Puah' is interpreted to mean that she cried out to the child and brought it forth; the more spiritual version of this explanation has her crying out through the Holy Spirit, saying 'My mother will bear a son, who will be the savior of Israel'.[22] The midrash praises Zipporah for her virtue and for her beauty, and around her name, which means 'bird', the rabbis weave several stories illustrating her piety and power.[23] The rabbis twice describe Zipporah as saving her husband from death. She feeds him during the years that he was kept in a pit, and she circumcises her second son when Moses is swallowed by Satan in the guise of a serpent, so that the serpent spits him out.[24] Some sources credit Jochebed the mother of Moses, rather than Serah, the role of guiding Moses to Joseph's bones: 'She led him to the very spot where Joseph's bones lay. As soon as he came near them, he knew them to be what he was seeking, by the fragrance they exhaled and spread

21. E. Schuller, 'Women of the Exodus in Biblical Retellings of the Second Telling', in P.L. Day (ed.), *Gender and Difference in Ancient Israel* (Minneapolis: Fortress Press, 1989), p. 178.

22. *b. Soṭ.* 12b; *Exod. R.* 1.13 onwards.

23. *Exod. R.* 1.17; *Midr. Ps.* 7.18.

24. Ginzberg, *Legends of the Jews*, II, pp. 293-95.

around.'[25] Other stories give Jochebed renewed youth, a happy remarriage to her husband and a painless birthing of Moses, and she is said to have entered the Promised Land with Joshua at the age of 250.[26]

Of all these women, Miriam provokes the most elaborate midrashic stories.[27] Miriam is said to have prophesied the birth of Moses and to have foretold his brilliant career as redeemer of Israel.[28] At the end of her life Miriam is described as dying by the kiss of God, and her corpse is 'not exposed to ravage', both signs of her favor with God.[29] The rabbis' identification of Miriam with Puah has several interesting consequences. They relate the name Puah to הופיעה (*hofi'ah*), 'lift up', and explain that this shows that on a number of occasions Miriam lifted her face in defiance. As a result of this etymology, the rabbis involve themselves in an extensive and quite feminist tale about Miriam and her father:

> [She was called Puah] because she dared to reprove her father, Amram, who was at that time the head of the Sanhedrin, and when Pharaoh decreed that 'if it be a son, then ye shall kill him', Amram said it was useless for the Israelites to have children. Further he ceased to have sexual relations with his wife Jochebed and even divorced his wife, though she was already three months pregnant. Whereupon all the Israelites arose and divorced their wives. Then said his daughter to him: 'Your decree is more severe than that of Pharaoh; for Pharaoh decreed only concerning the male children, and you decree upon males and females alike. Besides, Pharaoh being wicked, there is some doubt whether his decree will be fulfilled or not, but you are righteous and your decree will be fulfilled'. So he took his wife back and was followed by all the Israelites, who also took their wives back.[30]

Their identification of Miriam with Puah also leads the rabbis into another difficulty. God promised to give the midwives who disobeyed

25. Ginzberg, *Legends of the Jews*, III, p. 5.

26. *Gen. R.* 949; *Soṭ.* 12b, 1b. *S 'Ol. R.* 9.

27. The one instance of rebuke against her comes in connection with her criticism of Moses, which is used it as an example of women's talking too much (*Gen. R.* 45.5). This is part of the list of women's negative attributes that appears in rabbinic literature in several versions (*Gen. R.* 18.2; 45.5 and 80.5), each of which lists different biblical women as examples. For a more extensive discussion of Miriam, see L.L. Bronner, *From Eve to Esther: Rabbinic Reconstructions of Biblical Women* (Louisville, KY: Westminster/John Knox Press, 1994).

28. *Exod. R.* 1.13; *b. Soṭ.* 12b. A different version is given by Pseudo-Philo; see D.J. Harrington (trans. and introduction), 'Pseudo-Philo', in *OTP*, II, p. 329.

29. *b. M. Qaṭ.* 28a.

30. *Exod. R.* 1.13 -14.

Pharaoh households of their own (Exod. 1.21), but the Bible does not mention that Miriam has a husband or children. Thus, although Miriam is introduced simply as the sister of Aaron and Moses,[31] rabbinic sources identify her with Azubah (1 Chron. 2.18) and so supply her with a husband, Caleb; a son, Ḥur; and an illustrious great-grandson, Bezalael, who as the architect of the Sanctuary is said to have inherited the wisdom of his great-grandmother.[32]

Like Miriam, the daughter of Pharaoh is praised by the rabbis for her defiance. In explicating Exod. 2.5 the midrash says that by rescuing Moses she challenged her father, even though he had absolute power over her. The rabbis go on to reward the daughter of Pharaoh for her saving of Moses by identifying Pharaoh's daughter with the Bithiah who is mentioned in 1 Chron. 4.18. They explain that the name Bithiah shows that she was a daughter of God: 'The holy One, blessed be He, said to Bithiah the daughter of Pharaoh: "Moses was not your son, yet you called him your son; you, too, though you are not My daughter, yet I will call My daughter".'[33]

Feminist analysis of the midrash has taught us that, under certain circumstances, rabbis would construct narratives that recognize virtue and heroism in women. In commenting on the Exodus experience the rabbis present us with a rich galaxy of exemplary woman, an entire generation of wise women. The midrashic stories about Seraḥ bat Asher are the most astonishing, both in content and presentation. No other biblical woman sparks an equivalent interest in the rabbis. From three appearances of her name in the Scriptures, they fashion a multi-faceted woman who is without parallel in Jewish literature. But Seraḥ is not the only woman of the Exodus made exceptional in the midrash. We have touched on the rabbinic legends about Miriam, Jochebed, Zipporah, the midwives and Pharaoh's daughter; but the Talmud also claims heroism for every woman in the days of Exodus, saying that 'as the reward for the righteous women who lived in that generation [Exodus] were the Israelites delivered from Egypt'.[34] For women of our time, the legends of these women are a gift to reclaim.

---

31. In Exod. 15.21 only Miriam is mentioned; in Num. 12.1-15 and Mic. 6.4 all of the siblings are mentioned.

32. *Exod. R.* 1.16-17.

33. *Lev. R.* 1.3.

34. *b. Soṭ.* 11b.

BIBLIOGRAPHY

Abrahams, R.D., *Deep Down in the Jungle: Negro Narrative Folklore from the Streets of Philadelphia* (Chicago: Aldine Publishing, 1970).

Adelman, Penina V., *Miriam's Well: Rituals for Jewish Women Around the Year* (Fresh Meadows, NY: Biblio, 1986).

Adler, Jonathan, 'Dating the Exodus: A New Perspective', *JBQ* 23 (1995), pp. 44-51.

Alcoff, L., 'The Problem of Speaking for Others', *Cultural Critique* 20 (Winter 1991–92), pp. 5-32.

Alter, Robert, *The Art of Biblical Narrative* (New York: Basic Books, 1981).

—*The World of Biblical Literature* (New York: Basic Books, 1992).

Anderson, Ana Flora, and Gilberto Da Silva Gorgulho, 'Miriam and Her Companions', in Marc H. Ellis and Otto Madura (eds.), *The Future of Liberation Theology: Essays in Honor of Gustavo Gutiérrez* (Maryknoll, NY: Orbis Books, 1989), pp. 205-21.

Anderson, J.C., and J.L. Staley (eds.), *Taking it Personally: Autobiographical Biblical Criticism* (Semeia, 72; Atlanta: Scholars Press, 1995).

Angel, Leonard, *The Book of Miriam* (Mosaic Press, 1997).

Antonelli, Judith S., *In the Image of God: A Feminist Commentary on the Torah* (Northvale, NJ: Jason Aronson, 1995).

Aratangi, Canny, 'Born Into A Living Hope: The Role of the Midwives Shiprah and Puah: Exodus 1:15-21', *Pacific Journal of Theology* 4 (1990), pp. 41-44.

Assmann, Jan, *Moses the Egyptian: The Memory of Egypt in Western Monotheism* (Cambridge, MA: Harvard University Press, 1997).

Bach, Alice, 'With a Song in Her Heart: Listening to Scholars Listening for Miriam', in *idem* (ed.), *Women in the Hebrew Bible: A Reader* (New York: Routledge, 1999), pp. 419-27.

Bach, Alice, and J. Cheryl Exum, *Miriam's Well: Stories About Women in the Bible* (New York: Delacorte Press, 1991).

Bailey, Randall, ' "Is That Any Name for a Nice Hebrew Boy?" Exodus 2:1-10: The De-Africanization of an Israelite Hero', in Randall Bailey and Jacquelyn Grant (eds.), *The Recovery of Black Presence: An Interdisciplinary Exploration* (Nashville: Abingdon Press, 1995), pp. 25-36.

Baille, Gill, *Violence Unveiled: Humanity at the Crossroads* (New York: Crossroad/Herder & Herder, 1997).

Balentine, Samuel, *The Hidden God: The Hiding of the Face of God in the Old Testament* (Oxford: Oxford University Press, 1983).

Bellis, Alice Ogden, *Helpmates, Harlots, and Heroes: Women's Stories in the Hebrew Bible* (Louisville, KY: Westminster/John Knox Press, 1994).

Ben-Barak, Zafrira, 'Inheritance of Daughters in the Ancient Near East', *JSS* 25 (1980), pp. 22-33.

Ben-Hayyim, Z. (ed.), *Tibat Markeh: A Collection of Samaritan Midrashim* (Jerusalem: Academy of Sciences, 1988).

Ben Jehiel, A., *Sefer Hadar Zekainim* (B'nai Brak: Institute for Dissemination of the Commentaries of the Ba'alei Tosafot, n.d.).

Bergant, Dianne, 'Exodus as a Paradigm in Feminist Theology', in Iersel and Weiler (eds.), *Exodus*, pp. 100-106.

Berlin, Adele, 'Lexical Cohesion and Biblical Interpretation', *Hebrew Studies* 30 (1989), pp. 29-40.

Bernard, Mary, *Sappho: A New Translation* (Berkeley: University of California Press, 1958).

Bird, Phyllis, *Missing Persons and Mistaken Identities: Women and Gender in Ancient Israel* (Minneapolis: Fortress Press, 1997).

Bloom, Harold, 'Poetic Crossing: Rhetoric and Psychology', *The Georgia Review* 30 (1976), pp. 495-526.

Boadt, Lawrence, 'Divine Wonders Never Cease: The Birth of Moses in God's Plan of Exodus', in Holmgren and Schaalman (eds.), *Preaching Biblical Texts*, pp. 46-61.

Boyarin, D., ' "This We Know to Be the Carnal Israel": Circumcision and the Erotic Life of God and Israel', *Critical Inquiry* 18 (1992), pp. 474-505.

Braude, W.G. (trans.), *Pesikta Rabbati: Discourses for Feasts, Fasts, and Special Sabbaths* (New Haven: Yale University Press, 1968).

Braude, W.G., and I.J. Kapstein (trans.), *Pesikta de-Rav Kahana* (Philadelphia: Jewish Publication Society of America, 1975).

Brazilian Pastoral Workers, 'Miriam', *Estudos Bíblicos* 29 (1991), pp. 37-39.

Brenner, Athalya, *The Israelite Woman: Social Role and Literary Type in Biblical Narrative* (Sheffield: JSOT Press, 1985).

—'An Afterword: The Decalogue—Am I an Addressee?', in *idem* (ed.), *Exodus to Deuteronomy*, pp. 255-58.

Brenner, A. (ed.), *A Feminist Companion to Exodus to Deuteronomy* (Sheffield: Sheffield Academic Press, 1994).

Bronner, L.L., 'The Changing Face of Woman from Bible to Talmud', *Shofar* 7 (1989), pp. 34-47.

—'Biblical Prophetesses through Rabbinic Lenses', *Judaism* 40 (1991), pp. 171-83.

—*From Eve to Esther: Rabbinic Reconstructions of Biblical Women* (Louisville, KY: Westminster/John Knox Press, 1994).

Brook, George J., 'A Long-Lost Song of Miriam', *BARev* 20 (May–Jun. 1994), pp. 62-65.

Brueggemann, Walter, 'Exodus', in Leander E. Keck (ed.), *The New Interpreter's Bible: Genesis to Leviticus* (Nashville: Abingdon Press, 1994), pp. 703-705.

Buber, S., (ed.), *Pesikta de Rab-Kahana, Beshalah* (Vilna: Romm, 2nd rev. edn, 1925; repr. Lyck: Selbstverlag des Vereins Mekize Nirdamim, 1968).

Budd, Philip J., *Numbers* (WBC, 5; Waco, TX: Word Books, 1984).

Burns, Rita J., 'The Book of Exodus', in Iersel and Weiler (eds.), *Exodus*, pp. 11-21.

—*Has The Lord Indeed Spoken Only Through Moses? A Study of the Biblical Portrait of Miriam* (SBLDS, 84: Atlanta: Scholars Press, 1987).

Cassuto, Umberto, *A Commentary on the Book of Exodus* (trans. Israel Abrahams; Jerusalem: Magnes Press, 1983 [1967]).

Chefez, A.Z., *Midrash Avot* (Warsaw: n.pub., 1904) (Hebrew).

Childs, Brevard S., *The Book of Exodus: A Critical, Theological Commentary* (OTL; Philadelphia: Westminster Press, 1974).

Coats, George, *Moses: Heroic Man, Man of God* (JSOTSup 57; Sheffield: JSOT Press, 1988).

Copher, C.B., 'The Black Presence in the Old Testament', in Felder (ed.), *Stony the Road We Trod*, pp. 146-64.

Cotton, Hannah M., 'Deeds of Gift and the Law of Succession in the Archives from the Judaean Desert', *Eretz Israel* 25 (1996), pp. 410-16 (Hebrew).

—The Law of Succession in the Documents from the Judaean Desert Again', *SCI* 17 (1998), pp. 115-23.

Cotton, Hannah M., and Jonas C. Greenfield, 'Babatha's Property and the Law of Succession in the Babatha Archive', *ZPE* 104 (1994), pp. 211-21.

Cross, Edmond, *Theory and Practice of Sociocriticism* (Minneapolis: University of Minnesota Press, 1988).

Daly, Mary, 'The Women's Movement: An Exodus Community', *Religious Education* 67 (Sep.–Oct. 1972), pp. 327-35.

Davis, Eryl W., *Numbers* (NCBC; Grand Rapids: Eerdmans, 1995).

Derby, Josiah, 'Why Did God Want to Kill Moses?', *JBQ* 18 (1989), pp. 222-29.

De Vaux, Roland O., *Ancient Israel: Its Life and Institutions* (New York: McGraw–Hill, 1961).

Dijk-Hemmes, F. van, 'Some Recent Views on the Presentation of the Song of Miriam', in Brenner (ed.), *Exodus to Deuteronomy*, pp. 200-206.

Donaldson, L.E., 'Rereading Moses/Rewriting Exodus: The Postcolonial Imagination of Zora Neale Hurston', in *idem, Decolonizing Feminisms: Race, Gender, and Empire Building* (Chapel Hill: University of North Carolina Press, 1992), pp. 102-17.

Downing, Christine, *The Goddess: Mythological Images of the Feminine* (New York: Crossroad, 1981).

Dreyfus, Stanley A., 'The Burning Bush Through the Eyes of Midrash: God's Word Then and Now', in Holmgren and Schaalman (eds.), *Preaching Biblical Texts*, pp. 62-75.

Eilberg-Schwartz, Howard, *The Savage in Judaism: An Anthropology of Israelite Religion and Ancient Judaism* (Bloomington: Indiana University Press, 1990).

Ellmenreich, Renate, '2. Mose 1, 15-21: Pua und Schiphra—Zwei Frauen im Widerstand', in Schmidt, Korenhof and Jost (eds.), *Feministisch gelesen*, I, pp. 39-44.

Epstein, I. (ed.), *Babylonian Talmud* (London: Soncino , 1952).

Exum, J. Cheryl, 'Second Thoughts about Secondary Characters: Women in Exodus 1.8-2.10', in Brenner (ed.), *Exodus to Deuteronomy*, pp. 75-87.

—' "You Shall Let Every Daughter Live": A Study of Exodus 1.8–2.10', in Brenner (ed.), *Exodus to Deuteronomy*, pp. 37-61 (reprinted from *Semeia* 28 [1983], pp. 63-82)

Falk, Zeev, 'The Daughter and Widow's Inheritance in Bible and Talmud', *Tarbiz* 23 (1952), pp. 9-15.

Felder, C.H. (ed.), *Stony the Road We Trod: African American Biblical Interpretatation* (Minneapolis: Fortress Press, 1991).

Ficker, R., '*rkb* to ride, drive', in Ernst Jenni and Claus Westermann (eds.), *Theological Lexicon of the Old Testament*, III (Peabody, MA: Hendrickson, 1997), p. 1238.

Fischer, Irmtraud, *Tora für Israel: Tora für die Völker* (SBS, 164; Stuttgart: Katholisches Bibelwerk, 1995).

Fox, Robin, *Kinship and Marriage* (London: n.pub. 1967).

Frankel, Ellen, *The Five Books of Miriam: A Woman's Commentary on the Torah* (New York: Putnam's Sons, 1996).

Freedman, H., and M. Simon (trans.), *Midrash Rabbah* (7 vols.; New York: Soncino , 3rd edn, 1983).

Fretheim, Terence E., 'The Plagues as Ecological Signs of Historical Disaster', *JBL* 110 (1991), pp. 385-96.

Friedlander, G. (trans. and annotated), *Pirke de Rabbi Eliezer* (New York: Hermon, 1965).

Freud, Sigmund, 'The Aetiology of the Neuroses', SE III (1896c), pp. 189-224.

—'The Interpretation of Dreams', SE IV, pp. 1-338 and V(1900a), pp. 339-621.

—'On the History of the Psycho-Analytic Movement', SE XIV (1914d), pp. 3-68.

—*Introductory Lectures on Psycho-Analysis*, SE XV: 15-239 and XVI (1916-17), pp. 243-463.

—'The Question of Lay Analysis', SE XII (1926), pp. 183-250.

—'Female Sexuality', SE XXI (1931b), pp. 223-45.

—'Analysis Terminable and Interminable', SE XXIII (1937c), pp. 216-53.

—*Moses and Monotheism*. SE XXIII (1939a), pp. 3-140.

—*Moses and Monotheism* (New York: Knopf, 1939; repr., New York: Random House, 1987).

Frymer-Kensky, Tikva, 'Forgotten Heroines of the Exodus: The Exclusion of Women from Moses' Vision', *BR* 13 (December 1997), pp. 38-44.

Gaster, M. (trans.), *The Chronicles of Jerahmeel; or, The Hebrew Bible Historiale* (New York: Ktav, 1971).

Gates, H.L. Jr, 'Zora Neale Hurston: "A Negro Way of Saying" ', Afterword to Hurston, *Moses, Man of the Mountain*, pp. 289-99.

—*The Signifying Monkey: A Theory of African-American Literary Criticism* (Oxford: Oxford University Press, 1988).

Gates, H.L., Jr, and K.A. Appiah (eds.), *Zora Neale Hurston: Critical Perspectives Past and Present* (Amistad Literary Series; New York: Amistad, 1993).

Gebhardt, Esther, '2. Mose 2:1-10: Frauen für das Leben', in Schmidt, Korenhof and Jost (eds.), *Feministisch gelesen*, II, pp. 55-62.

Ginzberg, L., *Legends of the Jews* (trans. H. Szold; 7 vols.; Philadelphia: Jewish Publication Society of America, 1959–68).

Girard, René, *Violence and the Sacred* (Baltimore: The Johns Hopkins University Press, 1977).

—*The Scapegoat* (Baltimore: The Johns Hopkins University Press, 1986).

Görg, Manfred, 'Der Spiegeldienst der Frauen (Ex. 38:8)', *BN* 23 (1984), pp. 9-13.

Goldin, Judah, *Studies in Midrash and Related Literature* (Philadelphia: Jewish Publication Society of America, 1988).

Gowan, Donald E., *Theology in Exodus: Biblical Theology in the Form of a Commentary* (Louisville, KY: Westminster/John Knox Press, 1994).

Graves, Robert, and Raphael Patai, *Hebrew Myths: The Book of Genesis* (New York: Greenwich House, 1983).

Gray, George B., *A Critical and Exegetical Commentary on Numbers* (ICC; Edinburgh: T. & T. Clark, 1903).

Griffiths, J.G., *The Origins of Osiris and his Cult* (Leiden: E.J. Brill, 1980).

Gruber, Mayer I., 'Matrilineal Determination of Jewishness: Biblical and Near Eastern Roots', in David P. Wright, David Noel Freedman and Avi Hurvitz (eds.), *Pomegranates and Golden Bells: Studies in Biblical, Jewish, and Near Eastern Ritual, Law, and Literature in Honor of Jacob Milgrom* (Winona Lake, IN: Eisenbrauns, 1995), pp. 437-43.

Haber, Beth K., *Drawing on the Bible: Biblical Women in Art* (New York: Biblio Press, 1995).

Halpern, Baruch, 'The Exodus from Egypt: Myth or Reality', in Hershel Shanks *et al.* (eds.), *The Rise of Ancient Israel* (Washington, DC: Biblical Archaeology Society, 1992), pp. 86-117.

Hammer, Reuven (trans), *Sifre: A Tannaitic Commentary on the Book of Deuteronomy* (New Haven: Yale University Press, 1986).

Hammerton-Kelly, Robert, *Violent Origins: Walter Burkett, René Girard, and Jonathan Z. Smith on Ritual Killing and Cultural Formation* (Stanford, CA: Stanford Univerity Press, 1988).

—'Biblical Interpretation, Mythology, and a Theory of Ethnic Violence', *Scriptura* 50 (1994), pp. 23-40.

Harrington, D.J. (trans. and introduction), 'Pseudo-Philo', *OTP*, II, pp. 315-16.

Hauptman, Judith, *Rereading the Rabbis: A Woman's Voice* (Boulder, CO: Westview Press, 1998).

Hayes, Diana L., 'And When We Speak: To Be Black, Catholic, and Womanist', in Diana L. Hayes and Cyprian Davis, *Taking Down Our Harps* (Maryknoll, NY: Orbis Books, 1998), pp. 102-19.

Hebblethwaite, Peter, 'Let My People Go: The Exodus and Liberation Theology', *Religion, State and Society* 21.1 (1993), pp. 105-14.

Heinemann, J., *Agadot ve-Toldotehen* (Jerusalem: Keter Publishing House, 1974) (Hebrew).

Hemenway, R.E., *Zora Neale Hurston: A Literary Biography* (Urbana: University of Illinois Press, 1977).

Herodotus, *The Histories, Book 2* (trans. David Grene; Chicago: University of Chicago Press, 1987).

Hertz, J.H. (ed.), *The Pentateuch and Haftorahs: Hebrew Text, English Translation, and Commentary* (London: Soncino, 2nd edn, 1960).

Holender, Barbara K., *Ladies of Genesis: Poems* (New York: Jewish Women's Resource Center, 1991).

Holmgren, Frederick C, and Hermann E. Schalman (eds.), *Preaching Biblical Texts: Exposition by Jewish and Christian Scholars* (Grand Rapids: Eerdmans, 1995), pp. 62-75.

Howard, L., *Zora Neale Hurston* (Boston: Twayne Publishers, 1980).

Hoyt, T., Jr, 'Interpreting Biblical Scholarship for the Black Church Tradition', in Felder (ed.), *Stony the Road We Trod*, pp. 17-39.

Hurston, Zora Neale, *Moses, Man of the Mountain* (Chicago: University of Chicago Press, 1984 [1939]).

—'Book of Harlem', in Wall (ed.), *Novels and Stories*, pp. 979-84.

—'Dust Tracks on a Road', in Wall (ed.), *Folklore, Memoirs, and Other Writings*, pp. 558-808.

—'The Fire and the Cloud', in Wall (ed.), *Novels and Stories*, pp. 997-1000.

—'How It Feels to Be Colored Me', in Wall (ed.), *Folklore, Memoirs, and Other Writings*, pp. 826-29.

—'Jonah's Gourd Vine', in Wall (ed.), *Novels and Stories* , pp. 1-171.

—'Moses, Man of the Mountain', in Wall (ed.), *Novels and Stories*, pp. 335-595.

—'My Most Humiliating Jim Crow Experience', in Wall (ed.), *Folklore, Memoirs, and Other Writings*, pp. 935-36.

—'Their Eyes Were Watching God', in Wall (ed.), *Novels and Stories*, pp. 173-333.

Iersel, Bas van, and A. Weiler (eds.), *Exodus: A Lasting Paradigm* (Edinburgh: T. & T. Clark, 1987).

Ilan, Tal, *Jewish Women in Greco-Roman Palestine* (Tübingen: J.C.B. Mohr, 1995).

—*Mine and Yours are Hers: Retrieving Women's History from Rabbinic Literature* (Leiden: E.J. Brill, 1997).

—*Integrating Women into Second Temple History* (Tübingen: J.C.B. Mohr, 1999).

—"Daughters of Israel Weep for Rabbi Ishmael" (*mNedarim* 9:11): The Schools of Rabbi Aqiva and Rabbi Ishmael on Women', *Nashim: Journal of Jewish Women's Studies and Gender Issues* (in press).

Jackson, Blyden, 'Introduction' in Zora Neale Hurston, *Moses, Man of the Mountain* (Chicago: University of Chicago Press, 1984 [1939]), pp. xvi-xviii.

James, Henry, *The Art of the Novel* (ed. R. Blackmur; New York: Charles Scribner's Sons, 1934).

Janzen, J. Gerald, 'Song of Moses, Song of Miriam: Who Is Seconding Whom?', *CBQ* 54 (1992), pp. 211-20 (reprinted in Brenner (ed.), *Exodus to Deuteronomy*, pp. 187-99).

John, Cresy, *et al.*, 'An Asian Feminist Perspective: The Exodus Story (Exodus 1:8-22; 2:1-10): An Asian Group Work', in Sugirtharajah (ed.), *Voices from the Margin*, pp. 255-66.

Johnson, B., 'Threshholds of Difference: Structures of Address in Zora Neale Hurston', in Gates, Jr, and Appiah (eds.), *Zora Neale Hurston*, pp. 130-40.

Jost, Renate, *Frauen, Männer und die Himmelskönigin* (Gütersloh: Gütersloher Verlagshaus, 1994).

—'Die Töchter deines Volkes prophezeien', in Dorothee Sölle (ed.), *Für Gerechtigkeit streiten: Festschrift Luise Schottroff* (Gütersloh: Gütersloher Verlagshaus, 1994), pp. 59-65.

Kawash, S., *Dislocating the Color Line: Identity, Hybridity, and Singularity in African-American Narrative* (Mestizo Spaces/Espaces Métissés; Stanford: Stanford University Press, 1998).

Kee, H.C. (trans. and introduction), 'The Testaments of the Twelve Patriarchs', *OTP*, I.

Kerscher, Kristina, 'God's First Instrument of Liberation', *Bible Today* (1995), pp. 359-63.

Kessler, Rainer, 'Mirjam und die Prophetie der Perserzeit', in Ulrike Bail and Renate Jost (eds.), *Gott an den Rändern: Festschrift Willy Schottroff* (Gütersloh: Gütersloher Verlagshaus, 1996), pp. 64-72.

Kim, Ee-Kon, 'Who is Yahweh: Based on a Contextual Reading of Exodus 3:14', *Asian Journal of Theology* 3 (April 1989), pp. 108-17.

Kirk-Duggan, C., 'Hot Buttered Soulful Tunes and Cold Icy Passionate Truths: The Hermeneutics of Biblical Interpolation in Rhythm and Blues' in Vincent L.

Wimbush (ed.), *African Americans and the Bible: Sacred Text and Social Texture* (New York: Continuum), forthcoming 2000.

Kirsch, Jonathan, *Moses: A Life* (New York: Ballantine Books, 1998).

Kitzberger, I.R. (ed.), *The Personal Voice in Biblical Interpretation* (London: Routledge, 1999).

Kramer, Phyllis Silverman, *Sexual Stereotyping and the Manipulation of Female Role Models in Jewish Bible Textbooks: A Study in the History of Biblical Interpretation and its Application to Jewish School Curricula* (PhD dissertation, McGill University, 1994).

Kugel, J.L., *In Potiphar's House* (San Francisco: HarperSanFrancisco, 1990).

Lacan, Jacques, *The Four Fundamental Concepts of Psycho-Analysis* (trans. Alan Sheridan; London: Tavistock, 1977).

Lacks, Roslyn, *Women and Judaism: Myth, History, and Struggle* (Garden City, NY: Doubleday, 1980).

Lambdin, Thomas O., *Introduction to Biblical Hebrew* (New York: Charles Scribner's Sons, 1971).

Langer, Heidemarie, Herta Leistner and Elisabeth Moltmann-Wendel, *Mit Mirjam durch das Schilfmeer: Frauen bewegen die Kirche* (Stuttgart: Kreuz, 1982).

Lauterbach, J.Z., (ed.), *Mekhilta de-Rabbi Ishmael* (3 vols.; Schiff Library of Jewish Classics; Philadelphia: Jewish Publication Society of America, 1933–35).

Lehane, Terry John, 'Zipporah and the Passover', *JBQ* 24 (1996), pp. 46-50.

Leibowitz, Nechama, *Studies in Bamidbar (Numbers)* (trans. and adapted from the Hebrew by Aryeh Newman; Jerusalem: WZO, Department for Torah Education and Culture in the Diaspora, 1980).

Lichtheim, Miriam, *Ancient Egyptian Literature*. II. *The New Kingdom* (Berkeley: University of California Press, 1976).

Loader, James A., 'Exodus, Liberation Theology and Theological Argument', *Journal of Theology for Southern Africa* 59 (July 1987), pp. 3-18.

Lockyer, Herbert, *All the Woman of the Bible* (Grand Rapids: Zondervan, n.d.).

Lowe, J., *Jump at the Sun: Zora Neale Hurston's Cosmic Comedy* (Urbana: University of Illinois Press, 1994).

Lüneburg, Elisabeth, '2. Mose 15, 20f: Schlagt die Trommeln, tanzt und fürchtet euch nicht!', in Schmidt, Korenhof and Jost (eds.), *Feministisch gelesen*, II, pp. 45-52.

Magonet, Jonathan, 'The Attitude Towards Egypt in the Book of Exodus', in Wim Beuken, Sean Freyne and Anton Weiler (eds.), *Truth and Its Victims* (Edinburgh: T. & T. Clark, 1988), pp. 11-20.

McDowell, D., 'Lines of Descent/Dissenting Lines', Foreword to Z.N. Hurston, *Moses, Man of the Mountain* (New York: HarperCollins, 1991), pp. xv-xvi.

Meyers, Carol, 'Miriam the Musician', in Brenner (ed.), *Exodus to Deuteronomy*, pp. 207-230.

Milgrom, Jacob, 'Excursus 63: The Inheritance Rights of Daughters', in *idem*, *Numbers*, pp. 482-84.

—*Numbers* (JPS Torah Commentary; Philadelphia: Jewish Publication Society of America, 1989).

Monaco, James, *et al.*, *The Movie Guide: A Comprehensive, Alphabetical Listing of the Most Important Films Ever Made* (New York: Perigree, 1992).

Neeman, P. 'The Daughter's Inheritance in Torah and Halakhah', *Beth Mikra* 47 (1971), pp. 476-89 (Hebrew).

Neusner, J., and R.S. Sarason (eds.), *The Tosefta: Translated from the Hebrew*, III. *Nashim* (trans. J. Neusner; New York: Ktav, 1979).

Newsom, Carol A., and Sharon H. Ringe, *Woman's Bible Commentary: Expanded Edition with Apocrypha* (Louisville, KY: Westminster/John Knox, 1998).

Newton, John, 'Analysis of Programmatic Texts of Exodus Movements', in Iersel and Weiler, *Exodus*, pp. 56-62.

Noah, M.M. (ed.), *The Book of Jashar* (repr., New York: Hermon Press, 1972 [1840]).

Noth, Martin, *Numbers* (OTL; London: SCM Press, 1968).

Nunnally-Cox, Janice, *Foremothers: Women of the Bible* (San Francisco: Harper & Row, 1981).

Ochshorn, Judith, *The Book of the Goddesses: Past and Present* (New York: Crossroad, 1988).

Oosthuizen, M.J., 'Scripture and Context: The Use of the Exodus Theme in the Hermeneutics of Liberation Theology', *Scriptura* 25 (1988), pp. 7-22.

Ostriker, Alicia Suskin, *Feminist Revision and the Bible* (Oxford: Basil Blackwell, 1993).

Otto, Rudolf, *The Idea of the Holy: An Inquiry into the Non-rational Factor in the Idea of the Divine and its Relation to the Rational* (trans. John W. Harvey; repr., New York: Oxford University Press, 1958 [1917]).

Pardes, Ilana, *Countertraditions in the Bible: A Feminist Approach* (Cambridge. MA: Harvard University Press, 1992).

Parkinson, R.B., *Voices from Ancient Egypt: An Anthology of Middle Kingdom Writings* (London: British Museum Press, 1991).

Pixley, George V., *On Exodus: A Liberation Perspective* (Maryknoll, NY: Orbis Books, 1987).

Plaskow, Judith, *Standing Again at Sinai: Judaism from a Feminist Perspective* (San Francisco: Harper & Row, 1990).

Plastaras, James, *The God of Exodus: The Theology of the Exodus Narratives* (Milwaukee: Bruce Publishing, 1966).

Plaut, Gunther, *The Torah: A Modern Commentary* (New York: Union of American Hebrew Congregations, 1981).

Plutarch, *Moralia, Vol. 5* (trans. Frank Cole Babbitt; Cambridge, MA: Harvard University Press, 1936).

Praetorius, Ina, 'Androzentrismus', in Elisabeth Gössmann *et al.* (eds.), *Wörterbuch der feministischen Theologie* (Gütersloh: Gütersloher Verlag, 1991), pp. 14-15.

Pressler, Carolyn, 'Wives and Daughters, Bond and Free: Views of Women in the Slave Laws of Exodus 21.2-11', in Victor H. Matthews, Bernard M. Levinson and Tikva Frymer-Kensky (eds.), *Gender and Law in the Hebrew Bible and the Ancient Near East* (Sheffield: Sheffield Academic Press, 1998), pp. 147-72.

Raboteau, Albert J., *Slave Religion: The 'Invisible Institution' in the Antebellum South* (New York: Oxford University Press, 1978).

—'African-Americans, Exodus, and the American Israel', in Paul E. Johnson (ed.), *African-American Christianity: Essays in History* (Berkeley: University of California, 1994), pp. 1-17.

Ragland-Sullivan, Ellie, *Jacques Lacan and the Philosophy of Psychoanalysis* (Urbana: University of Illinois Press, 1986).

Rapp, Ursula, 'Das Buch Numeri', in Schottroff and Wacker (eds.), *Kompendium Feministische Bibelauslegung* (2nd edn, 1999), pp. 54-66.

Rashkow, Ilona N., *The Phallacy of Genesis: A Feminist-Psychoanalytic Approach* (Louisville, KY: Westminster/John Knox Press, 1993).

Reis, Tamarkin Pamela, 'The Bridegroom of Blood: A New Reading', *Judaism* 159.40 (1991), pp. 324-31.

Rose, Jacqueline, 'Introduction', in Jacques Lacan, *Feminine Sexuality* (trans. and ed. Juliet Mitchell and Jacqueline Rose; New York: W.W. Norton, 1982).

Rosen, Norma, *Biblical Women Unbound: Counter-tales* (Philadelphia: Jewish Publication Society of America, 1996).

Sakenfeld, K.D., 'In the Wilderness Awaiting the Land: The Daughters of Zelophehad and Feminist Interpretation', *Princeton Seminary Bulletin* 9 (1988), pp. 179-96.

—'Numbers', in Newsom and Ringe (eds.), *Women's Bible Commentary*, pp. 49-56.

Sarna, Nahum M., *Understanding Genesis* (New York: McGraw-Hill, 1966).

—*Exodus* (JPS Torah Commentary; Philadelphia: Jewish Publication Society of America, 1991).

Schmidt, E.R., M. Korenhof and R. Jost (eds.), *Feministisch gelesen*, I, II (Stuttgart: Kreuz, 1988, 1989).

Schneemann, Gisela, 'Die Deutung und Bedeutung der Beschneidung nach Exodus 4, 24-26', *Communio viatorum* 32.1-2 (1989), pp. 21-37.

Scholz, Susanne, 'Exodus: Was Befreiung aus "seiner" Sicht bedeutet...', in Schottroff and Wacker (eds.), pp. 26-39.

Schottroff, Luise, and Marie-Theres Wacker (eds.), *Kompendium Feministische Bibelauslegung* (Gütersloh: Gütersloher Verlag, 1997; 2nd edn 1999), pp. 26-39.

Schuller, E., 'Women of the Exodus in Biblical Retellings of the Second Telling', in P.L. Day (ed.), *Gender and Difference in Ancient Israel* (Minneapolis: Fortress Press, 1989), pp. 178-90.

Schwager, Raymund, *Must There Be Scapegoats? Violence and Redemption in the Bible* (San Francisco: Harper & Row, 1987).

Setel, Drorah O'Donnell, 'Exodus', in Newsom and Ringe (eds.), *Women's Bible Commentary*, pp. 30-39.

Shannon, D.T., ' "An Ante-bellum Sermon": A Resource for an African American Hermeneutic', in Felder (ed.), *Stony the Road We Trod*, pp. 98-123.

Siebert-Hommes, Jopie, 'Die Geburtsgeschichte des Mose innerhalb des Erzählzusammenhangs von Exodus I und II', *VT* 42 (1992), pp. 398-404.

—'But if She Be a Daughter...She May Live! "Daughters" and "Sons" in Exodus 1-2', in Brenner (ed.), *Exodus to Deuteronomy*, pp. 62-74.

—*Let the Daughters Live! The Literary Architecture of Exodus 1–2* (Leiden: E.J. Brill, 1998).

Silverman, Kaja, 'The Lacanian Phallus', *Differences* 4.1 (1992), pp. 84-115.

Smith, Theophus. H., *Conjuring Culture: Biblical Formations of Black America* (Oxford: Oxford University Press, 1994).

Smitherman, G., *Talkin' and Testifyin': The Language of Black America* (Boston: Houghton Mifflin, 1977).

Snaith, N.H., 'The Daughters of Zelophehad', *VT* 16 (1966), pp. 124-27.

Spiro, Melford E., 'An Overview and a Suggested Reorientation', in Francis I.K. Hsu (ed.), *Context and Meaning in Cultural Anthropology* (Homewood: Dorsey Press, 1961).

Staley, J.L., *Reading with a Passion: Rhetoric, Autobiography and the American West in the Gospel of John* (New York: Continuum, 1995).

Steinmetz, Devora, 'A Portrait of Miriam in Rabbinic Midrash', *Prooftexts* 8.1 (January 1988), pp. 35-65.

Stuermann, Walter, *The Divine Destroyer: A Theology of Good and Evil* (Philadelphia: Westminster Press, 1967).

Sturdy, J., *Numbers* (CBC; Cambridge: Cambridge University Press, 1976).

Sugirtharajah, R.S. (ed.), *Voices from the Margin: Interpreting the Bible in the Third World* (Maryknoll, NY: Orbis Books, 1995).

Tapia, Elizabeth S., 'The Story of Shiphrah and Puah: Disobedient or Subservient Women?', *CTC Bulletin* 10 (May-Dec. 1991), pp. 398–404.

Trible, Phyllis, 'Subversive Justice: Tracing the Miriamic Traditions', in Douglas A. Knight and Peter J. Paris (eds.), *Justice and the Holy: Essays in Honor of Walter Harrelson* (Atlanta: Scholars Press, 1989), pp. 99-109.

—'Bringing Miriam Out of the Shadows', in Brenner (ed.), *Exodus to Deuteronomy*, pp. 166-86

Veeser, H.A. (ed.), *Confessions of the Critics* (London: Routledge, 1996).

Vervenne, Marc, 'Current Tendencies and Developments in the Study of the Book of Exodus', in *idem* (ed.), *Studies in the Book of Exodus* (Leuven: Leuven University Press, 1996), pp. 21-59.

Voltaire, 'Ezekiel', in *Philosophical Dictionary*, IV (trans. William F. Fleming; Akron: Werner, 1906), pp. 305-11.

Wacker, Marie-Theres, 'Mirjam: Kritischer Mut einer Prophetin', in Karin Walter (ed.), *Zwischen Ohnmacht und Befreiung: Biblische Frauengestalten* (Frauenforum; Freiburg: Herder, 1988), pp. 44-52.

—' "Religionsgeschichte Israels" oder "Theologie des Alten Testaments": (k)eine Alternative?', *Jahrbuch für biblische Theologie* 19 (1995), pp. 129-55.

Walker, A., 'In Search of Zora Neale Hurston', *Ms.* 3.9 (March 1975), pp. 74-89 (reprinted as 'Looking for Zora', in *idem*, *In Search of Our Mothers' Gardens*, pp. 93-116).

—'Zora Neale Hurston: A Cautionary Tale and a Partisan View', Foreword to Hemenway, *Zora Neale Hurston*, pp. xi-xviii.

—*In Search of Our Mothers' Gardens: Womanist Prose* (San Diego: Harcourt Brace Jovanovich, 1983).

Walker, A. (ed.), *I Love Myself When I Am Laughing…and Then Again When I Am Looking Mean and Impressive: A Zora Neale Hurston Reader* (Old Westbury, NY: The Feminist Press, 1979).

Wall, C.A., *Women of the Harlem Renaissance* (Bloomington: Indiana University Press, 1995).

Wall, C.A. (ed.), *Zora Neale Hurston: Folklore, Memoirs, and Other Writings* (Library of America, 75; New York: Literary Classics of the United States, 1995).

—*Zora Neale Hurston: Novels and Stories* (Library of America, 74; New York: Literary Classics of the United States, 1995).

Warrior, Robert Allen, 'A Native American Perspective: Canaanites, Cowboys, and Indians', in Sugirtharajah (ed.), *Voices from the Margin*, pp. 287-95.

Weber, Beat, ' "Jede Tochter aber sollt ihr am Leben lassen!": Beobachtungen zu Ex. 1, 15–2, 10 und seinem Kontext aus literaturwissenschaftlicher Perspektive', *BN* 55 (1990), pp. 47-76.

Weems, Renita, 'The Hebrew Women Are Not Like the Egyptian Women: The Ideology of Race, Gender and Sexual Reproduction in Exodus 1', *Semeia* 59 (1992), pp. 25-34.

Weingreen J., 'The Case of the Daughters of Zelophchad', *VT* 16 (1966), pp. 518-22.

Whitelam, Keith W., *The Invention of Ancient Israel* (New York: Routledge, 1996).

Wildavsky, Aaron, *The Nursing Father: Moses as a Political Leader* (University of Alabama Press, 1984).

Williams, James G., *The Bible, Violence, and the Sacred: Liberation from the Myth of Sanctioned Violence* (Valley Forge, PA: Trinity Press International, 1995).

Willi-Plein, Ina, *Das Buch vom Auszug: 2. Mose (Exodus)* (Neukirchen–Vluyn: Neukirchener Verlag, 1988).

—'Ort und literarische Funktion der Geburtsgeschichte des Mose', *VT* 41 (1991), pp. 110-18.

Wright, M.J., ' "Sunk in Slavery… Snarled in Freedom": Recent Feminist Analysis of Exodus–Deuteronomy and Zora Neale Hurston's *Moses, Man of the Mountain*', *Biblicon* 2 (1997), pp. 39-49.

Yaron, Reuven, *Gifts in Contemplation of Death in Jewish and Roman Law* (Oxford: Clarendon Press, 1960).

Zeligs, Dorothy F., *Moses: A Psychodynamic Study* (New York: Human Sciences Press, 1986).

Zuckermandel, M.S. (ed.), *Tosephta: Based on the Erfurt and Vienna Codices* (Jerusalem: Wahrmann Books, 1970).

INDEXES

INDEX OF REFERENCES

OLD TESTAMENT

NEW TESTAMENT AND RABBINIC REFERENCES

OTHER ANCIENT SOURCES

INDEX OF AUTHORS

FEMINIST THEOLOGY TITLES

Individual Titles in Feminist Theology

Linda Hogan, *From Women's Experience to Feminist Theology*

Lisa Isherwood and Dorothea McEwan (eds.), *An A–Z of Feminist Theology*

Lisa Isherwood and Dorothea McEwan, *Introducing Feminist Theology*

Kathleen O'Grady, Ann L. Gilroy and Janette Patricia Gray (eds.), *Bodies, Lives, Voices: Gender in Theology*

Melissa Raphael, *Thealogy and Embodiment: The Post-Patriarchal Reconstruction of Female Sacrality*

Deborah Sawyer and Diane Collier (eds.), *Is There a Future for Feminist Theology?*

Lisa Isherwood (ed.), *The Good News of the Body: Sexual Theology and Feminism*

Alf Hiltebeitel and Kathleen M. Erndl, *Is the Goddess a Feminist? The Politics of South Asian Goddesses*

Introductions in Feminist Theology

Rosemary Ruether, *Introducing Redemption in Christian Feminism*

Lisa Isherwood and Elizabeth Stuart, *Introducing Body Theology*

Melissa Raphael, *Introducing Thealogy: Discourse on the Goddess*

Pui-lan Kwok, *Introducing Asian Feminist Theology*

Janet H. Wootton, *Introducing a Practical Feminist Theology of Worship*

Feminist Companion to the Bible (1st Series)

Athalya Brenner (ed.), *A Feminist Companion to the Song of Songs*

Athalya Brenner (ed.), *A Feminist Companion to Genesis*

Athalya Brenner (ed.), *A Feminist Companion to Ruth*

Athalya Brenner (ed.), *A Feminist Companion to Judges*

Athalya Brenner (ed.), *A Feminist Companion to Samuel and Kings*

Athalya Brenner (ed.), *A Feminist Companion to Exodus to Deuteronomy*

Athalya Brenner (ed.), *A Feminist Companion to Esther, Judith and Susanna*

Athalya Brenner (ed.), *A Feminist Companion to the Latter Prophets*

Athalya Brenner (ed.), *A Feminist Companion to the Wisdom Literature*

Athalya Brenner (ed.), *A Feminist Companion to the Hebrew Bible in the New Testament*

Athalya Brenner and Carole Fontaine (eds.), *A Feminist Companion to Reading the Bible: Approaches, Methods and Strategies*

Feminist Companion to the Bible (2nd Series)

Athalya Brenner and Carole Fontaine (eds.), *Wisdom and Psalms*

Athalya Brenner (ed.), *Genesis*

Athalya Brenner (ed.), *Judges*

Athalya Brenner (ed.), *Ruth and Esther*

Athalya Brenner (ed.), *Samuel and Kings*

Athalya Brenner (ed.), *Exodus to Deuteronomy*